Migration Law in Spain

Migration Law in Spain

Fernando Elorza Guerrero

This book was originally published as a monograph in the International Encyclopaedia of Laws/Migration Law.

Founding Editor: Roger Blanpain
General Editor: Frank Hendrickx
Volume Editor: Helen Oosterom-Staples

Wolters Kluwer

Published by:
Kluwer Law International B.V.
PO Box 316
2400 AH Alphen aan den Rijn
The Netherlands
E-mail: international-sales@wolterskluwer.com
Website: lrus.wolterskluwer.com

Sold and distributed in North, Central and South America by:
Wolters Kluwer Legal & Regulatory U.S.
7201 McKinney Circle
Frederick, MD 21704
United States of America
Email: customer.service@wolterskluwer.com

Sold and distributed in all other countries by:
Air Business Subscriptions
Rockwood House
Haywards Heath
West Sussex
RH16 3DH
United Kingdom
Email: international-customerservice@wolterskluwer.com

ISBN 978-94-035-0811-5

e-Book: ISBN 978-94-035-0812-2
web-PDF: ISBN 978-94-035-0813-9

Table of Contents

List of Abbreviations

AR	Autonomous Regions
Art.	Article
CCJ	Constitutional Court Judgment
EC	European Community
ECtHR	European Court of Human Rights
EU	European Union
FP	Final Provision
OJEU	Official Journal of the European Union
OL	Organic Law
OLJ	Organic Law 6/1985, of 1 July, on the Judiciary
OSG	Official State Gazette
RD	Royal Decree
RLD	Royal Legislative Decree
SC	1978 Spanish Constitution
SCC	Spanish Constitutional Court
SSC	Spanish Supreme Court
TFEU	Treaty on the Functioning of the European Union
UNHCR	United Nations High Commissioner for Refugees
VIS	Visa Information System

List of Abbreviations

Preface

Migration law is an area of law that is often placed outside the limelight of legal research and legal publications. It is a dispersed field of law, where national, regional as well as international legal sources provide binding rules and sometimes collide. At the same time, migration law is an area of law that is utterly commonplace in the everyday life of citizens and people in the modern world. Borders and boundaries are no longer perceived as obstacles to movement, and the practical impact of rules regarding immigration as well as emigration is important to acknowledge.

This volume aims at providing a structured overview of the rules applicable to immigration to Spain. Emigration is not included in this particular study of normative guidance. The volume also aims at providing sufficient and adequate information on how the rules are applied so that their context in the legal system, both theoretically and practically, becomes clear. Also, the volume aims at highlighting some of the challenges in the application of the rules both in their interpretation and their development.

As immigration law is a particularly dynamic field of law, the applicable legislation is ever-changing. In this volume, changes to the legislation have been followed until 31 March 2018.

General Introduction

§1. Immigration History and Statistical Information

1. Historically, Spain has been a country of emigration, as evidenced by the migration movements that occurred from the end of the nineteenth century to the 1980s. Only at the beginning of the 1990s did the country transform into the opposite: a country of immigration. In this sense, it is possible to identify four phases in the history of Spanish migration: (1) from 1830 to 1945: Spaniards emigrated mainly to Latin America; (2) from 1945 to 1973: the Spanish emigration movement shifted to Central and Northern Europe; (3) from 1973 to 1990: coinciding with the oil crisis and the first restrictions on intra-European migration movements, Spain gradually became a country of immigration, even if, during the 1980s, immigrants represented only 0.5% of the Spanish population; (4) since 1991: Spain has established itself as a country of immigration, to the extent that the immigrant population rose from being 1% of the Spanish population in 1991 to 12% in 2014.

2. There are two significant migration events in Spanish twentieth century history in which Spaniards played a major role. One of them is the Spanish Civil War (1936–1939), which caused the exodus of more than 0.5 million Spaniards, who then sought refuge mostly in France, Mexico, Argentina and Russia. The other is the great emigration movement that took place between 1945 and 1973, when workers from, particularly, Andalusia and the Spanish eastern coast moved to countries like Switzerland, Germany, France, the United Kingdom and the Netherlands, urged by the difficult economic situation and the need to provide themselves with decent means of subsistence. In fact, it is estimated that, in 1970, more than 1 million Spaniards out of a population of 34 million were living abroad. With the passing of years, particularly after the end of the dictatorship (1975) and during the 1980s, part of that population returned to Spain.

3. Nowadays, official statistics indicate that the Spanish population decreased by 220,130 people during 2013 so that on 1 January 2014 it reached a total of 46,507,760 inhabitants. This decrease in population was mainly caused by the severe economic crisis that has been affecting the country since 2008. In fact, during 2013, the number of foreigners established in Spain also decreased by 7.8% to 4,676,022. That same year, Spain had a negative migration balance of 256,849 people. This imbalance, which is 80.2% higher than it was in 2012, is mainly due to a reduction of the immigration flow, estimated at 4.3%, and to an increase of the emigration flow by 22.7%. Regarding the specific case of Spanish citizens, the migration balance in 2013 was also negative (-45,913) because 79,306 people emigrated and only 33,393 people returned to Spain.

4. On 1 January 2014, the foreign population in Spain consisted mostly of nationals from Romania (730,340), Morocco (714,221), the United Kingdom (311,774), Ecuador (212,970), Italy (182,249), Colombia (172,368) and China (164,555). The largest decrease in Spain's foreign population during 2013 took place among nationals from Ecuador and Colombia.

§2. Overview of National Legal Instruments

I. Historical Overview

5. The starting point for Spain's current migration policies is traditionally identified with the passing of OL 7/1985, of 1 July 1985, on the rights and freedoms of foreigners in Spain.[1] This led to the repeal, through the passing of an implementing regulation via RD 155/1996, of 2 February 1996,[2] of many lower-ranking provisions dating, in certain cases, from the middle and end of the nineteenth century and evidencing the lack of a migration policy in Spain for decades.

6. Thus, the passing of the above-mentioned OL 7/1985 represents the first act marking the beginning of the first out (1985–1990) of four phases in which the recent history of Spanish migration policies can be divided from a legal point of view. As expressed in its Explanatory Memorandum, the Constitutional mandate in Article 13 of the Spanish Constitution (SC) – 'Migrants in Spain shall enjoy the public freedoms guaranteed by the present Part, under the terms to be laid down by treaties and the law' – represents 'the first reason why it is necessary to adopt a regulation specifying its scope, something the present Organic Law [OL] attempts to do'. This OL 7/1985 was basically restrictive by nature, as manifested by its almost exclusive focus on defining the mechanisms to regulate the admission and control of foreigners in Spain, particularly the requirements for entering, exiting and staying in the country and the procedure for expulsion from the country. The drafting of the OL 7/1985 caused little controversy in the Spanish Parliament, in contrast with the later declaration of unconstitutionality and the subsequent declaration of nullity of several of its provisions by the Spanish Constitutional Court (SCC) in its judgment 115/1987.[3]

1. OSG 3 Jul. 1985, No. 158.
2. OSG 23 Feb. 1996, No. 47.
3. The Spanish Constitutional court declared the unconstitutionality of certain aspects of the Arts 7, 8 and 34 of OL 7/1985. The fundamental reason was related to the fact that Art. 13.1 of the Constitution empowers the legislator to establish additional constraints on the exercise of fundamental rights by foreigners, as long as these restraints are in line with, in any case, the rules in the Constitution. In this sense, according to the Constitutional Court Art. 13.1 does not give the legislator a free hand to determine the contents of a right, when this rights has already been granted to foreigners by the Constitution. The Court therefore appreciated the excessive zeal in the legislative action regarding the recognition of rights granted to foreigners by the Spanish Constitution.

7. The period 1990–1997 is identified as the second phase during which the Spanish government developed a more complex approach to immigration that went beyond the attempt to control it. For the first time in 1990, a governmental report was published under the title of '*About the situation of foreigners in Spain. Basic lines of the policy on foreigners.*' It addressed the need for a comprehensive immigration policy that would consider the integration of immigrants in the country. Around that time, a non-legislative proposal was approved by a large majority of the Spanish Parliament, which underlined the need to initiate, for the first time in Spanish history, an extraordinary procedure to regulate the situation of immigrants entering the country. This process started in 1991 and it was around that time that the decision was made to create a *Dirección General de Migraciones* (Directorate General for Migrations) attached to the Ministry of Social Affairs and in charge of centralising the administrative management of migration flows in Spain. In 1993, Spain approved of a recruitment agreement which enabled the admission of the first group of foreign workers, as a way of organising the arrival of foreign citizens whose professional activities were in demand to address the needs of its labour market.

8. In the three-year period 1995–1997 migration policies were incorporated into the EU agenda. Spain acceded to the Schengen (Implementing) Agreements – incorporated into the Union legal order by the 1997 Treaty of Amsterdam – and the Union institutions began to put pressure on the EU Member States to introduce certain changes in their migration policies and laws so that they would better comply with EU immigration policies. From a legal point of view, the most significant change came through the reform of the Implementing Regulation of OL 7/1985, which was passed while the Spanish Socialist Party was in office, but only entered into force when the Popular Party came to power. The reform came together with a new regulatory process that allowed legalising the situation of, presumably, 25,000 foreigners.

9. The third phase covers the five-year period between 1999 and 2003 and is remembered by a distinct and rapid reorientation of Spanish legislative action. In particular, while the beginning of the year 2000 saw the passing of OL 4/2000, of 11 January 2000, on the rights and freedoms of foreigners in Spain and their social integration,[4] after the general elections held in March 2000, the new government decided to reform the recently enacted OL, adopting a different, more restrictive, legislative approach, as reflected by OL 8/2000, amending OL 4/2000.[5] The initial text of OL 4/2000, which had been the product of wide social and political consensus, represented a change of the policy logic of OL 7/1985 as it meant the recognition of a migrant's social integration into Spanish society and the acknowledgement of equal rights for both national and foreign workers, whether or not the situation of the latter was regularised. Thus, the right of assembly, association, demonstration, to strike and to organisation and collective bargaining were

4. OSG 12 Jan. 2000, No. 20.
5. OSG 23 Dec. 2000, No. 299.

expressly acknowledged, while the right to health case or education were universalised – in this last case, for the population under 18 years – and the fight against discrimination became a legal objective. For the first time, the concept of 'act of discrimination' was defined, and behaviour that could be regarded as such was catalogued, as well as the corresponding legal sanctions. However, OL 8/2000 also brought a partial step backwards and the restoration of the legal approach to migration in OL 7/1985 as it determined the legal status of immigrants on the basis of their administrative situation. In this sense, where regular foreign workers enjoyed a considerable number of rights, irregular foreign workers had most of their rights denied and ended up not being considered subjects of law. A paradigmatic example of this change was the fact that both the right to organise and collective bargaining and the right to strike were now denied to them.

10. During the months following the passing of OL 8/2000, immigrant regularisation processes became even more important, given that legalising the situation of immigrants meant that as foreign workers they became subjects of law. Having a work permit and/or a residence permit became the key factor for immigrants to be considered citizens.

11. This reform was very much criticised for its restrictive vision of who was entitled or not to enjoy their fundamental rights, to the extent that two Constitutional challenges were brought against it in 2001. It was not until 200 that the SCC decided on both challenges in its judgments 236/2007 and 259/2007. The latter decision meant that during six years the legal regime established by OL 8/2000 was fully in force. However, once the judgments were delivered, they both had a great impact on the legal framework regarding the situation of immigrants because they both declared several articles in the law unconstitutional and became the reason and argument for the reform of the immigration policy implemented after 2007.

12. In the period between the adoption of OL 4/2000 and the rulings of the SCC that law was amended by the adoption – by agreement between the government and the opposition – of OL 14/2003, of 20 November 2003, amending OL 4/2000, of 11 January 2000, on the rights and freedoms of foreigners in Spain and their social integration.[6] This reform, which did not change the legal model of acknowledgement of rights laid down by OL 8/2000, focused on establishing a new visa policy. Visa was thus defined as the document that would from then on allow the entry and stay of foreigners in Spain, while a new type of visa, specifically for employment seekers, was created as a tool in the hands of the legislator willing to facilitate access to the Spanish labour market for migrants. In addition, there was a clear will to facilitate an immigrant's social integration, as long as he/she was in a regular situation. After this reform, the Spanish legal model remained stable and six years went by without any significant changes to it.

13. 2009 brought the beginning of a new phase for Spanish migration policy with the passing of OL 2/2009, of 11 December 2009, amending OL 4/2000, of 11

6. OSG 21 Nov. 2003, No. 279.

January 2000, on the rights and freedoms of foreigners in Spain and their social integration.[7] Even if, technically speaking, it was only a modification of OL 4/2000, this reform can actually be considered 'a new law on migration and migration policies'.[8] This becomes evident when the facts and reasons that motivated this legislative reform are analysed: (a) the social and economic changes that had occurred in Spain in previous years; (b) the need to incorporate into the Spanish legal system the legal obligations derived from the Council of Europe Convention on Action against Trafficking in Human Beings;[9] (c) the incorporation into the Spanish legal system of the principles contained in the European Pact on Immigration and Asylum; and (d) the need to also integrate the new doctrine of the SCC on the rights of foreign migrants and, in particular, CCJ 236 and CCJ 259/2007.

14. In short, as it has been sometimes pointed out, OL 2/2009 had 'as main recipients those foreign immigrants legally resident in Spain',[10] and only secondarily those who were in an irregular or illegal situation. In fact, the latter were granted only the fundamental human rights acknowledged to every human being for the mere fact of being one. It is significant that, for the first time, the law specifically regulated the legal situation of highly qualified foreign professionals, a group that was now the object of preferential treatment unknown before.

15. The 2009 reform was not the last one to amend OL 4/2000. In 2011 OL 10/2011, of 27 July 2017, amending Articles 31*bis* and 59*bis* of OL 4/2000 of 11 January 2000 on the rights and freedoms of foreigners in Spain and their social integration,[11] introduced changes to the above-mentioned articles for the purpose of extending:

(a) the protection offered to women who are victims of domestic violence and have reported this fact to their children who are now covered by their mother's application for a residence and work permit that is issued due to their exceptional circumstances, making the granting of the provisional residence and work permit to abused woman and her children automatic – therefore, no longer just optional; and
(b) the right to request the competent public authorities to guarantee their security accorded to victims of human trafficking, to the victim's children who are in Spain – in general, this right applies not just to the children but to any person with family ties or any other kind of bonds with the victim.

---

7. OSG 12 Dec. 2009, No. 299.
8. Monereo Pérez, J.L. & Triguero Martínez, L.A., 'Estudio preliminar: avances, retrocesos y perspectivas de futuro de inmediato en la regulación jurídico-legal de inmigración extranjera en España', in: Monereo Pérez, J.L., Fernández Avilés, J.A. & Triguero Martínez, L.A. (Dir.), 'Comentario a la Ley y al Reglamento de extranjería inmigración e integración social (LO 4/2000 y RD 557/2011)', Editorial Comares, Granada, 2012, p. 10.
9. Council of *Europe Treaty Series* No. 197.
10. Monereo Pérez, J.L. & Triguero Martínez, L.A., *supra*, p. 15.
11. OSG 28 Jul. 2011, No. 180.

16. Likewise, 2012 brought a new, albeit controversial, reform of OL 4/2000, which regulated a foreigner's right to sanitary assistance. Ultimately, this reform was an attempt to clearly limit the access to this kind of assistance to immigrants in an irregular situation, i.e., who are not in possession of a valid residence permit. In practice, the reform only granted emergency sanitary assistance to irregular immigrants, denying them any preventive primary assistance.[12] This amendment met with strong opposition of various sectors of Spanish society, including a significant number of the autonomous regional governments. The legal reform was incorporated into Spanish migration law through RLD 16/2012 of 20 April 2012 on urgent measures to guarantee the sustainability of the National Health Care System and improve its quality and the security of its benefits, of which the third and final disposition amended Article 12 of OL 4/2000.[13]

17. In 2013 the migration legal regime witnessed one of the most significant changes in the last decades with the passing of Law 14/2013, of 27 September 2013, on the support to entrepreneurs and their internationalisation.[14] This change is characterised by the establishment of a new, differentiated and selective channel for migrants to reside in Spain. Law 14/2013 was modified by Law 25/2015, of 28 July 2015, on the second opportunity mechanism, reduction of financial burden and other social measures[15] that provided an alternative to the ordinary regime that until then had been determined by OL 4/2000. This selective ground for admission mainly served investors, entrepreneurs, highly qualified professionals and workers making intra-corporate transfers. The most significant aspect of the 2013 law was that, for the first time in Spain since the adoption of the Constitution, the regulation of migration movements – with the exception of the asylum-related legislation – stopped being a monopoly of just one law, OL 4/2000, and that, especially and most importantly, this new regime was established with the purpose of improving the country's competitiveness and achieving greater economic rationality. A new legislative policy was thus adopted, one that was devoid of any consideration of the human rights, or even of the fundamental rights acknowledged in the SC, which would have required the drafting of an OL. In Spain OLs are legal instruments used to regulate matters related to fundamental rights, and, due to their significance, require

12. This legal reform is highly significant because, prior to the passing of RLD 16/2012, in Spanish law the right to sanitary assistance of all foreigners regardless of their legal situation was acknowledged. Only the person's registration of residence in the place where he resided was required in order to have access to this kind of assistance.
13. OSG 24 Apr. 2012, No. 98.
14. OSG 28 Sep. 2013, No. 233. This law introduced two new notions into OL 4/2000: Arts 38*bis* and 38*ter*, which defined a 'special regime for researchers' and a specific regime for the 'residence and work of highly qualified professionals', both of which ultimately transposed to Spanish legislation Council Directive 2009/50/EC, of 25 May 2009, on the conditions of entry and residence of third-country nationals for the purposes of highly qualified employment (OJEU, L 155/17 of 18 Jun. 2009).
15. OSG 29 Jul. 2015, No. 180. This reform was characterised by introducing a series of legal specifications into Law 14/2013, while amending the regime defined for investors. It also meant the transposing to Spanish legislation of Directive 2014/66/EU of the European Parliament and the Council, of 15 May 2014, on the conditions of entry and residence of third-country nationals in the framework of intra-corporate transfers (OJEC, L 157/1 of 27 May 2014).

a qualified majority in order to be approved by the Parliament. In short, a supposedly objective regime, with an economic rationale as its supreme value, was instituted, even though it is generally accepted that in migration matters the human dimension is unavoidable.

18. With regard to Spanish asylum policy, the first significant law since the adoption of the 1978 SC is Law 5/1984, of 26 March 1984, regulating the right to asylum and the status of refugee.[16] This law, drawn up with the purpose of complying with Article 13 of the SC, dealt with the regulation of the right to asylum to both politically persecuted asylum seekers in a broad sense – for reasons of race, religion, nationality, etc. – and to those having committed political crimes or other related offences, as long as these had occurred outside Spain. In this respect, asylum was defined as the protection offered by the State, which is committed not to return anyone to a country where they may face persecution, to the extent that, while the asylum application is being assessed, all extradition processes that are underway or pending will be suspended by the law, so that if the expulsion finally takes place it will never be to the country demanding extradition, except in those cases that are specifically and formally agreed upon. In addition, the concept of asylum included several other complementary measures as the authorisation to work or receive social assistance.

19. Ten years later, Law 9/1994, of 19 May 1994, amended Law 5/1984, of 26 March 1984, regulating the right to asylum and the status of refugee.[17] This law aimed at: (a) correcting certain malfunctions detected in the application of the norm in Law 9/1994 and amending Law 9/1994 to accommodate the requirements of certain international conventions, like the Convention determining the State responsible for examining applications for asylum lodged in one of the Member States of the European Communities, signed in Dublin on 15 June 1990; (b) redefining the status of refugee in order to adjust it to internationally approved principles and, particularly, to the 1951 Geneva Convention, so that thenceforward Spain was obliged to protect all foreigners who were considered refugees as per that Convention; (c) simplifying the procedure for the acknowledgement of the condition of asylum seeker; and (d) improving the implementability of the provisions in the subject of asylum, particularly in what concerns the removal from Spanish territory of those whose asylum application is turned down, while striking down the power of the Spanish Ministry of the Interior to stop the activity of foreigners associations in compliance with CCJ 115/1987 of 7 July 1987.

20. In 2009 a new law was passed: Law 12/2009, of 30 October 2009, regulating the right to asylum and subsidiary protection,[18] which entered into force on 20 November 2009, repealing the aforementioned Law 5/1984. The objective of this new law, as expressed in its Explanatory Memorandum, was to incorporate into the

---

16. OSG 27 Mar. 1984, No. 74.
17. OSG 23 May 1994, No. 122.
18. OSG 31 Oct. 2009, No. 263.

Spanish legal system the numerous EU standards on asylum and subsidiary protection, as well as to bring Spanish legislation in line with the European Union's (EU's) asylum policy, as developed since the signing of the 1997 Treaty of Amsterdam. As a result, several directives were transposed, amongst them Council Directive 2004/83/EC, of 29 April 2004, on minimum standards for the qualification and status of third-country nationals or stateless persons as refugees or as persons who otherwise need international protection and the content of the protection granted;[19] Council Directive 2005/85/EC, of 1 December 2005, on minimum norms on procedures in Member States for granting or withdrawing refugee status;[20] and Chapter V of Council Directive 2003/86/EC, of 22 September 2003, on the right to family reunification.[21] Thus, the first phase of the Common Asylum System was incorporated into the Spanish legal system in the terms established by the 1999 Tampere Conclusions, as confirmed in 2004 by The Hague Programme.

II. Current Applicable Legislation

21. All analyses of the current Spanish migration legislation must start with a consideration of Article 13 of the 1978 SC, which states that 'immigrants in Spain shall enjoy the public freedoms guaranteed by the present Part, under the terms to be laid down by treaties and the law' and ultimately refers to the need to determine a legal configuration, as underlined by the SCC (CCJ 107/1984, of 23 November 1984), in consonance with the principles and rights in the Constitution and, in all cases, respectful of the minimum standards imposed by international law, as inferred from Article 10 of the SC.

22. Today, the above-mentioned legal configuration is defined by OL 4/2000, of 11 January 2000, on the rights and freedoms of foreigners in Spain and their social integration. The first provision of this law established that, for the purpose of the law, foreigners are those 'who do not have Spanish nationality'. With regard to nationals from EU Member States and those to whom the EU regime is applicable, their position is governed by the EU norms regulating their situation. The present law therefore only applies to them in those instances in which it provides more favourable standards. This last consideration is not easy to comprehend.

23. As a development of the current OL and as a consequence of the third final provision (FP) of OL 2/2009, the corresponding RD 557/2011, of 20 April 2011, approves the regulation of OL 4/2000.[22] This royal decree is considered to be the main regulation developing OL 4/2000, but it is, in fact, much more than a simple development of the legal norm or a mere updating of the Spanish administrative procedures reforming the OL 4/2000, as implemented through OL 2/2009, which

19. OJEUEC, L 304/2012 of 30 Sep. 2004.
20. OJEUEC, L 326/13 of 13 Dec. 2005.
21. OJEUEC, L 251/12 of 22 Sep. 2003.
22. OSG 30 Jun. 2011, No. 103.

was its initial objective. In fact, specialists on the matter have emphasised its length and thoroughness, though it also has sometimes been described as too redundant and repetitive.[23]

24. Regarding the healthcare to which migrant workers are entitled, it is important to take into account RLD 16/2012, of 20 April 2012, on the urgent measures to guarantee the sustainability of the National Health Care System and improve its quality and the security of its benefits,[24] which amended Article 12 of OL 4/2000. Due to this amendment nowadays, 'foreigners have the right to healthcare in the terms specified in healthcare legislation'. In reality, as developed later in this work, this norm in practice meant the exclusion of immigrants in an irregular situation from the enjoyment of this right. Nevertheless, for the purpose that is relevant here, what needs to be underlined is that, in relation to this matter, the provisions of Article 3 of Law 16/2003, of 28 May 2003, on the cohesion and quality of the National Health Care System[25] are the ones that currently prevail.

25. In relation to the migration of highly qualified workers, Articles 61ff. of Law 14/2013, of 27 September 2013, on the support to entrepreneurs and their internationalisation[26] regulated, for the first time and separately from the usual migration flow into Spain, a series of cases in which, 'for reasons of economic interest, the granting of visas and work permits is facilitated with the object of attracting investment and talent to Spain'. It is a legal measure designed for investors, entrepreneurs, workers making intra-firm movements, highly qualified professionals and researchers, as well as their spouses and older children. This law was modified by the eleventh FP of Law 25/2015, of 28 July 2015, on the second opportunity mechanism, reduction of financial burden and other social measures, which is actually a new draft for the regime established by the 2013 law.[27]

26. Finally, the above-mentioned legislation must be applied taking into account the courts' decisions, which are especially interesting on this matter, in particular those of the Constitutional Court and the Supreme Court. This is not the place to discuss in detail all the case laws generated by these courts, but it is necessary to highlight the relevance of CCJ 236/2007 of 7 November 2007 for current Spanish migration legislation. In CCJ 236/2007 OL 8/2000, of 22 December 2000, amending OL 4/2000, of 11 January 2000, on the rights and freedoms of foreigners in Spain and their social integration was declared partially unconstitutional. This judgment is especially significant for the development of Spain's immigration legislation, because it states that certain administrative requirements, in particular the legal nature of a person's stay in Spain, cannot condition the enjoyment of certain rights linked to internationally acknowledged concepts like human dignity, which is also acknowledged in the SC.

23. Monereo Pérez, J.L. & Triguero Martínez, L.A., *supra*, p. 17.
24. OSG 24 Apr. 2012, No. 98.
25. OSG 29 May 2003, No. 128.
26. OSG 28 Sep. 2013, No. 233.
27. OSG 29 Jul. 2015, No. 180.

27. In what concerns asylum, the reference law is the already mentioned Law 12/2009, of 30 October 2009, regulating the right to asylum and subsidiary protection, which was amended by Law 2/2014, of 25 March 2014, on the External Action and Service of the State (third FP),[28] which modified Article 40 of the 2009 law, i.e. the provision that regulated the extension of a person's refugee status and benefits associated to the right to asylum or the corresponding subsidiary protection to family members.

III. Administrative and Judicial Authorities

28. Analysing Spanish administrative immigration jurisdiction requires taking into account the peculiar structure of the Spanish State, which is constitutionally configured as a decentralised State the actions of which must always take into consideration the existence of autonomous regions (AR) and of their competences. In this sense, Article 149.1.12 of the SC grants the central State exclusive authority on issues related to the immigrant and foreign population, so the debate on the possible competences of the AR over this matter was initially non-existent. However, with the passing of time, especially during the 1990s, the growth of the immigration flow evidenced the need for other administrations, i.e., AR and municipalities, to assume certain responsibilities in the matter.

29. OL 4/2000 had, among others, the objective of decentralising certain aspects related to the administrative management of immigration, acknowledging the competence of certain administrations – mainly AR and municipalities – to perform specific actions, such as issuing social integration reports and housing adequacy reports for the purpose of family reunification. The municipalities were granted the competence to register foreigners established in their territory. The *Consejo Superior de Política de Inmigración* (High Council on Immigration Policy) was created as a body in charge of coordinating the work of the State and that of the AR in this field, giving expression to a decentralisation process in the administrative management of immigration, as established by the Spanish legislator.

30. OL 2/2009 assigned new functions to the AR regarding initial work permits, unaccompanied foreign minors, social integration measures and the competence to make propositions and be consulted in decision-making processes related to immigration policy. The main determinant of the consolidation of the Spanish administrative decentralisation in matters concerning immigration was the action of the Constitutional Court, in particular CCJ 31/2010, which was handed down at the time when the constitutionality of the new 2010 Statute of Autonomy of Catalonia was being considered. From then on, the doctrine established by this judgment has to be taken into consideration whenever the distribution of competences between the State and the AR concerning immigration issues is being examined.

---

28. OSG 26 Mar. 2014, No. 74.

31. When considering the administrative management of immigration in Spain, setting aside the competence assumed by the AR and municipalities, consideration must also be given of the *Oficinas de Extranjería* (Migration Affairs Offices) (Article 67.2 of OL 4/2000) and the *Centros de Migraciones* (Migration Centres) – which include the Refugee Reception Centres and the Immigrant Temporary Stay Centres – which are the main units through which the central State administration implements the administration and management of immigration. The management of immigration is in the hands of various Ministries of the Spanish government. Even if, in principle, the responsibility in immigration matters lies with the Ministry of the Interior – including police competences – other bodies are also required to take on certain duties, like the Ministry of Foreign Affairs and Cooperation – for instance, in relation to the management of the Spanish consular offices – and the Ministry of Finances and Public Administrations, regarding the management of the staff and material resources to be used by the offices dealing with immigration issues.

32. As for legal actions in immigration matters Spain has four legal jurisdictional orders that deal with different legal aspects related to immigration. Thus, in the first place, there is the contentious-administrative jurisdiction, which deals with allegations related to the action of the different public administrations subject of administrative law (Article 9.4 of the OLJ). Administrative decisions adopted in immigration case will, in certain cases, automatically exhaust all administrative remedies, something that will grant the addressee of the action access to contentious-administrative jurisdiction and the possibility of lodging a contentious-administrative appeal, while other cases will require exhausting all appeals to the administration before having access to contentious-administrative jurisdiction.

33. The social jurisdictional order deals with allegations related to what is known as social law (Article 9.5 of the OLJ) and, in particular, to the different aspects of an immigrant's labour activity and the social protection provided by the Spanish Social Security.

34. As for the criminal jurisdiction, this takes place within the framework of criminal cases and trials (Article 9.3 of the OLJ). In this sense, the Spanish Criminal Code includes a series of criminal acts which linked to immigration that are classified as crimes, such as, the promotion or facilitation of illegal immigration to Spain (Article 313 of the Criminal Code) or the constitution of illegal associations with the purpose of doing wrong (Article 515 of the Criminal Code).

35. Finally, the civil jurisdictional order is concerned with all those legal actions related to civil legislation (Article 9.2 of the OLJ) and all matters that are not assigned to any other jurisdictional order. Thus, civil jurisdiction has a common and supplementary function in relation to the other jurisdictional orders.

36. Naturally, in a State like Spain, governed by the rule of the law, jurisdictional actions include a series of appeals that can be lodged against the judgments pronounced by the courts of first instance. In the case of legal actions related to ordinary legislation, the process could end by bringing a corresponding appeal to the Spanish Supreme Court (SSC) – the highest jurisdictional body in Spain for any of the above-mentioned jurisdictional orders. In cases where there is an alleged violation of Constitutional rights, an appeal can be lodged with the SCC, which is the body in charge of dealing with all litigation concerning the interpretation and violation of the Constitution.

§3. Overview of International Legal Instruments Applicable in Spain

37. Any consideration of the International Law applicable in Spain in the area of migration must be based on what is established in Article 1.2 OL 4/2000, which literally reads as follows: 'The provisions of this Law are understood to be, in all cases, without prejudice to those established in special laws and in the International Treaties to which Spain is a party'. The normative reference might be considered obvious, taking into account the terms in which they are expressed in Articles 96 and 97 of the SC. However, it is a normative reference that did not exist in the original version of the OL 4/2000, and that however recovered was reinstalled by OL 8/2000, amending the above-mentioned OL. In short, these provisions reaffirm Spain's commitment to respect the international standards relevant to migration, and ultimately remind legal operators that when applying the national legislation in this field they must respect the international standards which Spain has committed itself to observe and, ultimately, to the Universal Declaration of Human Rights.

38. From a general perspective, and with regard to the normative framework developed within the framework of the United Nations, Spain is a signatory of international instruments such as the Convention against Transnational Organized Crime, signed in New York on 15 December 2000, and the two supplementary Protocols: the Protocol to Prevent, Suppress and Punish Trafficking in Persons, especially Women and Children, and the Protocol against the Smuggling of Migrants by Land, Sea and Air, both signed in New York on 15 November 2003.[29] In the case of the International Labour Organization (ILO), Spain is party to the following Conventions that also govern its actions in the field of non-nationals and migration: Convention No. 19 of 1925, concerning Equality of Treatment for National and Foreign Workers as regards Workmen's Compensation for Accidents, which was ratified by Spain on 22 February 1929; Convention No. 97 of 1949, concerning Migration for Employment, which was ratified by Spain on 21 March 1967; and Convention No. 143 of 1975 concerning Migrations in Abusive Conditions and the Promotion of Equality of Opportunity and Treatment of Migrant Workers, entry in force, in the case of Spain, on 9 December 1978. Specific mention must also be made to the Convention relating to the Status of Refugees, made in Geneva on 28 July 1951, as well as the Protocol on it, made in New York on 31 January 1967,

29. However, like the other EU Member States, Spain has not ratified, and, therefore, it is not applicable, the International Convention on the Protection of the Rights of All Migrant Workers and Members of their Families, 18 Dec. 1990.

with regard to the international protection of refugees, and to which Spain acceded by Instrument of Accession of 22 July 1978.[30]

39. In the case of the Council of Europe, Spain, as a member of that organisation, is bound the European Convention on the Legal Status of the Migrant Workers, of 24 November 1977, which was ratified by Spain on 29 April 1980; and the European Convention on Action against Trafficking in Human Beings, of 16 May 2005, that, in the case of Spain, entered into force on 1 August 2009. Likewise, Spain, through its Instrument of Ratification on 26 September 1979,[31] is bound by the European Convention for the Protection of Human Rights and Fundamental Freedoms of 4 November 1950, and, at the same time, falls under the jurisdiction of the European Court of Human Rights (ECtHR).

40. With regard to the bilateral agreements and treaties with other countries, they are numerous, and of very diverse content. Without claiming to be exhaustive, I think that the following bilateral agreements and treaties addressing aspects such as the control of migratory flows, the entry into and work in Spain, the prevention of clandestine migration – and ultimately their repatriation, and on dual nationality signed with Latin American countries such as Colombia, the Republic of Argentina, Honduras, the Dominican Republic, Ecuador, Costa Rica, Bolivia, Guatemala, Nicaragua, Paraguay, Peru or Chile,[32] deserve being mentioned. In the case of the dual nationality, it should be noted that Spain, after the entry into force of its current Constitution, and in particular Article 11.3, the agreements signed with different Latin American countries, have been revised over the years, seeking to adjust these bilateral instruments to bring them in line with the Constitutional framework. Often, these international agreements and conventions contain equality clauses which apply the citizens of the contracting parties, or a provision on non-discrimination on grounds of nationality. If a most-favoured-nation status clause has been included this undoubtedly impacts on the Spanish foreigners and immigration legal framework, making it more flexible in different degree.

30. OSG 21 Oct. 1978, No. 272.
31. OSG 10 Oct. 1979, No. 243.
32. In addition, there are various partnership agreements concluded between third States and the European Union, which tend to enshrine the principle of non-discrimination. In this sense, in the field of Social Security, Spain has seen a fairly intensive use of the EEC-Morocco Agreement 27 Apr. 1976.

Part I. Border Control and Entrance

Chapter 1. Organisation of Border Control

41. From the point of view of immigration, the organisation of border control in Spain is based on the principle according to which the control of foreigners wishing to enter Spain regularly must do this at border crossing points located at the external borders of the Schengen Area. It is at these external border crossing points where the members of the Spanish security forces must ensure compliance with the requirements to enter Spanish territory as established in Article 25 and following of OL 4/2000.

42. When it comes to analysing the organisation of the Spanish border control, it is necessary to remember that Spain, as an EU Member State and signatory of the Schengen Agreement, has structured its border control system in accordance with the integral border management system created within the framework of the Area of Freedom, Security and Justice into which the EU is configured, as laid down by the current Title V of the Treaty on the Functioning of the EU (Articles 67 and following).[33] This has a number of significant implications. For instance the application of the Schengen Borders Code to the Spanish border control system,[34] the use by the

33. OJEU, C115 of 9 May 2008.
34. Enacted in its day by Regulation (EC) No. 562/2006 of the European Parliament and of the Council, of 15 March 2006, establishing a Community Code on the rules governing the movement of persons across borders (Schengen Borders Code) (OJEU, L 105 of 13 Apr. 2006). Nowadays, the existing rule is the Regulation (EU) No. 2016/399 of the European Parliament and of the Council on a Union Code on the rules governing the movement of persons across borders (Schengen Borders Code) (OJEU, L 77 of 23 Mar. 2016).

Spanish migration authorities and members of the police of the Schengen Information System (SIS-II Regulation);[35] and the cooperation between the Spanish border authorities with the European Border and Coast Guard Agency (still referred to as FRONTEX).[36]

43. Current Spanish legislation incorporates the differentiation made in the 2016 Schengen Border Code between land, sea and air borders (Annex VI), so that entry control is officially made through the common external borders of the Schengen Area and through airport and port transit zones. At the same time, there is a surveillance system in those border areas through which irregular immigration may enter. In the case of Spain, these areas are especially important, given that it is a country located on Europe's southern border, where institutions such as the European Border and Coast Guard Agency are working. For this same reason, in the last few years Spain has installed a complex system of electronic surveillance, which controls the southern and eastern coasts, including the Canary and Balearic islands, which is known as the '*Sistema Integrado de Vigilancia Exterior*' (SIVE, External Surveillance Integrated System). This system, operated by the Spanish Guardia Civil, provides the Spanish security forces with real-time information on irregular immigration activities at these coasts.

44. An aspect that should be taken into account in relation to the implementation of border control measures is that, technically speaking, foreigners are only considered to have effectively entered Spain after they have actually crossed the external border and entered Spain either at a land, sea or air border. However, the legal qualification of entry – and therefore its legal or irregular nature – cannot be made until foreigners have undergone the corresponding migration control and the administrative authority has issued an administrative decision allowing the entry in accordance to Article 25.1 of OL 4/2000, or denying it, thus proceeding to turn the person back at the border, as specified in Article 26.2 of OL 4/2000. As long as the

35. Regulation (EC) No. 1987/2006 of the European Parliament and of the Council, of 20 December 2006, on the establishment, operation and use of the second generation Schengen Information System (SIS II) (OJEU, L 381 of 28 Dec. 2006). EU legislation on border control is much 'richer' than it appears upon first reading of the text. Also note in this respect the following EU legislative measures: Regulation (EC) No. 863/2007 of the European Parliament and of the Council, of 11 July 2007, establishing a mechanism for the creation of Rapid Border Intervention Teams and amending Council Regulation (EC) No. 2007/2004 as regards that mechanism and regulating the tasks and powers of guest officers (OJEU, L 199 of 31 Jul. 2007), or Council Decision 2010/131/EU, of 25 February 2010, on setting up the Standing Committee on operational cooperation on internal security (OJEU, L 52 of 3 Mar. 2010).

36. Council Regulation (EC) No. 2016/1624 of the European Parliament and of the Council of 14 September 2016 on the European Border and Coast Guard and amending Regulation (EU) 2016/399 of the European Parliament and of the Council and repealing Regulation (EC) No. 863/2007 of the European Parliament and of the Council, Council Regulation (EC) No. 2007/2004 and Council Decision 2005/267/EC (OJEU EU, L 251 of 16 Sep. 2016).

corresponding control action has not been performed by the Spanish authorities, foreigners find themselves legally 'in suspense',[37] a status that is highly contestable because of the legal insecurity it creates for the person concerned who is de facto already in Spain.

45. After the incorporation into the EU legal order by the 1997 Treaty of Amsterdam of the Protocol integrating the Schengen *acquis* into the EU framework, controls at the internal borders of Spain have disappeared. Nowadays, only nationals of non-EU Member States must undergo stringent immigration controls, so the nationals of the EU Member States normally are only subject to minimum controls, related to the verification of their identity.

46. Like other EU Member States, Spain has not been spared the discussion on relation to the legal treatment that people in international areas, like airports and ports, should receive. Many States considered that certain spaces within those areas, like waiting rooms and hallways, are legally not part of their national territory. The Spanish judiciary decided on this complex matter by applying the case law of the ECtHR. According to the Spanish judiciary, once foreigners have entered Spain, meaning that they have physically crossed the Spanish border, they find themselves in national territory and, something which is still more important, under Spanish jurisdiction, and are, therefore, subject to the actions of its judges and courts.[38]

47. A greater difficulty is experienced with migration controls performed by Spanish authorities in international waters or in areas under the jurisdiction of third countries. Notwithstanding the legal complexity, any action of the Spanish authorities in these cases must always comply with international law and its principles, although in practice this is sometimes not the case.

48. In the case of Spain, when discussing border controls, the specific treatment given to the border cities of Ceuta and Melilla, located in the north of Africa and periodically claimed by the Kingdom of Morocco. They have a special legal relationship with the EU. In this respect, Article 41 of the 2016 Schengen Borders Code[39] states that: 'The provisions of this Regulation shall not affect the special rules that apply to the cities of Ceuta and Melilla, as defined in the Declaration by the Kingdom of Spain on the cities of Ceuta and Melilla in the Final Act to the

---

37. Moya Malapeira, D. & Hernández Calero, D., 'Los controles en frontera: denegación de entrada, orden de regreso y devolución', in Boza Martínez, D., Donaire Villa, F.J., & Moya Malapeira, D. (Coords.): 'La nueva regulación de la inmigración y la extranjería en España. Régimen jurídico tras la LO 2/2009, el Real Decreto 557/2011 y la Ley 12/2009', Tirant lo Blanch, Valencia, 2012, p. 195.
38. In this context, the ECtHR' judgment *Amuur v. France* of 25 Jun. 1996, Appl. No. 19776/92 is usually quoted. This doctrine was embraced by the Spanish Constitutional Court in CCJ No. 174/1999 of 27 Sep. 1999 and CCJ No. 174/2000 of 26 Jun. 2000.
39. Regulation (EU) 2016/399 of the European Parliament and of the Council, of 9 March 2016, on a Union Code on the rules governing the movement of persons across borders (Schengen Borders Code) (codified text), published in OJEU, L 77/1 of 23 Mar. 2016.

Agreement on the Accession of the Kingdom of Spain to the Convention implementing the Schengen Agreement of 14 June 1985'. In accordance with to this provision, and notwithstanding the controls that Spain performs at its border with Morocco, which is an external border of the Schengen Area, Spain has agreed to maintain border controls on people and goods on flights and sea transfers between these two cities and the Iberian peninsula – continental Spain. The purpose of these controls is to verify compliance with the conditions specified in Article 6 of 2016 Schengen Border Code.[40]

49. In accordance with Spain's Accession Agreement to the 1990 Convention implementing the Schengen Agreement, the specific visa exemption regime applies to small border traffic between Ceuta and Melilla and the Moroccan provinces of Tetuán and Nador (border crossings at these borders is possible with only an identity card for those living in the border area) has remained in force.[41] Along the same line, Moroccan citizens not living in the provinces of Tetuán and Nador and wishing to enter exclusively the cities of Ceuta and Melilla are still issued a 'multiple limited visa' restricted to these two cities, allowing them to enter and exit these cities multiple times.[42]

50. The Spanish media often cover situations related to the removal of persons which are implemented at borders without notice of the administration which do not comply with the procedure set out in Article 26 of the OL 4/2000. Independent of the considerations that can be made on the illegal nature of these actions, it is clear that they evidently cause a feeling of helplessness felt everybody who experiences them and may also entail a violation of their fundamental rights. It is thus necessary to realise that they may be declared null and void as administrative actions which do not comply with the conditions specified in Article 26 of OL 4/2000.

---

40. Final Act, s. III, of the Instrument of Ratification of the Accession Agreement of the Kingdom of Spain to the Convention implementing the Schengen Agreement of 14 June 1985 between the Governments of the States of the Benelux Economic Union, the Federal Republic of Germany and the French Republic, on the gradual abolition of checks at the common borders, signed at Schengen on 19 June 1990, to which the Italian Republic acceded by the Agreement signed at Paris on 27 November 1990, implemented on 25 June 1991 (OSG 5 Apr. 1994, No. 81).
41. Final Act, s. 1 b) III.
42. Small border traffic is a concept that refers to the regular crossing of the external land border of the European Union by border residents in order to remain in the EU border area on economic, social, cultural or family grounds during a period that in no case shall exceed the one specified by the European regulation. In Spain, the admission as a cross-border worker, by decision of the legislator (Art. 43 of OL 4/2000), is regulatory by nature, meaning that the requirements and conditions which apply to foreign workers residing in the Spanish border areas, and allow them to develop an economic activity in the border area, Arts 182 & 183 of RD 557/2011 must be observed. Authorisation may be given to develop both labour activities as an employed and as a self-employed person (Art. 182 of RD 557/2011). The conditions are enforceable in each individual case (Art. 183 of RD 557/2011). The duration of the initial permit coincides with that of the labour contract that is agreed upon, with a minimum duration of three months and a maximum of one year – this time limit also applies to the self-employed – and its validity is limited to the territorial scope of the Autonomous Region or Autonomous City – Ceuta and Melilla – in whose border area the foreign worker resides (Art. 184 of RD 577/2011). The rules in s. III of this Final Act are a legal exception to the regime established by the RD 557/2011, which finds its origin in the historic agreements between the Kingdom of Spain and of Morocco in immigration matters.

51. Finally, Article 10 of Regulation (EC) No. 1031/2006 of the European Parliament and of the Council, of 20 December 2006, laying down rules on local border traffic at the external land borders of the Member States and amending the provisions of the Schengen Convention,[43] states that the provisions in this regulation shall not affect the specific rules which apply to the cities of Ceuta and Melilla. This provision reflects the already mentioned declaration made by Spain on the occasion of its accession to the 1990 Convention implementing the Schengen Agreement.[44]

43. OJEU, L 405/I of 30 Dec. 2006.
44. Final Act, s. 1 c) III.

Chapter 2. Right to Enter the Country

§1. Conditions for the Right to Enter

52. All analyses on the entry of foreigners into Spain must start by considering that the right to emigrate, defined in Article 13 of the 1948 Universal Declaration of Human Rights, is not mirrored in international law by an equivalent right to immigrate. This is why States are not obliged to receive and welcome all those having decided to emigrate to their country. This vision on the phenomenon of migration was embraced by the SCC years ago, through CCJ 94/1993 of 22 March 1993, where it is stated that 'the freedom to move across the borders of the State and the concomitant right to live within those borders, are neither indispensable rights to guarantee human dignity (Article 10 of the SC and CCJ 107/1984), nor do they belong to every person as such regardless of their capacity as a citizens'. Along the same line, Article 13.1 of the SC does not include the right to enter Spain as a right of the foreigner, although the SCC has acknowledged that the legislator may grant this right to foreigners who comply with certain requirements specified by law (CCJ 72/2005 of 4 April 2005).

53. For years, OL 4/2000 and RD 2393/2004 – the regulation implementing OL 4/2000, no longer in force – regulated entry of foreigners into Spain. Ever since Spain's accession to the Convention implementing the Schengen Agreement (1985) on 25 June 1991, all Spanish legislation regulating external border crossing is entirely conditioned by and subjected to the aforementioned Convention. In accordance with international law, the requirements that are detailed below are not applied to asylum seekers (Article 25.3 of OL 4/2000). They also do not apply to EU citizens and their family members, who are the subject of the preferential regime defined by RD 240/2007, of 16 February 2007 on the entry, free movement and residence in Spain of citizens of the Member States of the EU and other States signatories of the Agreement on the European Economic Area.[45]

54. Taking into account what has already been indicated, the provisions regulating admission into Spain, as part of the Schengen territory, of non-EU citizens requires, in the first place, that they prove that they are not to be refused entry permission in accordance with a series of exclusion clauses in Article 6 of the Schengen Borders Code (codified)[46] Thus, first of all, whoever wishes to enter Spain should not be the subject of an explicit entry ban, represent a danger for public order, internal security, public health or the international relations of any of the Member States, or be registered as a person not to be granted entry permission by

45. OSG 28 Feb. 2007, No. 57.
46. Article 6 of the currently in force Regulation (EU) 2016/399 reproduces Art. 5 of repealed Regulation (EU) 562/2006.

a Member State in the Schengen Information System (SIS) (Articles 25 of OL 4/2000 and 4 g) and f) of RD 557/2011).[47]

55. Second, entry into Spain must be sought using any of the border crossing points set up for this purpose and during its opening hours, holding one's valid passport or any other travel document ready as proof of identity as provided for by the provisions in the international conventions to which Spain is a party (Article 24.1 of OL 4/2000). If entry is sought not using a border crossing point specifically set up for the purpose of crossing the external border or out of opening hours, the person in question must inform the Spanish authorities of that their presence in Spain within three days from the moment of entry (Articles 25 of OL 4/2000 and 2, 3, 12 and 13 of RD 557/2011). If Spain is entered by crossing an internal border, then the above-mentioned regime does not apply.[48] As an example, that illustrates this point, both non-EU citizens and EU citizens alike, usually cross the Spanish borders with Portugal and France without being subjected to any measure of border control given that those are internal borders of the Schengen Area where the Schengen Borders Code only allows controls on persons under certain circumstances and which are temporary by nature.[49]

56. One aspect that needs to be considered in relation to entry controls are the so-called carriers' sanctions which find their origin in Article 26 of the Convention Implementing the Schengen Agreement and two EU directives: (a) Council Directive 2001/51/EC, of 28 June 2001, supplementing the provisions of Article 26 of the Convention implementing the Schengen Agreement of 14 June 1985, which defines the responsibility of carriers in relation to those passengers who wish to enter the EU;[50] and (b) Council Directive 2004/82/EC, of 29 April 2004, on the obligation of carriers to communicate passenger data of persons carried.[51] Article 26 SIA and these two directives have been implemented by the Spanish authorities through Article 66 of OL 4/2000 and Articles 16 and 18 of RD 557/2011. This means that any carrier is legally obliged to check the documents of all passengers – be it a passport, travel documents or visa – to ascertain that they will be allowed to enter Spain. When required by the Spanish authorities, the carrier will also have to provide passenger data after boarding is finished and before the departure of the vehicle by air, sea or land. If a passenger is denied leave to enter at the corresponding border crossing point due to deficiencies in the documents submitted, the carrier is obliged to take charge of him/her by providing that passenger with adequate living conditions and to cover the cost of repatriating him/her to the country from which he/she came

47. Article 4 g) of RD 557/2011 uses different terminology that that used in the Schengen Borders Code, such as 'national security' or a rather explicit reference to the 'international relations of Spain or other States with which Spain may have signed an agreement in that direction'.
48. This area is defined in contrast with those areas known as internal borders, which are the common land borders, including river and lake borders, of the Member States, as well as those airports and ports for internal flights and regular ferry connections within the States participating in Schengen (Schengen Borders Code II, Art. 2.1).
49. *See*: Arts 25 ff. of Regulation (EU) 2016/399 (Schengen Borders Code II).
50. OJEU EC, L 187/45 of 10 Jul. 2001.
51. OJEU EC, L 261/24 of 6 Aug. 2004.

or to a third country that will guarantee that person's admission and ensure a treatment compatible with human rights. Non-compliance with these legal obligations will lead to the imposition of significant economic sanctions to be imposed on the carrier.

57. The task entrusted to carriers by Spanish legislation to check their passenger's documents, which has its origin in the above-mentioned EU directives and the SIA, has raised criticism amongst Spanish experts, because it effectively means giving the responsibility for migration controls to a private agent where it should be assumed by public authorities.[52] This shifting of responsibility to private actors is qualified as 'an externalisation of document checking obligations' leading to an 'extra-territorialisation of border control', as documents are checked by a carrier before the journey starts, i.e., in another country outside the EU. Moreover, it hinders, in practice, the possibility of, for instance, a potential asylum seeker making the corresponding application, as they will be at a border crossing point that does not comply with the terms of national and EU legislation for the purpose of lodging an asylum application.[53] In addition, it is also a controversial issue that the Spanish authorities requiring the communication of passenger data in advance. It is a complex rule, halfway between the need to prevent irregular immigration and the fight against terrorism. As a matter of fact, this is a legal disposition that the EU adopted at the request of Spain.

58. Together with the previous elements, it is important to remember that entering Spain is usually conditioned upon the possession of a visa by the person wishing to enter the country. This is a classical legal requirement and ultimately an instrument with which gives the States a tool that allows them to exercise a kind of remote control over those wishing to enter their territory, as visa has to be applied for in the country of departure. The Spanish visa requirement is thus a general rule, rather than an exception for those who are not EU citizens. Article 25.2 of OL 4/2000 is clear in this sense: 'except in those cases in which the contrary is established through international agreements "subscribed" to by Spain or through an EU regulation, a visa will, in addition, be required'.[54] In this sense, although EU Member States are entitled to regulate so-called type D visas – allowing stays over ninety days –[55] the competence of regulating type A and type C visa lies with the EU.[56] Everything concerning these two types of visas is set out in Regulation (EC) No.

52. Iglesias Sánchez, S.: 'El régimen de entrada en España: entrada, visados, tránsito y salida del territorio español. Estancias de corta duración: visitas personales, turismo, negocios', in Boza Martínez, D., Donaire Villa, F.J., & Moya Malapeira, D. (Coords.): 'La nueva regulación de la inmigración y la extranjería en España. Régimen jurídico tras la LO 2/2009, el Real Decreto 557/2011 y la Ley 12/2009', Tirant lo Blanch, Valencia, 2012, p. 173.
53. Iglesias Sánchez, S., *supra.*, p. 173.
54. The countries whose citizens are required to hold a visa to enter the European Union are specified on Regulation (EC) No. 539/2001 of the Council, of 15 March 2001, listing the third countries whose nationals must be in possession of visas when crossing the external borders and those whose national are exempt from that requirement (OJEU EC, L 81, of 21 Mar. 2001).
55. Intended for the following purposes: adoption, health care, diplomacy, accompaniment of a relative, self-employment, employment, mission, voluntary work, religious reasons, re-entering, elective residence, family reunification, studies or vacations.

810/2009 of the European Parliament and of the Council, of 13 July 2009, establishing a Community Code on Visas.[57] Nevertheless, OL 4/2000 acknowledged that its provisions in relation to transit and stay visas are valid 'notwithstanding those of Regulation (EC) No. 810/2009, of 13 July, establishing a Community Code on Visas'.[58]

59. These are the seven types of visa defined, in general terms, by Article 25*bis* of OL 4/2000:

a) Transit visa: allows travelling through the international transit zones of Spanish airports or the transit across Spanish territory.
b) Stay visa: allows an uninterrupted stay during a specific period of time or a series of successive stays during a given period, the total length of which must not exceed three months per six months from the date of the first entry.
c) Residence visa: allows living in the country without having to develop a work or professional activity.
d) A residence and work visa: allows its holder to enter the country and reside in Spain for a maximum period of three months for the purpose of starting, during that period, a work or professional activity for which the person has been previously authorised.
e) A temporary residence and work visa: allows its holder to be employed by others for up to nine months within a period of twelve consecutive months.
f) Study visa: allows residence in Spain to attend courses, follow study plans, do research or training work, as well as attending a student exchange programme, gaining work experience or conducting voluntary work, for none of these activities can the holder of the visa be remunerated.
g) Research visa: allows residence in Spain to develop research projects within the framework of a hosting agreement with a research centre.

However, Spanish law establishes that a visa is not required when foreigners are in possession of foreign identity cards or, exceptionally, a 'return authorisation' (Art. 25.2 second paragraph of OL 4/2000). Also, it is not applicable to asylum seekers when they enter Spain. The granting of asylum is regulated by specific asylum rules (Art. 25.3 of OL 4/2000).

In any case, OL 4/2000 also states that it is possible to grant permission to enter Spain to foreigners who do not comply with the requirements established in Art. 25 of that law 'for exceptional humanitarian or public interest reasons or in compliance with the commitments undertaken by Spain' (Art. 25.4 of OL 4/2000).

56. Type A visas are: airport transit visa, valid only in international transit zones in airports. Type C visas are intended for various purposes (business, health care, sport events, invitation, self-employment, employment, mission, religious reasons, studies, transport and tourism) and allow a stay of up to 90 days within a 180-day period.

57. OJEU EU, L 243/I of 15 Sep. 2009. The EU Visa Code cancelled transit visas (known as Type B visas) some time ago.

58. Final provision 5 *bis*.

60. As for the effect that the granting of a visa has on the situation of its holder, Article 27.2 of OL 4/2000 is clear: (a) it allows foreigners to turn up at border crossing points and request permission to enter the country; and (b) it allows them, once their entry into Spain has been effectuated, to stay in Spain under the purpose for which the visa was granted, notwithstanding the obligation to obtain, when required, a 'foreigners identity card'.

61. Finally, Spanish legislation requires foreigners to submit the documents stipulated in the regulation for the purpose of justifying 'the object and conditions of their stay and to prove that they have the necessary financial means to support themselves during their stay in Spain, or that they are capable of legally obtaining those means' (Article 25.2 of OL 4/2000).

§2. Administrative Procedures and Documents

62. Non-EU citizens, when entering Spain, must submit the following documents (Articles 25 of OL 4/2000 and 4 of RD 557/2011): (a) passport or travel document; (b) visa, if it is compulsory to be in possession of it; (c) justification of the object and conditions of entry and stay; (d) proof, if required, of having the necessary means of subsistence – or of being capable of obtaining them – required for their stay and to cover the expenses of their return trip or trip to a third country; (e) when required, a health certificate, as specified in Spanish legislation.

63. Notwithstanding the above, Article 8.2 of RD 557/2011 states that the request of those documents by public officers at the border crossing point is a decision, not a legal duty, which can be adopted depending on the motive and length of the person's stay.

64. The regulation (Article 8.2 of RD 557/2011) provides for differentiated treatment regarding the submission of documents, meaning that the rules which apply, depends on the kind of stay or journey. For all situations a return or tourist ticket may be required, together with:

(a) For business trips, alternatively: an invitation from a company or authority in the terms established by Spanish law to participate in commercial, industrial or any other business meetings;[59] documents proving the existence of commercial or business links with the country; access cards to fairs and conferences.
(b) For tourist or private trips, alternatively: documents issued by the establishment providing accommodation or, in the terms established by the Spanish law, a letter of invitation from a private person acting as a host for the person concerned. The content of these documents must exclusively confirm the existence of

59. *See* Order PRE/1282/2007, of 10 May 2007, on the economic resources that foreigners must demonstrate in order to enter Spain (OSG 11 May 2007, No. 113).

accommodation that will be used by the person concerned, and provide information establishing whether the host will cover, partially or totally, the person's living expenses or not.[60] The confirmation of a booking of an organised trip may also be submitted.

(c) Stays for the purpose of study or vocational training: a certificate of enrolment or documents proving admission by the corresponding education centre.

(d) Journeys for other purposes, alternatively: invitations, bookings or programmes; a certificate of participation in events related to the journey; access cards or receipts.

65. As regards the issuing of visa, they can be requested from and are issued by Spanish consular offices and diplomatic missions, even if OL 4/2000 (Article 27.1) states that there may be exceptions to this rule as per the corresponding regulation (*see* RD 557/2011). There is also the possibility, envisaged by the Union Visa Code (Article 8), that the Spanish State agrees to represent another EU Member State for the purpose of issuing transit or stay visa or being represented by the consular authorities of any one of the twenty-seven other EU Member States. The issuing of visa, rather than being considered arbitrary, must be classed as the exercise of discretion by the administration that may be subject to legal control, just as every administrative action is.[61] Nevertheless and notwithstanding the fact that prior to the 2009 reform of OL 4/2000 this law limited the administration's obligation to substantiate its decisions to those concerning residence, work and family reunification visa refusals;[62] a restriction that is by now already one of the past., Nevertheless, the situation is still far from being fully satisfactory, considering the fact that defending a foreigner's interest is still a difficult matter. Visa refusals are nowadays considered an administrative action that exhausts all administrative remedies. In this sense, only a judicial appeal is possible against them, if the foreigner concerned does not choose to lodge an appeal for revocation, to which they are entitled, before the administrative body that refused to issue the visa in the first place. Considering that a judicial appeal must be filed while outside Spanish territory, the reader will easily understand the difficulty of such enterprise. This is the reason why some experts have suggested the need to carry out a legislative reform that will allow filing an appeal with a higher administrative instance, given that, in such cases, it is deemed more appropriate that a higher administrative body should resolve the matter, rather than the administrative body that issued the refusal in the first place.[63]

---

60. *See* Order PRE/1283/2007, of 10 May 2007, establishing the terms and requirements for the issuance of a letter of invitation by private individuals in favour of foreigners willing to enter the national territory for tourism or private reasons (OSG 11 May 2007, No. 113).
61. In relation to the motivation of visa refusals, the doctrine established by the Spanish Supreme Court (Contentious-Administrative Division) in its judgments of 24 June 2008 (appeal No. 11565/2004) and 28 October 2011 (appeal No. 730/2010) should be taken into consideration.
62. This rule was, however, declared to be unconstitutional according to Art. 24 of the Spanish Constitution by several Constitutional Court judgments (CCJ 236/2007 and CCJ 239/2007 of 19 Dec. 2007; CCJ 260, CCJ 261, CCJ 263 and CCJ 267/2007 of 20 Dec. 2007).
63. Boza Martínez, D., 'Los derechos de los extranjeros en el procedimiento administrativo', in Aja, E. (Coord.), 'Los derechos de los inmigrantes en España', Tirant lo Blanch, Valencia, 2009, pp. 247–278.

66. As for the proof of having sufficient means of subsistence for themselves and the people travelling with them for whom they are responsible, the regulation (Article 9 of RD 557/2011) specifies that this should be regulated by the corresponding ministerial order.[64] According to the above-mentioned provision this regulation, which will in fact determine the level of the required means of subsistence and the way to prove their availability, should provide that the authorities, when assessing the means of subsistence should take into consideration whether the accommodation comprises totally or partially the living expenses of the foreigner and those travelling under their responsibility.

67. In relation to the health requirement, RD 557/2011 (Article 10) establishes that, when thus determined by the Spanish Ministry of the Interior foreigners wishing to enter Spanish territory shall a health certificate issued in their country of origin by medical services appointed for that purpose by the Spanish diplomatic mission or consular office submit at border crossing points. Alternatively, the Ministry will be authorised to subject foreigners and those under their responsibility, upon their arrival at the border crossing point, to a medical examination performed by the competent Spanish health service. The object of this medical examination is to establish that the foreigner is not affected by 'any of the diseases that may have an impact on public health in accordance with the provisions of the 2005 International Health Regulations and the international agreements subscribed by Spain on this respect, notwithstanding the provisions of the EU regulations on the matter'.

68. In any case, Spanish legislation, in line with the provisions of the 2016 Schengen Borders Code (Article 6, section 5 c) establishes that the Spanish authorities – in particular, the *Comisaría General de Extranjería y Fronteras* (Commissioner General for Alien Affairs and Borders)– can, by way of exception, authorise the entry into Spain of foreigners who do not satisfy the requirements specified in Article 25 of OL 4/2000 whenever there are 'extraordinary humanitarian or public interest reasons or the need to comply with international commitments acquired by Spain'. In these cases, the foreigner will be given the corresponding documents. In this respect Spanish legislation, in particular RD 557/2011 (Article 4.2), determines that leave to enter Spain under such circumstances does not in itself irrespective of other circumstances that might be alleged, amount to compliance with the requirements to obtain a residence permit under exceptional circumstances. In brief, it states that entering the country for exceptional reasons does not imply residence under exceptional circumstances. In order to enjoy the latter, the corresponding requirements, as defined in the above-mentioned RD, will have to be satisfied.

69. If foreigners and those travelling with them are in possession of the necessary documents and satisfy the requirements to enter Spain, their entry will actually take place, in which case, their passport or travel document will be stamped or marked as established, unless, according to Spanish law or an international agreement, documents do not need to be stamped. Once the documents have been given

64. *See*: Order PRE/1282/2007, of 10 May 2007, on the means of subsistence the availability of which shall be proved by foreigners in order to enter Spain (OSG 11 May 2007, No. 113).

back to their bearers, they can actually enter the country officially (Article 12.2 of RD 557/2011). If the identity document carried by the foreigner cannot be stamped, the foreigner will have to fill out a form that, once stamped, will be returned to them as confirmation of their lawful entry into the country. Foreigners have to keep this form during their entire stay and submit it, together with their identity documents, when thus required. The stamp includes the date of entry into the country.

70. Despite the abolition of controls at the internal borders between Schengen Member States, Article 13 of RD 557/2011 still obliges every foreigner to personally inform the Spanish police authorities –'entry declaration'– when entering Spanish territory from a country with which Spain has signed a border control removal agreement (Schengen Area). This is, however, a legal obligation that is frequently breached in practice. In any case, the regulation specifies that, in case the declaration is not made at the moment of entry, the foreigner has three more working days to make it at any national police station or an Aliens Affairs Office.

71. The insertion into OL 4/2000 (Article 25.5), via OL 2/2009 of the possibility for the Spanish authorities to register nationals from non-EU States entering Spanish territory, for the purpose of controlling the duration of their legal stay in the country, was new to Spanish legislation. Nevertheless, it is a legal provision that has not yet been effectively developed through the corresponding ministerial order of the Ministry of Presidential Affairs (Article 14.2 of RD 557/2011).

Chapter 3. Entry Refusal

72. When addressing the issue of entry refusal one must be aware that this may have its origin not in the foreigner's non-compliance with the above-mentioned legal requirements, but also in the circumstances described in Article 26 of OL 4/2000 – *see also* Article 11 of RD 557/2011– under the heading 'refusal of entry to Spain'. The following two circumstances are, in fact, the circumstances considered by the law:

(a) foreigners who have previously been expelled from Spain, for as long as an entry ban is valid; and
(b) foreigners whose entry is forbidden 'for another legally established cause or by virtue of international agreements signed by Spain'.

73. In relation to the entry ban, Article 11 of RD 557/2011 specifies that it affects foreigners who:

(a) have previously been the subject of a return action and are presently the subject of an entry ban for the period determined by the corresponding return agreement;
(b) are known, through diplomatic channels, Interpol or any other international cooperation organisation, whether judiciary or police-related, to be claimed, in relation to a criminal law decision following a sentence for a serious non-political crime, by the legal or police authorities of another country, as long as the events that are the reason for this claim are also considered a crime in Spain, notwithstanding their arrest, when applicable;
(c) have been the subject of an explicit entry ban by decision of the Minister of the Interior, due to activities contrary to the interest of Spain, that are contrary to human rights standards, or in connection with criminal organisations, whether national or international, or to any other legal or administrative reason that can justify such decision, notwithstanding their arrest, when applicable;
(d) are forbidden to enter the country according to an international agreement signed by Spain or a provision of Union law unless it is deemed necessary to make an exception on humanitarian or national interest grounds.

74. As can be seen, the capacity of the Ministry of the Interior to impose an entry ban is quite ample, as a consequence of the terms established by the above-mentioned Article 11 of RD 557/2011. Along the same line, the possibility to make an exception to this ban because of humanitarian or public interest reasons or the need to comply with international agreements is formulated in broader terms that are subject to the discretionary power of the corresponding governmental body, in this case the Commissioner General on Alien Affairs and Borders (Article 24.4 of OL 4/2000). In this last case, leave to enter the country does not imply the acknowledgement of a right of residence. Therefore, a foreigner benefiting from this leave will have to initiate the procedure to obtain a residence permit for exceptional reasons after having been granted leave to enter (Article 4.2 of RD 557/2011). This issue is the subject of harmonisation within the EU through a controversial rule, known as the 'Return Directive', actually Directive 2008/115/EC, of the European Parliament and of the Council, of 16 December 2008, on common standards and procedures in Member States for returning illegally staying third-country nationals.[65]

75. Title II of the 2016 Schengen Borders Code (codified text) specifically addresses the crossing of external borders, as well as entry conditions and the refusal to grant entry permission.

76. The 2016 Schengen Borders Code (Article 8) provides for two basic types of border checks on persons, in the case of cross-border movements at the external borders: (a) minimum check,[66] and (b) thorough check.[67] In the case of people enjoying the right of free movement according to EU law, the minimum check is the normal procedure. In the case of third-country nationals, and independent of them undergoing a minimum check, a thorough check will be compulsory, both when entering and leaving the Schengen Area. In the case of Spanish legislation, this thorough check is linked to the so-called refusal to grant entry permission and the return procedure, as regulated by Articles 26.2 and 60 of OL 4/2000 and Article 15 of RD 557/2011. This procedure also applies to those enjoying the right of free movement when a minimum check proves to be insufficient. This thorough check allows the Spanish security forces to carry out a further investigation on a person wishing to enter the country.

77. A refusal to grant entry permission is actually an administrative procedure despite its special characteristics, in the sense that, because it affects the foreigner's freedom and autonomy, the Spanish legislator attaches to it a series of guarantees that are not common in other ordinary administrative procedures defined in accordance with the provisions of the 2016 Schengen Borders Code, particularly those included in Article 14. To that end, the current regulation establishes that foreigners who do not comply with entry requirements will actually be refused entry permission through a substantiated decision that will inform them of the possibility to lodge an appeal against it, the period for doing it and the authority before which the

---

65. OJEU EU, L 348/98 of 24 Dec. 2008. *See* Art. 11.
66. This check includes verifying the person's identity and the validity and authenticity of their identity and travel documents. Nevertheless, Art. 8.2, third paragraph, of the 2016 Schengen Borders Code states that, on a non-systematic basis, border police may, during minimum check, consult national and European databases with the purpose of ensuring that those persons are not a genuine, present and sufficiently serious threat to internal security, public policy, international relations with other Member States or public health.
67. The thorough check requires the authorities to verify whether the conditions governing entry laid down in Art. 6.1 of the 2016 Schengen Borders Code, are satisfied as well as thoroughly scrutinising the documents authorising that person's stay and their pursuit of a professional activity, including the authenticity of their visa, submitted if required. At the same time, this provision considers the possibility of, by way of exception, checking with the Visa Information Service, using the number of the visa sticker in all cases and, on a random basis, the number of the visa sticker in combination with a verification of fingerprints.

appeal should be formalised.[68] At the same time, the rule establishes the right to legal assistance provided by a lawyer, who may be a public defender, and as well as an interpreter. These professionals are allowed to intervene from the moment that the check is being performed at the border crossing point (Articles 26.2 of OL 4/2000 and 15 of RD 557/2011). This last legal provision differs from the general terms in which the 2016 Schengen Borders Code provides for professional assistance: 'A written indication of contact points to provide information on representatives competent to act on behalf of the third-country national in accordance with national law shall also be given to the third-country national' (Article 14.3 of the Schengen Borders Code).

78. Foreigners who are refused permission to enter the country are obliged to return to their point of origin (Article 60.1 of OL 4/2000). According to the 2016 Schengen Borders Code (Article 14.3, second paragraph), lodging an appeal does not have suspensive effect for the decision to refuse entry permission. In this sense, from the moment the decision to refuse entry permission is issued, the foreigner passes from a situation of detention, while the corresponding migration check is being performed, to a situation of actual deprivation of liberty. This circumstance is made evident by the Spanish rule, which establishes that the decision to refuse entry permission entails the immediate adoption of the necessary measures to facilitate the foreigner's return within the shortest possible period. If return is delayed for more than seventy-two hours, the authority having refused entry permission will have to ask the investigating judge to determine the place where the person must be detained before departure from the country (Article 60.1, second paragraph of OL 4/2000). Moreover, it states that 'detention of the foreigner following a refusal to grant entry permission for the purpose of effectuating his return, must be communicated to the Ministry of Foreign Affairs and to the embassy or consulate of his country of origin' (Article 60.4 of OL 4/2000).

79. From a conceptual point of view, it is important to differentiate between refusals to grant entry permission and return orders. A refusal to grant entry permission is a declarative act by virtue of which the foreigner cannot enter Spain due to legal reasons. This act is a fundamental requirement to issue a return order, which is, in brief, the administrative act that establishes the compulsory return of the foreigner to his country of origin, although practice shows that these two acts are usually issued together. There is a conceptual difference between the return order and other orders, such as those imposing a removal or an expulsion order, which is that, in the latter two, return to the country of origin or departure also entails a re-entry ban for a specified period of time (*see* Article 58 of OL 4/2000).

---

68. The administrative decision to refuse entry permission and the order to return the foreigner to his country of origin does not exhaust all administrative remedies (fourteenth additional provision of RD 557/2011). Therefore, it is possible to lodge an administrative appeal against that decision, as a first step before resorting to a judicial remedy.

80. Finally, it has already been mentioned that, in the case of the Spanish cities of Ceuta and Melilla, access to and border control from Morocco is subject to a special regime, laid down in Article 41 of the 2016 Schengen Borders Code. This regime determines a different dynamic in border checks that lead, for instance, to refusing entry permission at the border without a corresponding administrative decision, notwithstanding the provisions of Article 26 of OL 4/2000. This is a consequence of the intense cross-border traffic of persons at these borders, which prevents an exhaustive control of those entering and leaving the two cities.

Part II. Right of Residence: General Provisions

Chapter 1. Short Stay

§1. Conditions for Short Stay

81. The generally assumed circumstance that not every foreigner wishing to cross the borders of a country has the intention of staying and residing in that country lies at the heart of Spanish law, which is in line with the Union rules, that conceptually differentiate between the two distinct legal situations of stay and residence (Article 29 of OL 4/2000). Thus, Spanish law defines stay, understood as a short-time stay, as the presence on Spanish territory for a period of time no longer than ninety days in one hundred and eighty days period, starting from the date of the foreigner's first entry into the country (Articles 30.1 of LO 4/2000 and 28.1 of RD 557/2011).[69] In addition, the legal norm recalls the existence of a special legal regime envisaged for stays for the purpose of study, student exchange, non-remunerated internship or volunteer service grounds, as set out in Article 33 of OL 4/2000. Residence is identified as cases in which foreigners live in Spain as holders of a residence permit (Article 30 of OL 4/2000).

82. The way in which Spanish law has defined the concepts of stay and residence is not at all ideal, because there are numerous cases in which foreigners remain in the country for quite a long time – certainly not for a short stay – without residing there. The classical example is precisely the above-mentioned case of students, exchange students, trainees and volunteers, all of whom are the subject of a

69. As regards the concept of 'first entry', the doctrine established by the European Court of Justice judgment of 3 October 2006 (C-241/05) (Bot case), in Art. 20 of the Convention implementing the Schengen Agreement, in a case concerning the entry of a Romanian citizen into the European Union before Romania became an EU Member State, should be taken into account. The court concluded that this concept must be interpreted as meaning that it 'refers, besides the very first entry into the territories of the Contracting States to that agreement, to the first try into those territories taking place after the expiry of a period of six months from that very first entry and also to any other first entry taking place after the expiry of any new period of six months following an earlier date of first entry'.
Article 6.2 of the 2016 Schengen Borders Code establishes that 'the date of entry shall be considered as the first day of stay on the territory of the Member States and the date of exit shall be considered as the last day of stay on the territory of the Member States. Periods of stay authorised under a residence or a long-stay visa shall not be taken into account in the calculation of the duration of stay on the territory of the Member States'.

special regime. Nevertheless, it should not be forgotten that the Spanish legal perspective finds its origin in the harmonisation achieved by the 2016 Schengen Borders Code, in particular by Article 6. Notwithstanding the fact that short stays are defined by using only the time factor, the Spanish rule states that all foreigners must, when required, specify and justify the reason for applying for permission to enter and stay in Spain (Article 8 of RD 557/2011).

§2. Administrative Procedures and Documents for Short Stay

83. Article 6 of the 2016 Schengen Borders Code establishes that the entry conditions for third-country nationals in the event of short stays are the following:[70]

(a) being in the possession of a valid travel document entitling the holder to cross the border:
   (i) the validity of which extends at least three more months after the intended date of departure from the territory of the Member States. In a justified case of emergency, this obligation may be waived; and
   (ii) that has been issued within the previous ten years.
(b) being in possession of a valid visa, when required according to Council Regulation (EC) No. 539/2011, except when the foreigners hold a valid residence permit or a valid long-stay visa;
(c) being in possession of documents that justify the purpose and conditions of the intended stay and having sufficient means of subsistence, both for the duration of the intended stay and for the return to their country of origin or transit to a third country into which they are certain to be admitted, or being in a position to obtain those means lawfully;
(d) not being a person for whom an alert has been issued in the Schengen Information System;
(e) not representing a threat to public policy, internal security, public health or the international relations of any of the Member States, in particular, where no alert has been issued in a Member State's national databases on the same grounds.

84. In relation to short-stay visas, RD 557/2011(Article 29) defines two categories:

(1) Uniform visa: valid for either transiting the Schengen Area for a period no longer than the time necessary to make such a journey or staying within the

70. The refusal of third-country nationals under these circumstances has occasionally generated diplomatic tensions between Spain and some Latin American countries, like Mexico or Brazil. It must be remembered that Spain is the main entry to Europe for citizens of that region of the world. Those diplomatic tensions have finally been resolved through dialogue and negotiation. However, in the case of Brazil, ever since mid-2012 Spanish citizens willing to enter that country have to comply with similar entry requirements as Brazilian citizens wishing to enter Spain in accordance with the 2016 Schengen Borders Code (Martí Martí, X. & González García, G.J.J., 'La política común de visados de corta duración de la Unión Europea: el camino hacia una política inteligente', *Revista de Derecho Migratorio y Extranjería*, No. 41, 2016, pp. 31–32).

Schengen Area for a maximum of ninety days in one hundred and eighty days period. The regulation specifies that this visa may allow one, two or multiple entries or stays, the total duration of which cannot exceed ninety days per semester.

(2) Visa with limited territorial validity: this allows crossing or staying in the territory of one or more States within the Schengen Area, but not all of them.[71] Again the Spanish norm establishes that the total duration of the transit or stay may not exceed ninety days in one hundred and eighty days period.[72]

85. The entry into force of Council Regulation (EC) No. 539/2001, of 15 March 2001, listing the third countries whose nationals must be in possession of visas when crossing the external borders and those whose national are exempt from that requirement unless they hold a valid residence permit,[73] has obliged Spain to terminate, in certain cases, or to suspend, in others, various bilateral agreements regarding an exemption of short-stay visa that Spain had signed with certain Latin American countries, like Barbados and Jamaica (1986), Colombia (2001), Peru (1992), Ecuador (2003) and Bolivia (2007). Likewise, several other agreements on the exemption of short-stay visas had to be signed with various countries to comply with Article 1.2 and Annex II of Regulation (EC) 539/2001. Spain participates very actively in negotiations the purpose of which is to update the list of countries whose nationals are subjected to or exempted from the obligation of to hold a visa when visiting the EU. Spain's interest is to improve the situation of some Latin American countries. Thus Spain has realised that, for instance, Peru and Colombia were being placed on the list of countries exempted from that obligation in 2014.

86. The Spanish law specifies that any short-stay visa application must be examined and decided upon, in a substantiated manner, by the diplomatic missions or consular offices appointed by the Spanish government (Article 30.3 of RD 557/2011). If the decision is a refusal to issue a visa, this must be notified to the applicant and justified using the form in Annex VI of the Union Visa Code. This decision must also inform the administrative appeal procedures that the person may lodge against the decision.[74]

---

71. While the uniform visa is inspired by the provisions of the Schengen Borders Code, visas with limited territorial validity are regulated by Art. 25 of the Community Visa Code and have the purpose of providing EU Member States with a tool that allows them to respond, with greater discretionary power, to situations deemed to be exceptional for humanitarian, national interest, international obligations or whatever other valid reason, even when the applicant has already enjoyed a three-month stay within that 180-day period. A visa with limited territorial validity is only valid for the territory of the issuing Member State and only exceptionally for those Schengen Member States that authorise it.
72. In accordance with Arts 25*bis* of OL 4/2000, entitled 'Types of visa', Spanish law, as is customary practice in all the countries of the European Union, and in line with the Art. 3 of the Regulation (EC) No. 810/2009 (Visa Code), introduces airport transit visa, a document that finally allows the transit of a foreigner, who is not a citizen of the European Union, through the international area of the Spanish airports, without entering Spanish territory. *See also*: Art. 25 and following of RD 557/2011.
73. OJEU EC, L 81/1 of 23 Mar. 2001.
74. As regards the management of visa, it the rules in Regulation (EC) No. 767/2008 of the European Parliament and of the Council, of 9 July 2008, concerning the Visa Information System (VIS) and

87. A variation of this type of procedure is described by Article 31 of RD 557/2011, which includes the granting of a so-called visas issued at the external borders.[75] These visas, which may be issued both as uniform visa or visa with limited territorial validity, are granted, under duly justified exceptional circumstances – the reader will observe the broad legal formula – or by appointment of the Ministry of Foreign Affairs and Cooperation, directly by the members of the police service of the Ministry of the Interior in charge of controlling the entry of people to the Spanish territory. A transit visa granted to seamen wishing to embark or disembark at a port where they must work or have already worked also falls into this category.

88. The possibility envisaged by Article 36 of RD 557/2011 in relation to certain entry circumstances or documents qualified as irregular is also exceptional. In particular, this provision establishes that, by way of exception, 'and as long as there are humanitarian or public interest reasons or international obligations', the head of the Ministry of the Interior or the head of the Ministry of Labour may authorise the stay in Spanish territory for a maximum period of three months within a one hundred and eighty days period to foreigners who have entered the country holding incorrect documents or no documents at all or through places not designated for this purpose.

89. In any case, independent of Union and Spanish legislation on short stays, a series of agreements which the EU has concluded with several countries – Albania, Azerbaijan, Bosnia and Herzegovina, Cabo Verde, Russia, etc. – on political grounds and for the purpose of facilitating the issuing of visa to their citizens are to be considered. These agreements operate under the principle of reciprocity in Regulation (EC) 539/2001 (Article 1.4) and allow Spain to issue visa to the nationals of those countries for stays of ninety days within a one hundred and eighty days period. Although these agreements help to promote economic, cultural and other relations, they ultimately make the management of visa more complicated for the Spanish authorities, who are obliged to work with different norms.

---

the exchange of data between Member States on short-stay visas (OJEU EU, L 218 of 13 Aug. 2008), which envisages the creation of a database of granted and refused visa applications, known as the VIS must also be taken into account. This database provides the States of the Schengen Area with a variety of information on visa applicants. Data are preserved for a period of fifty-nine months.

See also: Council Regulation (EC) No. 1683/95, of 29 May 1995, laying down a uniform format for visas (OJEU EC, L 164 of 14 Jul. 1995) and Council Regulation (EC) No. 333/2002, of 18 February 2002, on a uniform format for forms for affixing the visa issued by Member States to persons holding travel documents not recognised by the Member State drawing up the form (OJEU EC, L 53/4 of 18 Feb. 2002).

75. In any case, The Spanish regulation refers to the procedures established by EU law to grant this type of visa, in particular the Schengen Borders Code and the Union Visa Code (Art. 31.3 of RD 557/2011). More specifically, Art. 35 of the Union Visa Code includes the possibility of issuing visa at border crossing points in exceptional cases if the applicant fulfils the conditions laid down in Art. 6 of the Schengen Borders Code, his return is guaranteed, he has not been in a position to apply for a visa in advance and they submit supporting documents substantiating unforeseeable and imperative reasons for entry are submitted. If the conditions of Art. 6 2016 Schengen Border Code are not complied with, a visa with limited territorial validity may, nevertheless, be granted.

§3. LEGAL POSITION IN THE EVENT OF SHORT STAY

90. The general principle is that foreigners authorised to stay in Spain find themselves in a legal position that is different to that of foreigners who have been issued a residence permit. In fact, in terms of rights, OL 4/2000 differentiates between those granted to 'foreigners' – a term that includes persons in an irregular situation, for instance, those who are neither in the possession of a short-stay visa nor a residence permit – and those granted to 'foreigners who are legally in Spain' or 'residents'. Undoubtedly, foreigners with a short-stay visa are individuals who belong to either one of the two first legal categories – (1) foreigners and (2) foreigners legally in Spain. They benefit from the rights that are granted to them by Spanish law, even if neither their status, nor their rights are comparable to those enjoyed by residents.

91. Article 3.1 of OL 4/2000 states that 'foreigners' in Spain are entitled to all the rights and freedoms acknowledged in Title I of the SC, in the terms established by international agreements, OL 4/2000 and the laws that implement it. The general interpretative criterion is that foreigners enjoy the rights granted to them by OL 4/2000 on equal terms with Spaniards. Over the years, as a consequence of the frequent changes seen in Spanish migration legislation, as mentioned previously in this work, the list of rights in the above-mentioned OL has not remained unaltered. Initially, the right to the necessary documentation, freedom of movement, education, healthcare and basic social services and benefits were all granted to foreigners. The reform of the OL realised with the passing of OL 2/2009 increased the number of rights and modified the terms in which the rights already included in the OL 4/2000. As a result of this amendment amongst others the following rights were included in OL 4/2000: the right of assembly, demonstration, association and the right to organise and to strike. A foreigner holding a short-stay visa is therefore entitled to all those rights. The fact that some of these rights cannot be easily exercised in practice, given the limited validity of this type of visa and the fact that they do not entitle their holders to a residence or work permit, is a different matter.

92. After ninety days from the foreigner's date of entry into Spain or the Schengen Area, the general criterion in relation to short-stay visa is that the foreigner will have to leave Spain, given that their permit will have expired. Nevertheless, if they wish to stay longer than those ninety days, this is only possible under the following two circumstances: (a) obtaining an extension of authorised stay; or (b) obtaining a residence permit.

93. In relation to an extension of a short stay, Spanish law provides differently depending on whether the previous stay was subject to the visa regime or not. If a visa was required for a short stay and if this visa was valid for less than three months, a stay may be extended up to ninety days, within a one hundred and eighty days period (Article 30.3 of OL 4/2000). Foreigners who are subject to the visa regime can never extend their stay in Spain beyond those ninety days. In relation to visa renewal this is not only determined by Spain's law, for instance Article 34 of RD 557/2001 on Spanish authorities in charge of examining and deciding upon extension applications, but also by EU law and, particularly, the Union Visa Code.

More specifically, Article 33 of that Code that includes the possibility for the Member State authorities to authorise an extension of a stay in two different situations: (a) when the competent authority of the Member State considers that the visa holder has provided proof of humanitarian or force majeure reasons preventing them from leaving the country before the expiry of the period of validity or of the duration of the stay authorised by the visa; and (b) when the visa holder provides proof of serious personal reasons justifying that extension. Curiously enough, in this second case extension requires the payment of a EUR 30 fee, whereas it is totally free of charge in the first situation.

94. In the event of short stays for which no visa is required, the general rule is that, when 'exceptional circumstances occur to justify it', it is possible to authorise the stay of a foreigner in Spain beyond the initial three months (Article 30.4 of OL 4/2000). Being a legal action with great discretionary power for the administration – see the reference to 'exceptional circumstances' – the Spanish government chose to establish quite a complex administrative procedure (Article 32 of RD 557/2011). An important aspect of this procedure is that it is not possible to extend a visa for employment purposes and that the documents that must be submitted by the foreigner allow him to provide proof of the above-mentioned exceptional circumstances justifying the extension. In the case that the extension of stay is refused, the reasons for this decision of the Spanish authorities must be specified. Additionally, foreigners applying for an extension of their stay must not be the subject of a return or expulsion administrative procedure or an entry ban.

95. As for the possibility of obtaining a residence permit, which, in brief, implies a change in the legal position of the person, who would move from a situation of stay to a situation of residence, the general principle is that, generally speaking, short-stay visa cannot be transformed automatically into residence permits when a foreigner is already present in Spain. Thus, moving from one legal status to another – i.e., from stay to residence – is only possible by applying for a residence permit under the exceptional circumstances regime, which, amongst other aspects, requires a foreigner to be in an irregular residence situation. Again, the underlying principle is that of an impossibility of automatically transforming a short-stay visa into a residence permit. By excluding any connection between the stay regime and the residence regime foreigners are informed that in no way will authorisation to stay in the country help them in obtaining a residence permit, which is far more demanding in terms of requirements to be met. The purpose is to avoid a so-called call effect, which might lead certain groups of immigrants to believe that residence in Spain or the EU is more easily attainable if there is a previous authorisation to stay.

96. The following exception to the above-mentioned principle has been included in the Spanish law: the collective management of hiring in the country of origin, regulated by Article 39 of OL 4/2000. In effect, Article 29 a) second paragraph of RD 557/2001 establishes that, in the case envisaged in the above-mentioned provision of the OL, a stay visa will authorise the holder to look for employment and to apply for a residence and work permit in Spain during its period of validity and under the terms specified in Spanish law.

§4. Position of Family Members

97. In relation to the family members of short-stay visa holders, the logic behind Spanish migration law, as provided for by Union law, is that of allowing the accompaniment of the by the latter. A different issue is whether they are required or not to be in possession of short-stay visa, something that depends on the provisions of Regulation (EC) 539/2001, which is the Union norm law listing the countries whose citizens are and which are not compelled to hold a short-stay visa. If the abovementioned relatives present themselves at the border crossing point without the corresponding visa, they are given the best possible conditions to obtain it.[76]

98. Nevertheless, from a factual point of view, and considering that a stay is a legal situation that only allows a person to remain in Spain for a period of less than ninety days, family reunification – an issue that will be examined in detail in § 4 of the next chapter, where the residence regime is analysed – is not really an option for these family members. Article 41 of RD 557/2011 legally acknowledges this possibility in relation to foreigners who have applied for a stay permit for study, student exchange, non-remunerated internship or volunteer service grounds, which, as mentioned before, is a type of permit that can exceptionally exceed the duration of ninety days. On this issue, *see* Chapter 2 of Part III.

76. In this sense, the main reference is the doctrine of the European Court of Justice's judgment of 25 July 2002 (Case C-459/99, *MRAX*, ECLI:EU:C:2002:461). Likewise, the Union court has established that, in those cases, family members shall not be required to be in possession of residence visas (European Court of Justice (Second Chamber), judgment of 6 April 2005, Case C-157/03, *European Commission v. Spain*, ECLI:EU:C:2005:225).

Chapter 2. Residence

§1. Conditions for Residence

99. Although residence is classified by Article 29 of OL 4/2000 as one of the two situations in which a foreigner can be lawfully in Spain – the other one being a stay, analysed in the previous chapter – the distinctive legal treatment that the Spanish law gives to one legal concept and the other distinguishes residence from stay. Thus, while 'stay' is defined by Article 30 of OL 4/2000, 'residence' is not defined at all in Spanish law. The law only states that residents are foreigners who are in Spain and hold a residence permit (Article 30 bis of OL 4/2000). Section 2 of this provision clarifies that residents may be in a situation of either temporary or long-term residence.

100. Despite the lack of legal definition in Spanish law, it is important to notice from a conceptual point of view that, within the field of Spanish migration law, the status of residence does not require a foreigner's desire to stay in Spain indefinitely, though this is the factor that differentiates residence from stay. Stay necessarily implies residing in Spain for less than ninety days, whereas residence is usually identified by a certain desire to remain permanently in the country.

101. Article 21 of OL 4/2000 defines temporary residence as a situation in which the foreigner is authorised to stay in Spain for a period of more than ninety days and less than five years. RD 557/2011 (Article 45.1) specifies that this will be so notwithstanding the rules on stays for the purpose of study, student exchange, non-remunerated internship or to provide a volunteer service, which will be analysed later.[77] There are two basic categories of temporary residence: (a) temporary residence as a general category, which is thoroughly regulated in Title IV of RD 557/2011 (Articles 45–122); and (b) temporary residence under exceptional circumstances, as defined by Articles 31 and 31*bis* of OL 4/2000 and developed in

77. The temporary residence regime in Spain witnessed a significant change through the amendment of OL 4/2000 implemented by OL 2/2009, as a consequence of Spain's obligation to transpose a whole series of EU directives on migration issues, the deadlines of which had long passed in many cases. Some of those directives were: (a) Council Directive 2005/71/EC, of 12 October 2005 (OJEU EU, L 289/15 of 3 Nov. 2005), on a specific procedure for admitting third-country nationals for the purposes of scientific research, which led to the incorporation to OL 4/2000 of a new article, number 38*bis*, as well as to a new regulatory development in RD 557/2011 (Arts 73–84); (b) Council Directive 2004/114/EC, of 13 December 2004 (OJEU EU, L 375/12 of 23 Dec. 2004), on the conditions of admission of third-country nationals for the purposes of studies, pupil exchange, unremunerated training or voluntary service, according to which Art. 33 of OL 4/2000 and its regulation were modified; (c) Council Directive 2009/50/EC, of 25 May 2009 (OJEU, L 155/17, of 18 Jun. 2009), on the conditions of entry and residence of third-country nationals for the purposes of highly qualified employment, which led to the incorporation of a new Article, number 38*ter*, to OL 4/2000 and to its regulatory development; (d) Council Directive 2004/81/EC, of 29 April 2004 (OJEU EU, L 261/19 of 29 Apr. 2001), on the residence permit issued to third-country nationals who are victims of trafficking in human beings or who have been the subject of an action to facilitate illegal immigration, who cooperate with the competent authorities; (e) Directive 2008/115/EC of the European Parliament and of the Council, of 16 December 2008 (OJEU EU, L 348/98 of 24 Dec. 2008), on common standards and procedures in Member States for returning illegally staying third-country nationals.

Title V of RD 557/2011 (Articles 123–146). In relation to the legal treatment of this concept, the brief specifications included in the Spanish law – basically two provisions – are, at the very least, noteworthy, especially when compared to the extensive regulatory covering 101 provisions.

102. Article 32 of OL 4/2000 defines long-term residence as the legal situation that authorises foreigners to reside and work in Spain indefinitely and under the same conditions as Spaniards. With regard to this legal situation, the temporary nature of residence is a legal configuration in Spanish law as a prerequisite for long-term residence. It is not possible to acquire the status of long-term resident in Spain without having lived temporarily, during a specified period of time, in Spain or any other EU Member State. As provided for by law, a long-term resident is a person who, in all that concerns residing and working in Spain, is on an equal footing with Spaniards. This equality has very important practical consequences, which notably differentiate this legal situation from that of persons who are only authorised to reside temporarily in Spain. Holders of a long-term residence and work permit: (a) will not have to periodically apply for a permit renewal; (b) are entitled to public housing support under the same conditions as Spaniards (Article 13 of OL 4/2000); and (c) can apply for family reunification (Article 18.1 of OL 4/2000), something that temporary residents cannot do (unless they are researchers or holders of the EU blue card).

§2. Administrative Procedures and Documents for Residence

103. The acquisition of both temporary and long-term residence status requires the Spanish administrative authorities to issue a permit that entails the processing of a so-called administrative record. When processing an administrative record, the Spanish authorities will have to take into consideration not only the corresponding dispositions of OL 4/2000 and its regulations, but also, in all that concerns the record and is not specified in those laws, the relevant provisions of the current Law on the Administrative Procedure – Law 39/2015, of 1 October 2015, on the common administrative procedure of public administrations.[78]

104. Another point that has to be taken into consideration in all situations regarding the administrative procedure that has to be followed in order to obtain a residence permit is that acquiring a resident status does not necessarily mean that previously a visa has been applied for and obtained. In effect, and even though Article 25.2 of OL 4/2000 makes the entry into Spain conditional on the issuing of a visa, which is thus necessary for the foreigner to obtain before presenting himself at the Spanish border, the truth is that the law acknowledges a number of situations in which this requirement is not enforceable or where residence permission may be granted to persons having entered the country with a visa that does not authorise them to reside or to reside and work in Spain. It is possible to enter Spanish territory with a job search visa or a study visa, which are both of a different nature from

78. OSG 2 Oct. 2015, No. 236.

those mentioned above. Likewise, as indicated before, there are a number of situations in which Spanish law does not require a person to obtain a visa, as a visa can neither be required according to an international agreement to which Spain is a party, nor by EU law. More specifically, Article 25.4 of OL 4/2000 specifies an number of situations in which the obligation to obtain a visa or even supply documentary evidence to justify the stay in Spain cannot be imposed on a person due to various extraordinary humanitarian or public interest reasons or the need to comply with international commitments entered into by Spain. These situations will be analysed in Chapter 5 of Part III.

105. Visa applications have to be made with the Spanish diplomatic mission or consular office in the territory where the applicant lives. As a general rule an application has to be submitted in person by the applicant (third additional disposition, second section, of OL 4/2000). Exceptions to this requirement, which dates back to the reform of OL 4/2000 by OL 14/2003, are provided for in certain situations. In these cases, the application may be made by a legally authorised representative. These situations include an applicant who lives a long way from the place where the diplomatic mission or consular office is located and who is unable to travel for justified reasons – as, for instance, when the geographical distance makes the trip very costly – or that of applicants living in Spain who are applying for family reunification.

106. Having said this, Spanish law does include the possibility for the diplomatic mission or consular office to request the applicant to appear before the Spanish authorities in person in order to be interviewed (tenth additional disposition of RD 557/2011). This personal interview is recorded in the corresponding minutes, signed by those present at the meeting. The object of this interview is to allow the authorities to verify the applicant's identity, the validity of the documents submitted and the veracity of the person's motives to apply for the visa. If, in the course of the interview, the representatives of the Spanish administration conclude that the person's identity, the documents' validity or the veracity of the motives to apply for the visa is not sufficiently proved, they can refuse to issue a visa. The procedure is also considered to be terminated when, having been called for a personal interview, the applicant does not appear before the authorities, unless there is a duly justified reason that explains the applicant's absence.[79]

107. Once the visa has been issued, the holder can enter Spanish territory during the document's validity period, which is never beyond three months. Once in the country, a foreigner has to apply in person and within one month from entry for a foreign identity card with the competent Spanish office. This card is issued for the duration of the temporary residence permit and has to be collected by the applicant

79. It should be taken into account that the granting of the visa has a discretionary character. In this sense, the ninth additional disposition of RD 557/2011 establishes that the decision on whether to grant a visa or not will respond to the interests of the state and the implementation of international commitments on these matters undertaken by the Kingdom of Spain.

in person. When the residence period is longer than six months and, exceptionally, in those cases in which envisaged residence is shorter than that, it is obligatory to apply for the card.

108. Residence authorisation is granted or denied by the Government Delegate's or sub-delegate's Office in Spain where the foreigner is applying for residence permission. An application for residence authorisation has to be sent by telematic means to the aforementioned Government Delegate or sub-delegate by the diplomatic mission or consular office where the foreigner started the administrative procedure to reside in Spain. A residence visa includes the initial residence authorisation granted by the above-mentioned Government Delegate's or sub-delegate's Office, which is valid from the date that the foreigner enters Spain.

§3. Legal Position of Residents

109. The first temporary residence permit granted to a foreigner is valid for a period of one year (Article 49.2 of RD 557/2011) and may be renewed for another two years, with the exception of situations in which a long-term or EU long-term resident permit has to be applied for (Article 51.7 of RD 557/2011). Once the granting of the renewal has been notified, the permit holder has one month to apply for the renewal of his foreign identity card (Article 51.9 of RD 557/2011).

110. An interesting aspect of Spanish law is that it does not preclude foreigners who have violated Spanish law from applying for the renewal of their temporary residence permit. In particular, the current norm (Article 51.5 of RD 557/2011) provides for the possibility of renewing the residence permit issue to foreigners: (a) who have been convicted for having committed an offence and have served their sentence, (b) who have been pardoned and (c) who are the subject of conditional remission or a suspended sentence. However, the norm also specifies that, while evaluating the possibility of renewal, the administration should take into consideration, among other aspects, the foreigner's 'non-compliance with their tax and Social Security obligations' or 'their criminal record' (Article 37.7 of OL 4/2000).

111. If the renewal application is submitted in time – i.e., within sixty days prior to the expiry date of the current permit – the validity of the current permit will be extended until the administration decides on the requested renewal. This norm obviously intends to avoid a situation in which the applicant would be living in Spain without a valid permit to do so. This extension is effective even if the renewal is applied for three months after the current permit expires, although, in such cases, the administration has three months to issue a decision on the application. Consequently, the norm expressly indicates that, should the renewal not be decided upon within this period, the 'silence' will be understood as favourable to the granting of the renewal (Article 51.8 of RD 557/2011).

112. On a final note, administrative competence in migration affairs is not necessarily a State competence in Spain. Thus, RD 557/2011 concerns the executive competence of the autonomous regional governments to grant work permits whenever their Statutes of Autonomy thus provide.[80]

113. Notwithstanding the time that has passed since the adoption of and the successive reforms of OL 4/2000, the Spanish legislator has never found it necessary to regulate the transition from authorised temporary residence to long-term temporary residence. The absence of integral legal treatment of this issue means that, sometimes, a foreigner wishing to change his temporary resident status for a long-term residence permit will have to leave Spain in order to obtain a visa, which he did not need when he first entered the country.

114. Notwithstanding the above, RD 557/2011 does regulate the transition between certain administrative situations of foreigners living in Spain – in Title XII, specifically denominated entitled 'Modification of the situation of foreigners in Spain' – so that they do not the need to obtain a visa first. Four situations are provided for:

(1) From the situation of stay for the purpose of study, research, training or internship to the residence and work situation, or to the residence situation excluding a work permit (Article 199 of RD 557/2001). The employer hiring the foreigner must submit a permit application, specifying that the foreigner complies with the requirements specified in Article 64 of RD 557/2011 – which are those established for the granting of the initial temporary residence and employment permit – and that the foreigner can prove that he has: (i) lived in Spain for at least three years as a holder of a stay permit; (ii) finished his studies or satisfactorily concluded his research work, training or internship; (iii) not received a grant or been subsidised by public or private institutions as part of a cooperation or development programme financed by Spain or his country of origin. The permit that is issued is considered to be an initial permit. A foreigner, who does not satisfy the requirements to acquire a work permit, will nevertheless be granted a residence permit as long as he satisfies the requirements for this purpose (Article 199.6 of RD 557/2011).
(2) From the residence situation to the residence and work situation, or to the residence situation excluding a work permit (Article 200 of RD 557/2011). This change in situation may be considered for a foreigner who has been in Spain during at least one year as a holder of a residence permit. Exceptionally it is possible to acquire a residence and work situation without them having to comply with the above-indicated residence period if a foreigner can prove a

80. Spain is a highly administratively decentralised country. The central State administration coexists with seventeen regional administrations, identified as autonomous regions, with their own executive and legislative competence. Only the autonomous regions of Andalusia and Catalonia have to date assumed competence regarding immigration, initial temporary residence and employment permits. For a better understanding of the distribution of competences on migration issues between the autonomous regions and the State, *see*: VV.AA., 'Las Comunidades autónomas y la inmigración', Tirant lo Blanch, Valencia, 2006, and Alonso-Olea García, B., 'Extranjería y trabajo', Thomson-Reuters Civitas, Madrid, 2011, in particular pp. 111 ff.

'need to work, due to unexpected circumstances, in order to guarantee his survival'. For this purpose, the employer offering the job must apply for the corresponding permit and the foreigner has to satisfy the above-mentioned requirements which are specified in Article 64 of RD 557/2011 – with the exception of the dispositions of Article 3 a). In any case, Article 200.4 of RD 557/2011 provides that the requirements for the change of administrative situation as described, also have to be satisfied to move from the situation of residence to the situation of: residence and employment, residence without the right to work, residence and research work, or residence and highly qualified employment permits.

(3) From the situation of residence under exceptional circumstances to the residence, residence and work, or residence without the right to work situations (Article 202 of RD 557/2011). In this situation, the foreigner has to have lived in Spain under exceptional circumstances (Article 130 of RD 557/2011) for at least one year. If the foreigner is allowed to work, he must submit, in person, an application to obtain a residence and work permit. If granted, the permits will have a two-year validity period and will be considered to be an initial authorisation. In the rest of the situations, it is the employer who applies for the permit and that, as before, the foreigner satisfies the requirements in Article 64 of RD 557/2011 – with the exception for the conditions in section 3 a). The Spanish norm establishes that the conditions in Article 202 of RD 557/2011 also apply in order to acquire one of the following residence statuses: residence and employment, residence without the right to work, residence and research work, or residence and highly qualified professional work permits.

(4) A combination of the residence and employment situation and the residence and self-employment situation, or of a self-employment authorisation in a different geographical area (Article 201 of RD 557/2011). Combining these situations requires obtaining the corresponding permits to be employed and self-employed at the same time. In order to obtain these permits, it is necessary to prove that one can exercise both economic activities with regard to their object and characteristics, their duration and working hours. The administrative authorisation evidencing the approval of compatibility has the same validity duration as the foreigner's work permit, unless it is granted on the basis of a contract or activity of shorter duration.

§4. Position of Family Members of Residents

115. Any consideration of the legal situation of the family members of foreigners with a temporary residence permit should start with the acknowledgement that OL 4/2000 recognises a foreigner's right to live with their family members and to enjoy family intimacy (Article 16 of OL 4/2000). This right is defined in accordance with the provisions of OL 4/2000 and those in the international agreements to which Spain is a party. Even though it may seem, from what has been said, that the legal treatment of the situation of a foreigner's family members has not changed in the last years, the truth is that the reforms implemented on their legal regime since 1985 have been remarkable. OL 4/2000 brought the most significant transformation of the legal treatment of a foreigner's family members. Before the year 2000, family reunification was seen as an issue on which only the Spanish administration could decide, but with the passing of the above-mentioned law family reunification became one of the foreigner's rights.[81] Although nowadays the holder of the right to family reunification is the foreigner living in Spain, this has been the case when OL 4/2000 was amended by OL 8/2000, because in the original draft of the law the holders of that right were the family members requesting reunification.

116. Article 16 of OL 4/2000 cannot be considered a technically perfect norm as strangely it connects the right to family reunification and the right to family intimacy, where the first one seems to be instrumental in the realisation of the second one. Probably the most reasonable option would have been to simply entitle the provision 'Right to family reunification'. Even if its basic meaning can be drawn from Articles 16–19 of OL 4/2000, the absence of a definition of the concept 'family reunification' is another deficiency in the law on family reunification. For this purpose, the definition in Article 2 d) of Council Directive 2003/86/EC, of 22 September 2003, on the right to family reunification, defines family reunification as 'the entry into and residence in a Member State by family members of a third-country national residing lawfully in that Member State in order to preserve the family unit, whether the family relationship arose before or after the resident's entry'.[82]

117. The family members who benefit from the right to reunification are not, in principle, all who could be considered as family members if the concept of extended family were to be used for this purpose. In this sense, it is possible to say that basically the Spanish law accord the right to family reunification to those family members who are an integral part of the 'nuclear family', defined as the couple and their children. Although Spanish law does recognise the ascendants of the foreigner living in Spain and their partners as family members, they have to satisfy more restrictive conditions to be reunited. These conditions are a way to discourage reunification with these family members Family reunification with an unmarried partner was not explicitly considered by OL 4/2000, but was included in that law through the reform implemented by OL 2/2009. The law now establishes that family members who can apply for family reunification include 'any person having a relationship of affection equivalent to the conjugal relationship with the foreign resident in Spain' (Article 17.4 of OL 4/2000).

118. In order to ensure that the Spanish rules on family reunification comply with those in Directive 2003/86/EC, the Spanish legislator established the status of temporary residence for the purpose of family reunification. The legal regime comprises, not only of Articles 16–19 of OL 4/2000, but also of Articles 57–61 of RD

81. A foreigner's right to family reunification is not included in the Spanish Constitution, hence the importance of the acknowledgement made in OL 4/2000. This absence in the constitutional text is explained by the fact that the Spanish Constitution was drafted at the end of the 1970s, when Spain was not a host country for immigrants, but rather a country of emigration. The Spanish Constitution does, nevertheless, acknowledge the right to personal and family intimacy (Art. 18.1).

82. OJEU EU, L 251/12 of 31 Oct. 2003.

557/2011. This legal status applies to foreigners who are allowed to stay in Spain by virtue of the right to family reunification exercised by a foreign resident in Spain.

119. For the purpose of obtaining this temporary residence permit, the Spanish regulations have established the following legal framework:[83]

(a) It is only possible to be reunited with the following family members:
  - The foreigner's spouse – only one spouse is allowed, even if the foreigner's personal law allows for marital relations with more than one spouse –[84] as long as they are not legally or de facto separated and the marriage is not one of convenience.
  - The person who has a relationship with the foreign resident in Spain that is equivalent to the conjugal one;[85] as mentioned before, this refers to unmarried partners as well as domestic relationships.

  For a relation to be classed as 'equivalent to the conjugal one', the relationship must be duly proved and meet the necessary requirements to produce these effects in Spain. In accordance with the legal treatment of polygamous marriages, Spanish law establishes that 'marriage situations and situations of equivalent affection shall be considered mutually incompatible', in the same way as 'it shall not be possible to reunite more than one person with an equivalent relationship of affection, even if the foreigner's personal law recognises these family ties'.
  - The foreigner's children and those of the spouse or partner, including adopted children, as long as they are younger than 18 years old at the moment when the application for their residence permit is submitted or if they are disabled and objectively unable to provide for their own needs due to the state of their health.

---

83. Additionally, Spanish legislation requires the submission of the following documents (Art. 56.3 of RD 557/2011): (a) documents certifying family ties that give the right to reunification (marriage certificate, the children's birth certificates, etc.); (b) an affidavit stating that the foreigner applying for family reunification does not live in Spain with another partner or spouse, in the case of reunification with the spouse or partner; (c) for reunification of the children of the parents, the properly legalised and translated document that proves the exclusive exercise of parental authority over the children, of whom they are the legal guardian, or otherwise the express legal authorisation of the other parent.

84. On this issue, Directive 2003/86/EC, on the right to family reunification, expressly establishes in Art. 4.4 that: 'In the event of a polygamous marriage, where the sponsor already has a spouse living with him in the territory of a Member State, the Member State concerned shall not authorise the family reunification of a further spouse'.

85. According to Spanish law there is 'a relationship of affection that is equivalent to the conjugal one' when (Art. 53 of RD 557/2011): first, the relationship is filed with the public registry and the registration has not been cancelled; or, second, evidence is provided, mainly through documents issued by a public authority, of an unregistered relationship, entered into before the start of the sponsor's residence period in Spain.

In relation to this matter, Art. 5.2, third paragraph, of Directive 2003/86/EC establishes that: 'When examining an application concerning the unmarried partner of the sponsor, Member States shall consider, as evidence of the family relationship, factors such as a common child, previous cohabitation, registration of the partnership and any other reliable means of proof'.

- Those legally represented by the foreigner, who are younger than 18 at the moment that the application for their residence permit is submitted or if they are disabled and objectively unable to provide for their own needs due to the state of their health, as long as the legal action of representation complies with the principles in the Spanish law.
- The foreigner's ascendants in the first degree, and those of their spouse or partner, who depend on the applicant foreigner, are over 65 years and if there is an objective justification to authorise their residence in Spain.[86]

(b) The foreigner must have sufficient economic means to provide for the needs of the family, including healthcare, if this is not covered by the Social Security system to the amount established by law (Article 54 of RD 557/2011).[87]

(c) The foreigner shall provide evidence of adequate housing to meet his needs and those of his family members, as established in Article 55 of RD 557/2011.

(d) The foreigner must have lived in Spain for at least one year and be in possession of a permit that allows his to reside in the country for at least one more year.[88] The one-year continued legal residence does not apply in the following cases: (a) when the person to be reunified is the foreigner's ascendant, because in this case it will be necessary to wait until the applicant acquires the long-term resident status; (b) when the applicant is the holder of a stay permit for the purpose of study, because in this case family members may accompany the student when he enters the country – on this case, *see* Chapter 2 of Part III in this work; (c) if the foreign resident in Spain is an EU long-term resident in another Member State of the Union, a holder of the EU blue card, or a beneficiary of the special regime for researchers.

120. One exception to the temporary residence status for family reunification is the independent temporary residence status (Article 19 of OL 4/2000 and Article 59 of RD 557/2011). The independent residence and work permit can be obtained by

---

86. Article 53 of RD 557/2011, s. e), paras 2–4, exceptionally considers that, when humanitarian reasons concur, it is possible to reunite ascendants who are younger than 65 and are not first-degree relatives. Humanitarian reasons concur when the ascendant lived with the applicant foreigner in their country of origin before the latter obtained a residence permit. Humanitarian reasons also occur, if the ascendant is disabled and the applicant foreigner or his spouse or partner are granted custody over that person by the competent authority in the country of origin; if the ascendant is objectively unable to provide for his own needs; or if the ascendant, be it the applicant's or that of the spouse or partner, is the spouse or partner of another ascendant, the latter being over 65 years of age.

    It is assumed that 'the applicant is in charge' of a family member when it is established that, at least during the last year of residence in Spain, the applicant has transferred funds or supported the family member, to an amount that is equivalent to at least the 51% of the GDP per capita of the family member's country of residence (Art. 53 e), fifth paragraph, of RD 557/2011).

87. According to Art. 54.1 of RD 557/2011, if the family unit, including the applicant foreigner and, once in Spain, the reunited person, is formed by two people, the monthly amount required accounts for 150% of the IPREM – an indicator established by the Spanish legislator (Public Income Rate of Multiple Effects), which, for 2017, was EUR 798.76. However, if the family unit, on arrival of the reunited person, includes more than two family members, the monthly amount required is 50% of the IPREM (EUR 266.25 for 2017) for each additional member of the family.

88. It is not necessary to wait until the renewal of the residence permit is granted to apply for reunification, because renewal and reunification can be simultaneously applied for, although, in this case, reunification will depend on the granting of the residence renewal.

a spouse or partner who, not having any outstanding obligations with the tax administration or the Social Security authorities, satisfies any one of the following requirements:[89]

(a) Having sufficient economic means for the granting of a non-lucrative temporary residence permit.
(b) Having one or several work contracts, of a minimum duration of one year from the moment the application is submitted, and from which a retribution of no less than the monthly full-time national minimum wage (in fourteen payments) is derived.
(c) Meeting the requirements demanded for the granting of a temporary residence and self-employment permit.

121. In addition, the reunited spouse or partner can obtain an independent residence and work permit if one of the following circumstances occurs (Article 59.2 of RD 557/2011):

(a) The marriage that was the reason to grant the residence situation has been dissolved due to a legal separation, divorce, cancellation of the registration, or termination of life as a couple, and evidence is provided of cohabitation with the applicant for at least two years.
(b) If they are victims of domestic violence and a protection legal order has been issued in their favour or if there is a report from the Public Prosecutor's Office providing evidence of domestic violence.
(c) If the applicant has passed away.

122. In the cases mentioned in the previous paragraph, whenever the reunification of other family members has also taken place, these family members will retain their residence permit. When these family members apply for a renewal of their residence permit their situation will be assessed in the light of the family member with whom they live. Children and minors for whom the applicant acts as legal representative will obtain an independent residence permit when they become of age if the can provide evidence that there situation is one of the situations mentioned in Article 59.1 of RD 557/2011. Children are also entitled to an independent residence permit when they reach the legal age of majority if they have lived in Spain during a period of five years.

123. The current law (Article 59.5 of RD 557/2011) allows reunited ascendants to obtain an independent residence permit when they are issued a work permit. In relation to these ascendants, the law also establishes that they may exercise their right to family reunification, subject to the conditions provided by law. For this purpose, they must have obtained the long-term resident status and provide evidence of their economic and financial solvency. Exceptionally, if they are responsible for one

89. According to Art. 59.6 of RD 557/2011, the validity of the independent residence and work permit will depend on the validity period of the previous residence permit for family reunification. In all cases an independent permit will be valid for a minimum of one year.

or more minor children or disabled children who are objectively unable to provide for their own needs due to the state of their health, they are entitled family reunification before they have obtained the long-term resident status.

124. The Spanish immigration regulations do not deal with family relationships from the exclusive point of view of family reunification. On the contrary, there are special rules that apply to the residence of minors in Spain due to family reasons other than reunification, as provided for in RD 557/2011, which distinguishes between the following two situations: (a) that of a resident's child born in Spain (Article 185 of RD 557/2011); and (b) that of a resident's child born outside Spain (Article 186 of RD 557/2011). A distinction is thus made according to the child's place of birth, within or outside Spain.

125. In the case of a child born in Spain, the law acknowledges the baby's automatic acquisition of a residence permit issued to one of the parents. It is either the father or mother that must apply in person for the child's residence permit after the child is born, or, should this be the case, at the moment when one of them is granted a residence status. In both cases, the parents must submit the both the child's original birth certificate and a copy of it. When a child who has been issued a residence permit reach the legal working age – 16 in Spain – that they will be authorised to work without having to obtain permission (Article 185.5 of RD 557/2011).

126. There are two very specific situations. The first one is that of a child born in Spain to a father or mother who is a refugee or a beneficiary of subsidiary protection. In this case, Spanish law establishes that the parents may choose between applying for the extension of the right to international protection to that child or for a minor's residence permit, in accordance with the 'minor's interest' – which will normally be that of the parents (Article 185.2 of RD 557/2011).

127. The second situation is that of a child born in Spain from a foreigner holding a residence permit for the purpose of family reunification as a descendant of another resident. In this case, the minor will be granted a residence permit for family reunification dependant on that of the parent (Article 185.3 of RD 557/2011).

128. When the child is born outside of Spain, just like in the case of minors under the legal guardianship of a Spanish citizen or institution or of a legal foreign resident in Spain, they can obtain a residence permit if evidence has been provided of their continuous presence in Spain during at least two years, and if their parents or guardians satisfy the requirements regarding to sufficient economic means and adequate housing as required by Spanish law on the right to family reunification. If the minor is a school-age child, the parents or guardians must submit a certificate proving that the child has been in education while residing in Spain. As in the previous case, children who have been issued a residence permit who reach the legal working age, are authorised to work without having to follow any other administrative procedure (Article 186.5 of RD 557/2011).

129. The last situation, concerns a minor who was born in a third country and is living in Spain on an irregular basis. It is in this light that the reference to residence in the country for at least two years must be understood. Article 186 of RD 557/2011 has therefore established a way to legalise the situation of these minors through their social and family ties, which is different and less demanding, because the subjects are minors, than the one provided for in Article 124.2 of RD 557/2011 which provides a general procedure to obtain temporary residence permits on social ties grounds.

Chapter 3. Long-Term Residence

§1. Conditions for Long-Term Residence

130. Article 32 of OL 4/2000 defines 'long-term residence' as the legal situation authorising the foreigner to reside indefinitely in Spain under the same conditions as a Spaniard. As established by RD 557/2011, acquiring this legal status involves being the holder of a permit not only to reside in Spain but also to work in the country. Compared to the temporary residence status, it is possible to conclude that the long-term residence status in Spain is one that is granted for more than five years, as opposed to a temporary residence status, which allows the foreigner to reside in the country for a period of more than ninety days but less than five years.

131. Legally speaking, Spanish law distinguishes between two types of long-term residence:[90]

(a) Long-term residence (Articles 147–150 of RD 557/2011): this permit allows the holder to remain permanently in Spain and is only valid in this country, so the foreigner will not be able to move to another Member State of the Union.
(b) EU long-term residence (Articles 151–154 of RD 557/2011): this permit allows the holder to remain permanently in Spain, but also enables them to live in another Member State of the Union, exercising their right to move between the Member States.

132. In the case of long-term residence (Article 14 of RD 557/2011), the corresponding permit can be obtained by the following persons:

(a) Foreigners who have legally and continuously lived in Spain for five years.
(b) Foreigners who can prove that they have lived continuously in the EU as holders of the EU blue card – issued to highly qualified professionals – for five years, as long as they have lived in Spain during the two consecutive years prior to the moment when the application is submitted.
(c) Foreigners who have 'a special connection with Spain'.[91] The interpretation of this legal notion is both broad and peculiar at the same time. According to the law, the beneficiaries are: (i) residents who receive a contributory retirement

---

90. In accordance with Directive 2003/109/EC, of 25 November 2003, concerning the status of third-country nationals who are long-term residents (OJEU EU, L 16/50 of 23 Jan. 2004), which establish the issuing in the territory of the Union of a 'long-term resident's EC residence permit' and at the same time states (Art. 13) that 'Member States may issue residence permits of permanent or unlimited validity on terms that are more favourable than those laid down by this Directive. Such residence permits shall not confer the right of residence in the other Member States as provided by Chapter III of this Directive'.
91. Article 32.4 of OL 4/2000 points to the possibility of determining, through the regulation, the criteria for the granting of other long-term residence permits for the reasons mentioned. Attending to this legal mandate, Art. 148.3 of RD 557/2011 specified the additional cases in which, in the framework of the above-mentioned special connection with Spain, certain foreigners may obtain a long-term residence in Spain.

pension, which is part of the protective action provided by the Spanish Social Security system; (ii) residents who benefit from a contributory full permanent incapacity or severe disability pension, which is part of the legal protection provided by the Spanish Social Security system, or from subsidies obtained in Spain that are equivalent to those pensions and provide a life annuity that cannot be capitalised and is sufficient to pay for their subsistence; (iii) residents who were born in Spain and who, having reached the legal age of majority, have legally and continuously lived in Spain during at least the three consecutive years immediately prior to the moment when the application is submitted; (iv) foreigners who were originally Spanish and have lost their Spanish nationality; (v) residents who, having reached the legal age of majority, were placed under the guardianship of a Spanish public institution during the five consecutive years immediately prior to the submission of the application;[92] (vi) stateless persons, refugees and beneficiaries of subsidiary protection resident in Spain, whose status has been acknowledged by the Spanish authorities; (vii) foreigners who have prominently contributed towards the economic, scientific or cultural progress of Spain or to the promotion of Spain abroad.

(d) Foreigners holding an EU long-term residence permit issued by the authorities of another Member State of the EU. This legal status, addressed in Article 32.3 of OL 4/2000, is nothing more than the acknowledgement of any foreigner's right to reside in Spain, if they apply for it, when they have been issued an EU long-term residence permit.

133. Spanish law recognises the right to obtain an EU long-term residence permit as a foreigner who finds himself in one of the following situations (Article 152 of RD 557/2011):[93]

(a) Foreigners who have legally and continuously lived in Spain for five years.
(b) Foreigners who can prove that they have lived continuously in the EU as holders of an EU blue card – issued to highly qualified workers – for five years, provided that they have lived in Spain for two years immediately prior to submitting their application.
(c) Foreigners living in Spain after having been EU long-term residents in another Member State of the EU – a situation considered in Article 157 of RD 557/2011. For the purpose of avoiding a double legal status, it is expressly established that 'the granting of an EU long-term residence permit in Spain will entail the loss of the right to keep the EU long-term residence status in the previous Member State of residence'.

---

92. This seems to be quite a paradoxical case for it requires minor to be a temporary resident for five years, which is the same requirement imposed on any foreigner wishing to obtain a long-term residence permit. It is thus unclear what the special nature of this legal situation is.
93. In this case, Spain has already transposed Directive 2011/51/EU of the European Parliament and of the Council, of 11 May 2011, amending Council Directive 2003/109/EC to extend its scope to beneficiaries of international protection (OJEU EU, 1/132 of 19 May 2011). This transposition was made through the modification of Arts 152 and 153 of RD 557/2011 by RD 844/2013, of 31 October 2013, amending Organic Law 4/2000, of 11 January 2000, on the rights and freedoms of foreigners in Spain and their social integration, approved by RD 557/2011 (OSG 1 Nov. 2013, No. 262).

§2. Administrative Procedures and Documents for Long-Term Residence

134. Foreigners who want to obtain a long-term permit must submit the corresponding application, using the official form, to the immigration affairs office in the province where they live or, when no previous residence in Spain is required, to the immigration affairs office in the territory where they wish to establish their residence. Applications made by foreigners who have prominently contributed towards the economic, scientific or cultural progress of Spain are treated differently in the sense that their application shall be forwarded ex officio to the Ministry of Employment at the request of the corresponding authority, given that the Ministry is the competent body to decide on the granting of the permit.

135. The decision on long-term resident permits applications are issued within three months from the moment that they are recorded by the competent authority. In the absence of a decision within this time limit, the application is deemed to be accepted and a permit is issued (Article 149.4 of RD 557/2011). Once the permit is obtained by the foreigner, an application for a foreigner identity card must be made in person within one month from the notification. This card is renewed every five years.

136. The following documents shall be submitted together with the permit application (Article 149.2 of RD 557/2011): (a) a photocopy of the whole passport or travel document, acknowledged as valid in Spain, to be checked against the original document; (b) a receipt that the fee for the processing of the application has been paid; (c) a report issued by the competent authority certifying the schooling of any school-age minors for whom the foreigner is responsible – if there are any – for applications based on previous residence periods; (d) documents certifying previous residence periods as a holder of an EU blue card in another Member State of the EU; (e) when required, documents certifying being in a situation that allows applying for a residence permit because of a special connection with Spain; (f) the foreigner's criminal record or some equivalent document issued by the authorities of their country of origin or of the country or countries where he has lived during the past five years, if no sentences for offences or crimes as provided for by Spanish laws are recorded.

137. When applying for an EU long-term residence permit, the foreigner will be additionally required (Article 152 of RD 557/2011): (a) to have sufficient stable and regular means for his own support and, where appropriate, that of their family – the terms and amounts of which are similar to those established for family reunification; (b) to have a public or private health insurance policy issued by an insurance company authorised to operate in Spain.

§3. LEGAL POSITION OF LONG-TERM RESIDENTS

138. The issuing of either one of the two types of long-term residence permits described above – long term and EU long term – implies that the foreigner, as the Spanish law indicates (Article 32.1 of OL 4/2000), is authorised to reside and work in Spain indefinitely and under the same conditions as a Spaniard.[94]

139. In the case of EU long-term residents, the granting of the corresponding permit places them in a special legal situation that guarantees that they cannot be expelled from Spanish territory if they commit a criminal offence. As mentioned before, the holders of this permit have the right to reside, if they wish to, in another EU Member State.

140. Termination of the long-term resident status, is specified as follows in the law (Article 166 of RD 557/2011): (a) when the permit has been obtained by fraudulent means; (b) when an order of expulsion is issued in the cases determined by the law; (c) when the foreigner is absent from the territory of the EU for twelve consecutive months;[95] (d) when the permit is obtained by someone who was granted international protection by another EU Member State and the authorities of that State decide to terminate, deny the renewal of or revoke that protection. Additionally, the EU long-term residence permit may be terminated in the following cases: (a) when the person has been granted an EU long-term residence permit by another Member State and (b) when the foreigner is absent from Spanish territory during six years.

141. The long-term resident status – and the EU long-term resident status can be reacquired as set out in Article 160 of RD 557/2011 and in certain other cases, such as (Article 158 of RD 557/2011): (a) when the permit is terminated due to absence from the territory of the EU for twelve consecutive months or when the foreigner has been granted an EU long-term residence permit in another Member State of the Union; (b) when the foreigner returns to Spain upon the expiration of the

94. In any case, it must be borne in mind that although Directive 2003/109/EC (Art. 13) recognises a Member State's competence to issue residence permits of a permanent or unlimited validity on terms that are more favourable than those laid down by this Directive, such residence shall not confer the right of residence in another Member States as provided for by Chapter III of this Directive.
    Within this context the rule, established by Art. 32.3 of OL 4/2000, allows a foreigner who enjoys a long-term resident status in another EU Member State and wishes to retain his status of long-term resident acquired in the first Member State, to request and obtain a temporary residence permit in Spain.

95. This law excludes the holders of temporary residence and work permits employed as voluntary workers by non-governmental organisations, foundations or associations that are registered in the corresponding general registry and are officially acknowledged as being of public interest, for which they perform research, development cooperation or humanitarian aid tasks overseas.

period during which they agreed not to come back in accordance with the provisions of Chapter X of Title V of RD 557/2011, provided that at the moment of their voluntary return to their country of origin they were legally a long-term resident in Spain.[96]

142. The procedure to reacquire the long-term residence status (Article 159 of RD 557/2011) is very similar to the one already described for the granting of this residence status. After its submission, the application will be examined by the competent administration that will, depending on the application itself and on the reports that may have been collected in relation to it, issue a motivated decision within a three-month period. If a decision is not adopted within this period, the application is considered favourably in any case.

§4. Position of Family Members of Long-Term Residents

143. As mentioned, the status of the family members of holders of a long-term residence permit or of an EU long-term residence permit is mainly determined by the right to family reunification and the regime established for these persons in Articles 16–10 of OL 4/2000. The reader is referred to the observations made in §4 of Chapter 2, Part II, of this work, regarding the status of temporary resident's family members.

144. However, Article 18 of OL 4/2000 contains certain particular rules, linked to the situation of long-term residence, which also have to be taken into account. Thus, it is only possible, according to Spanish law, to apply for family reunification for the applicant's ascendants once the applicant has acquired the long-term resident status himself. This is a legal condition that ultimately serves the purpose that the legislator wants to discourage family reunification for those family members who are not considered members of the nuclear family and, in brief, who are not the foreigner's direct descendants. In this sense, it is important to differentiate family reunification of ascendants, as mentioned here, from family reunification with foreigners who enjoy a temporary resident status, because, as mentioned before (§4 of Chapter 2, Part II, of this work), in this last situation, reunification is only possible on humanitarian grounds.

145. However, the foreigner does not necessarily have to wait to acquire the long-term resident status before applying for reunification with his ascendants. As in other cases, already discussed, the Spanish law establishes that the foreigner may apply for family reunification at the same time as he applies for a long-term residence permit (Articles 18*bis* of OL 4/2000). The granting of the former will, obviously, depend on the issuing of the latter. Likewise, it must be taken into account

96. This chapter (Arts 120–122 of RD 557/2011) addressed the situation in which a foreigner may decide to return to his country of origin, whether on their own initiative or within the framework of a voluntary return programme fostered, financed or acknowledged by the general administration of the Spanish State.

that, if the right to family reunification has been exercised by a long-term resident in another EU Member State who then moves and lives in Spain, an application for family reunification can be submitted by the family member. This application will have to include proof of residence in that Member State of the Union as a family member of the long-term resident (Articles 18.2*bis* of OL 4/2000).

Part III. Right of Residence for Special Categories of Persons

Chapter 1. Nationals with Preferential Treatment

146. Up to now, this work has shown how legal permanence in Spain depends on the granting of, in some cases, a residence permit and, in other cases, of a residence and work permit, whether the permit is temporary or just a first step towards long-term residence status, and whether the objective is to be employed or self-employed. In this sense, it has been emphasised that the Spanish administration uses two basic methods to regulate migration flows of those who intend to enter and reside in Spain and, ultimately, intend to access the national labour market. One of them is the collective management of hiring in the countries of origin (Article 39 of OL 4/2000), and the other one is the assessment by the Spanish administration of applications submitted by foreigners personally, in both cases according to what is known as the 'national employment situation'.

147. When using the first mechanism – the collective management of hiring in the countries of origin – the administration makes a general assessment of the above-mentioned national employment situation for the purpose of identifying the professions and, when convenient, the estimated number of position that will not be filled by the national labour market, i.e., by Spaniards, EU citizens and foreigners with residence and work permits, and which can, therefore, be offered to foreign workers not living in Spain. The question is that, from 2012 onwards – and this was still the case in 2018–,[97] the collective management of hiring has been limited by the Spanish government to seasonal agricultural campaigns and workers from countries with which Spain has signed an agreement for the regulation of migration flows.

148. Through the second mechanism – the assessment by the Spanish administration of individual applications for residence and work permits – the administration adopts a decision after taking into account the applicant's situation and the above-mentioned national employment situation. In this case, the question is whether Spanish law precludes consideration of the national employment situation

---

97. Such is the provision of Order ESS/1309/2017, of 28 December, extending the validity of Order ESS/1/2012, of 5 January 2012, regulating the collective management of hiring in the countries of origin for 2012 (OSG 12 Dec. 2016, No. 314).

when the person who will ultimately be the holder of the labour contract and, consequently, of the work permit is one of the following subjects (Article 40 of OL 4/2000):[98]

(a) The reunified working-age family members, spouse or child, of a foreign resident in Spain holding a renewed permit, as well as the child of a Spanish national or of citizens of another Member State of the EU or another State belonging to the European Economic Area, provided that they have lived in Spain lawfully for a minimum of one year and that the Union regime does not apply to the child.
(b) Holders of a work permit who intend to renew it.
(c) Workers necessary for the renovation of an installation or productive equipment.
(d) Those who have had the status of refugees, during the year following the cessation of the application of the Geneva Convention of 28 July 1951 on the Status of Refugees – for the reasons described in point 5, section C, of Article 1.
(e) Those who have been recognised as stateless persons and those who may have lost that status during the year following the termination of such status.
(f) Foreigners who are in responsible for ascendants or descendants of Spanish nationality.
(g) Foreigners who were born and live in Spain.
(h) The children and grandchildren of a native Spaniard.
(i) Foreign working-age minors holding a residence permit who have been placed under the guardianship of a competent minor protection institution, for those activities which, according to the criteria of the aforementioned institution, favour their social integration, and after the impossibility of the child returning to his family or country of origin has been established.
(j) Foreigners who have been issued a residence permit due to exceptional circumstances as determined by law and, in any case, when they are victims of domestic violence or human trafficking.
(k) Foreigners who have been holders of work permits for seasonal activities during two years and have returned to their countries of origin or habitual residence.

---

98. The list of cases included in Art. 40 of OL 4/2000 is incomplete, because according to Spanish law three are some additional cases where the national employment situation is also not to be taken into account, as for example is the case for: (a) nationals of States with which international agreements have been signed for this purpose – basically Chile and Peru; (b) nationals of States not belonging to the European Union or the European Economic Area, working on Spanish ships by virtue of international sea fishing agreements – the copy of the boarding notification or the renewal of the contract as a foreign member of the crew on Spanish ships are valid and can be used as work permits (Art. 64.4 of RD 557/2011); (c) long-term residents; (d) foreigners whose activity is interesting from an economic, social or labour point of view, or the object of which is the performance of research, development or teaching that require high qualifications, or artist with a special cultural interest as established in Art. 178 of RD 557/2011, as well as their family members – as established in Art. 181 of RD 557/2011; (e) foreigners with a stay permit for the purpose of study, research, training or internship, who obtain the residence and work status (Art. 199 of RD 557/2011); (f) foreigners who, from a situation of temporary residence under exceptional circumstances, move to a regular temporary residence and work status.

(l) Foreigners who have given up their residence and work permit by virtue of a voluntary return programme.
(m) Finally, as provided for by law, the national employment situation will also not be considered in the case of: (i) persons filling a position of trust or management in a company; (ii) highly qualified professionals, including technicians and scientists, hired by public institutions, universities and research, development or innovation centres dependant on companies, notwithstanding the application of the specific permit regime specified in the current law for this kind of workers; (iii) the staff of a firm or group of firms in one country who intend to develop their working activity for the same firm or group in Spain; and (iv) renown and prestigious artists.

149. This is the first exception to the ordinary treatment of migration flows intending to access the Spanish labour market, to which it is now the time to add a second one. The second exception concerns those exempted from applying for a work permit, as established by the Spanish legislator in Article 41 of OL 4/2000. An exemption is possible for, amongst others, the following activities:

(a) Foreign technicians and scientists, whether invited or hired by the State, the AR, local bodies or institutions that have the object of promoting and developing research projects and are supported by the former administrations or in which these administrations have a major stake.
(b) Foreign professors invited or hired by Spanish universities.
(c) The foreign management staff and professors of prestigious cultural and teaching institutions, whether dependant on other States or private organisations, which are officially acknowledged by the Spanish authorities and develop their own cultural and teaching programmes in Spain, as long as the activities are limited to the implementation of those programmes.
(d) Civil servants and military staff of foreign administrations who come to Spain to perform activities under cooperation agreements with the Spanish administration.
(e) Foreign media correspondents duly accredited for the exercise of information dissemination activities.
(f) Members of international scientific missions who work and carry out research activities in Spain with the authorisation of the State.
(g) Artists who come to Spain to perform specific activities that are not a continuous activity.
(h) Ministers, clergymen or representatives of different churches and confessions, duly registered in the '*Registro de Entidades Religiosas*' (Religious Entities Registry), as long as their activity is limited to strictly administrative tasks.
(i) Foreign working-age minors placed under the guardianship of a competent minor protection institution, for those activities which, according to the criteria of the aforementioned institution, favour their social integration, and for as long as they remain in that situation.

150. This list of activities provides the context for and introduces Part III of this monograph, which will provide, as indicated by its title, an analysis of the right to residence of persons belonging to certain special categories. From a general perspective, the special treatment of migration flows in Spain – these are not exceptions, like the above-specified cases, but rather preferential legal treatment regime – as in many other countries, is a response to different situations. In some cases, it is justified by the historical ties that Spain has developed with certain nations (as with the Latin American countries), or by its present and current ties (as with the Member States of the EU), which explain the preferential treatment of the nationals of these countries. In other cases, the reasons are purely economic (for instance the preferential treatment provided to investors and entrepreneurs), linked to the revitalisation of the economy (as is the case of highly qualified professionals or the staff of multinational companies), or related to the improvement of the innovation and knowledge capacities of Spain, or to attract human talent (for instance, students, researchers and university professors) or address humanitarian causes (asylum seekers, unaccompanied minors, etc.).

151. In recent years, the EU has in fact shown a special preoccupation for the adoption of policies to attract human talent and investments to its territory and counteract the strong leadership in this area exercised by both the United States and Asia, particularly China, Japan, South Korea and India. This is the context that explains the reform of OL 4/2000 implemented by OL 2/2009, and the passing of Law 14/2013, of 27 September 2013, on the support to entrepreneurs and their internationalisation, which defines, as mentioned at the beginning of this work, a very specific migration channel, distinct and differentiated from the general migration regime that is established by OL 4/2000.

152. It is thus possible to affirm – and so the focus turns to the central object of this title – that preferential treatment due to nationality, with the obvious exception being the legal regime that applies to EU citizens, is not nowadays one of the factors driving Spanish legislative action. Having said this, it is evidently possible to refer to third-country nationals who are the object of preferential treatment in Spanish legislation.

153. The starting point to analyse the preferential treatment given to certain third-country nationals is Article 1 of OL 4/2000, a provision that determines the scope of this OL and establishes that 'foreigners are, for the purpose of the application of the present law, those who do not have the Spanish nationality'. The definition is interesting, particularly in relation to the issue analysed here, because it is wrong to fully identify the term 'foreigner', in the sense given to it by the Spanish law, with persons 'who do not have the Spanish nationality', since the former and the latter have different legal statuses as a consequence of, precisely, the differential treatment provided to certain third-country nationals. It is within this context that section 2 of this provision must be situated, where it states that 'in all cases, the dispositions of this Law shall be understood notwithstanding the provisions of special laws and international agreements signed by Spain', which is the reason why section 3 reads that 'the nationals of Member States of the EU and those to whom the Union regime is applied shall be governed by the norms that regulate this regime, while the present Law shall be applied to them in those aspects that could be more favourable for them'. Nowadays, it is difficult to argue, for instance, that an EU citizen is a foreigner, for the purposes of Spanish migration legislation, in the same way as a national of Nigeria or Thailand is.

154. Nationals of the Member State are EU citizens, according to Article 20(1) of the TFEU. As EU citizens they have, *inter alia:* a) 'the right to move and reside freely within the territory of the Member States, subject to the limitations and conditions laid down in the Treaties and by the measures adopted to give them effect' (Article 21). The most important legislative measures adopted in which the conditions and limitation for the exercise of this right to free movement are specified, is Directive 2004/38/EC, of the European Parliament and the Council, of 29 April 2004, on the right of citizens of the Union and their family members to move and reside freely within the territory of the Member States, amending Regulation (EEC) No. 1612/68 and repealing Directives 64/221/EEC, 68/360/EEC, 72/194/EEC, 73/148/EEC, 75/34/EEC, 75/35/EEC, 90/364/EEC, 90/365/EEC and 93/96/EEC.[99] This Directive applies to any EU citizen, whether or not he is engaged in active employment. This Directive was implemented by the Spanish authorities in RD 240/2007 of 16 February 2007, on the entry, free movement and residence in Spain of citizens of the Member States of the EU and other States, signatories of the Agreement on the European Economic Area.[100]

155. The legal regime that applies to EU citizens also benefits the nationals of States outside the EU like Liechtenstein, Norway or Iceland, by virtue of the Agreement on the European Economic Area, of 2 May 1992.[101] Likewise, the regime established for citizens of the EU also applies to Swiss citizens, as provided for by the Agreement of 21 June 1999, signed by the EU and the Swiss Confederation, on the free movement of persons, which entered into force on 1 June 2002.[102] In fact, the above-mentioned RD 240/2007, as it is possible to deduce from its title, also applies to the nationals of those countries.

156. Spanish migration law not only grants a preferential and differentiated treatment to the citizens of the Member States of the EU, countries of the European Free Trade Area (EFTA), or Swiss citizens, who, according to what has been just said, cannot technically be classed as foreigners. There are multiple bilateral agreements and treaties ratified by Spain, which include a differentiated and, to a certain extent, also preferential treatment for citizens of States outside the EU with which

99. OJEU EU, L 158/77 of 30 Apr. 2004.
100. OSG 28 Feb. 2007, No. 51. This RD, must be implemented taking into consideration, among others, Instruction DGI/SGRJ/03/2010, of 4 November 2010, implementing the Supreme Court judgment, of 1 June 2010, on the repeal of various sections of RD 240/2007, which, among other aspects, established that the right to remain for family members of Spanish nationals, including their ascendants, is governed by the rules on free movement and, therefore, fall outside the scope of the general regime on immigration, contrary to what the royal decree and, evidently, the Spanish government expected.
101. OJEU, L 1 of 3 Jan. 1994.
102. OJEU, L 114/6 of 30 Apr. 2002.

Spain has special historical, economic or commercial ties. These bilateral agreements or treaties can be classified into five basic categories:

(1) Agreements on the regulation of migration flows, signed with States like Cape Verde, Colombia, Peru, Dominican Republic, Ecuador, Gambia, Guinea, Guinea Bissau, Mali, Mauritania, Niger, Nigeria and Morocco.
(2) Right of entry and work agreements, signed with Andorra, Algeria, Morocco and New Zealand.
(3) Agreements on the prevention of clandestine migration – allowing the repatriation of emigrants who illegally enter the territory of the other Contracting Party – signed with France, Estonia, Cape Verde, Slovenia, Bulgaria, Switzerland, Romania, Portugal, Poland, Morocco, Macedonia, Lithuania, Latvia and Italy.
(4) Agreements on double nationality, especially signed with Latin American countries like Honduras, Chile, Peru, Nicaragua, Paraguay, Guatemala, Bolivia, Ecuador, Costa Rica, Colombia, Venezuela, Dominican Republic and Argentina. After the promulgation of the SC – which in its Article 11.3 acknowledges a Spaniard's right to become citizens of another country without losing his Spanish nationality, irrespective whether that other country acknowledges a reciprocal right to its own citizens – these agreements lost all relevance for Spaniards. This explains why they are gradually being revised; a process that started in the 1990s. In any case, those agreements often establish a migration regime that is more favourable for Latin American citizens than the one generally established by Spanish law – as is the case with the agreements signed with Ecuador, Peru and Chile.
(5) Additionally, there are bilateral agreements on issues as diverse as the waiver of visa obligations or visa fees, Social Security benefits,[103] or the participation of foreign citizens in Spanish political life. Examples of agreements that allow the participation of foreigners in local elections which have been signed with the following States: Bolivia, Chile, Colombia, Ecuador, Paraguay, Peru, Uruguay, Cape Verde, Iceland, Norway and New Zealand, are especially significant.

---

103. Spain has signed bilateral agreements regarding Social Security matters with Andorra, Argentina, Australia, Brazil, Cape Verde, Canada, Chile, Colombia, Dominican Republic, Ecuador, Japan, Morocco, Mexico, Paraguay, Peru, the Philippines, Russia, South Korea, Tunisia, Ukraine, United States, Uruguay and Venezuela.

Chapter 2. Students

157. As mentioned – particularly in §1 of Chapter 2, Part II, of this work – OL 4/2000 provides a special regime for the admission of foreigners for the purpose of study, student exchange, non-remunerated training or internship, and voluntary work.[104] Because in these cases the reason that justifies the foreigner's presence in Spain is temporary by nature, the Spanish law provides that the status derived from this regime is one of legal stay. This means that only after a person has been granted a stay permit, can they apply for, when possible, a resident status, without having to apply for a visa first – as established in Article 199 of RD 557/2011.

158. An interesting aspect of the differentiated regime for this specific group of persons is the recent evolution which the concept of 'student' has experienced in Spanish migration legislation. The concept that was normally used in Spain has become broader as a consequence of the transposition of Council Directive 2004/114/EC, of 13 December 2004, on the conditions of admission of third-country nationals for the purposes of studies, pupil exchange, unremunerated training or voluntary service,[105] into Spanish law via OL 2/2009 and the corresponding amendment to OL 4/2000. As a result, the Spanish legislator disregarded the very concept of 'student' when it came to listing the subjects to whom the special regime defined in Article 33 of OL 4/2000 was to be applied. In fact, 'student' as it is used in the Spanish law is broader than the concept of 'student' used in the above-mentioned Union directive,[106] because it also allows the application of this regime to those coming to Spain to receive secondary education, outside any exchange programme, and to those entering the country to perform research or training work in teaching or research centres.

159. The key provision is Article 33 of OL 4/2000 that addresses the issuing of residence permits to a foreigner whose only purpose to be in Spain, or at least the main one, is to perform one of the following non-remunerated activities:

(a) To pursue a study. The Spanish implementing rule explicitly includes those who wish to pursue specialised healthcare studies and training in Spain in of Law 44/2003, of 11 November 2003, on healthcare professions[107] and in accordance with a decision of the Spanish administration that goes beyond the standards in Directive 2004/114/EC – a Union standard that, nevertheless, does provide the possibility for a Member State to regulate this particular issue.

104. Articles 33 of OL 4/2000 and 37 to 45 of RD 557/2011 are the ones regulating this issue.
105. OJEU, L 375/12 of 23 Dec. 2004.
106. Student, as it is used in the Student Directive, means: 'a third-country national accepted by an establishment of higher education and admitted to the territory of a Member State to pursue as his/her main activity a full-time course of study leading to a higher education qualification recognised by the Member State, including diplomas, certificates or doctoral degrees in an establishment of higher education, which may cover a preparatory course prior to such education according to its national legislation' (Art. 2 b)).
107. OSG 22 Nov. 2003, No. 280.

(b) To carry out non-remunerated research or training activities – remunerated activities are regulated by Articles 38*bis* of OL 4/2000, entitled *'Régimen especial de los investigadores'* ('Special regime for researchers').
(c) To participate in a student exchange programme in officially recognised teaching or scientific centres, either public or private.
(d) To work on an internship.
(e) To perform voluntary services.

160. In addition to what has just be said, the following also applies in relation to the regime established by Article 33 of OL 4/2000:[108] (a) the application of this special regime depends not so much on the actual performance of the above-mentioned activities, but on the objective of the person's stay in Spain, which shall be related, whether mainly or exclusively, to the performance of one or more of those activities;[109] (b) notwithstanding the wording of Article 33 of OL 4/2000, in all five situations the performance of the activity justifying the issuing of a stay permit must take place in a teaching or scientific institution, either public or private; (c) the teaching or research centres need not be Spanish – they may be foreign – but they must be authorised or officially recognised centres by the Spanish authorities; (d) the activity performed must be non-remunerated, if not, as mentioned before, the applicable regime would be that of researchers (Articles 38*bis* of OL 4/2000) or employed workers (Article 38 of OL 4/2000).

161. In order to enter and stay in Spain, the Spanish law defines the obligation to apply for a stay permit, which can only be obtained by requesting the corresponding visa, which is identified as a study visa, even though the regime established by Article 33 of OL 4/2000 includes people who are not strictly speaking students. Obtaining a study visa is possible by satisfying two kinds of requirements (Article 38 of RD 557/2011):[110]

---

108. Section 6 in Art. 33 of OL 4/2000 reads: 'the entry and presence in Spain, in the terms regulated by the law, of foreign students participating in EU programmes designed to favour mobility towards or within the Union will be facilitated'. However, RD 557/2011 has not determined anything on the matter. This is, therefore, a non-developed legal provision, despite the legislative interest initially manifested. In this sense, the lack of action of the Spanish legislator can be seen as non-compliance with Directive 2004/114/EC, which supports this kind of processes.

In accordance with Art. 19 of the above-mentioned Directive, the Spanish State has decided not to facilitate the entry of foreigners on the grounds of agreements that could be signed by the immigration affairs authorities of the host countries of students who are third-country nationals and the teaching centres or organisations responsible for the student exchange programmes for the purpose of accelerating the admission procedure.

109. Therefore, this special regime is not applicable to those arriving in Spain for other reasons than the ones included in Art. 33 of OL 4/2000, even if they finally carry out those activities. This would be the case of those who, living in Spain, or holding a residence and work permit, decide to pursue their studies in Spanish teaching centres, to work in non-remunerated internships or to perform voluntary activities whilst in Spain. Neither is it applicable, for instance, to the children of foreigners living in Spain who, after being reunified or born in Spain, are enrolled in school.

110. The rules on applications for a study visa include a legal exception for foreigners who have been admitted as students by another EU Member State and request to pursue or complete their studies in Spain. These foreigners will be able to apply for a stay permit without having to obtain a visa first (Art. 33.7 of OL 4/2000).

(a) General requirements, to be assessed by the Spanish diplomatic mission or consular office: (i) when the foreigner is still a minor and is not accompanied by his parents or guardians, and as long as the minor does not lack of protection and the parents or guardians have given their permission for the minor to travel to Spain to perform the activity concerned and the centre, organisation, institution or body responsible for the activity and the stay have been duly informed; (ii) has the necessary economic means to cover his living expenses and a return ticket guaranteeing the return to the country of origin and, when required, those of their family members, to the amount expressly established by the law;[111] (iii) has paid the fee for the processing of the application; (iv) has taken out a public or private health insurance with an insurer authorised to operate in Spain; (v) when the duration of the stay exceeds six months, not having any of the diseases that may have serious public health implications as set out in the 2005 International Health Regulations, and, in the case that the applicant has reached the age of criminal accountability, not have a criminal record in the countries where he has lived during the past five years, for offences or crimes as laid down in Spanish law.

(b) Specific requirements, to be assessed by the corresponding immigration affairs office, depending on the reason for admission the following applies:
   (i) if the person's purpose is to pursue a study: admission to an authorised teaching centre in Spain to follow a full-time programme leading to a degree or study certificate;
   (ii) if the purpose is to perform research or training activities, admission to an officially recognised centre in Spain;
   (iii) if the foreigner aims at participating in a student mobility programme – to pursue a secondary education and/or high school course in an officially recognised teaching or scientific centre: admission to the corresponding centre and evidence that the officially recognised organisation coordinating the programme will select a host family or institution to host the student during his stay and is responsible for the payment of study fees, living expenses and a return ticket to the student's country of origin;
   (iv) in the case of a non-remunerated internship: an agreement signed with a public or private company or an officially recognised professional training centre establishing the internship relationship; and
   (v) in the case of voluntary work: an agreement signed with the organisation in charge of the voluntary work programme which includes a description

111. The amounts required are the following: (a) for the student's subsistence, an amount that monthly represents 100% of the IPREM – as mentioned before, this is an indicator (the Public Income Rate of Multiple Effects) defined by the Spanish law, which was fixed at EUR 532.51/month for 2017–, except when it is duly proved that the accommodation for the whole stay period has been paid beforehand; (b) if the foreigner participates in a student mobility programme, to pursue a secondary education or high school course in an officially recognised teaching or scientific centre, the evidence of the availability of the above-mentioned amount will be substituted by the fact that the mobility programme provides the means to guarantee the subsistence of the foreigner enrolled in it; (c) for the subsistence of family members, of whom the foreigner is in charge during their stay in Spain, an amount representing 75% of the IPREM, for the first family member, and 50% of the IPREM for each of the following persons that will conform the family unit in Spain, except when the accommodation for the whole stay period in Spain is proved to have been paid beforehand.

of the activities to be performed by the foreigner, the conditions in which they will be performed, the time schedule and the resources available to pay for the person's travel expenses, costs of living and accommodation during his stay as well as evidence that the organisation coordinating this voluntary work programme has taken out a civil liability insurance to cover those activities.

162. The diplomatic mission or consular office has seven days, from the moment the visa application is received, to adopt a decision on the application. If this period expires without a decision of the administration, it is assumed that the decision is favourable to the applicant (Article 39.3 of RD 557/2011).[112] A visa may be refused without being motivated for any one of the following circumstances (Article 39.5 and tenth additional disposition of RD 557/2011): (a) if the applicant has a criminal record in any of the countries where he has lived during the past five years for offences and crimes which are also offences and crimes according to Spanish law; (b) when false documents have been submitted, incorrect statements have been made, or certain actions were made in bad faith; and (c) if there is a legal justification for a dismissal or rejection of the application that was not recognised as such when the application was submitted.

163. As for the validity period of the stay permit, it shall coincide with the duration of the activity for which it was requested, although the law establishes a maximum period of one year. If the activity for which the visa was requested has a duration that exceeds this period, a foreigner can apply for and obtain an extension of the permit for successive one-year periods (Article 33.3 of OL 4/2000).[113] Here, Spanish law is more favourable than Directive 2004/114/EC, which restricts the possibility of extending a stay permit in relation to certain activities (*see* Articles 14 and 15).

164. As far as family reunification is concerned Spanish law acknowledges the right of the family members of foreigners who have applied for a study visa, or who are in Spain as participants in a student mobility programme or performing a non-remunerated internship or voluntary services, to apply for the corresponding stay visa to enter and remain in Spain during the validity period of the foreigner's stay, without requiring the holder of the study visa to provide evidence of a previous stay period (Article 41 of RD 557/2011). For this purpose, the law considers as a family

112. It should also be taken into account that, once the stay is authorised, should its duration exceed six months, the foreigner has to apply for a foreign identity card, a legal obligation that they have to comply with within one month from their entry into Spain (Art. 30.7 of RD 557/2011).

113. Spanish law also acknowledges the right of foreigners admitted as students by another EU Member State, who request to pursue or complete their studies in Spain, to apply for a stay permit on study grounds and to obtain it as long as they meet the corresponding legal requirements, amongst which being granted a visa is in this case non-compulsory (Art. 33.7 of OL 4/2000). For foreign students who have been admitted in Spain who wish to pursue or complete their studies in another EU Member State, the Spanish law establishes the obligation of Spanish authorities to provide information on the person's stay in Spain whenever the competent authorities of that Member State thus request.

member: the foreigner's spouse, unmarried partner, and children under the age of eighteen or who have a disability that objectively prevents them from providing for their own needs due to the state of their health. An application made by a family member will be processed if the holder of the stay permit satisfies the following requirements:

(a) holds a valid stay permit, i.e., the permit must have been granted before family reunification is applied for;
(b) has sufficient economic means of subsistence for the family members; and
(c) provides evidence of the family or kinship ties between the foreigner and their family members.

165. The duration of residence of the family members in Spain is, by law, linked to the duration of the stay permit granted to the foreigner. Article 41.3 of RD 557/2011 specifies that they are allowed to stay legally in Spain 'during the same period and in with an identical status as the holder of the main permit'. In any case, should the stay of the family members exceed six months, the Spanish law requires them to apply for a foreigner identity card within a month from their entry into Spain. This is an obligation that the foreigner who is granted a stay permit for the purpose of study also needs to fulfil. It is forbidden for these foreigners to apply for a permit to perform economic activities. This prevents them from developing a professional and labour career (Article 41.4 of RD 557/2011).

166. As mentioned before, Spanish legislation includes the possibility of a change of the legal status of a foreigner who is in the country for reasons related to study, research, training or non-remunerated internship. This is not the case for foreigners admitted in a student exchange programme or wishing to perform voluntary services. This means that there is no need for them to request a visa and as long as they meet the legal requirements, they may apply for one of the following residence permits:[114] (a) residence and employment; (b) residence and research work; (c) residence and highly qualified employment; (d) residence and self-employment; and (e) residence without the right to work.

114. For this purpose, the requirements in Arts 41 of OL 4/2000 and 64, 76, 87, 105 or 117 of RD 557/2011 need to be taken into account – though in this case the national employment situation, to which, for example, Art. 64.3 a) of RD 557/2011 refers, will not be taken into consideration.
The legal requirement of having a work permit reflects the legal exception in Art. 43, first paragraph, of RD 557/2011, which concerns foreigners who are pursuing a specialised health care training. For these foreigners, Spanish law establishes that, if they wish to work, they do not need to apply for a work permit – although they will be obliged to communicate this circumstance to the competent immigration affairs office – if they have obtained a Spanish degree in Medicine, Pharmacy, Nursery or any other university degree enabling them to participate in the annual calls for selective tests to obtain a specialised health care training position (subject to the regime defined by RD 1146/2006, of 6 October 2006, regulating the special employment relationship of trainee Health specialists in residency (OSG 7 Oct. 2006, No. 240), and if they obtain one of those positions within the context of such calls. This legal exception also benefits those holding a duly recognised or approved of foreign degree in one of the above-mentioned studies (Art. 43, third paragraph, of RD 557/2011).

167. In general terms, a foreigner will, in this case, be requested to provide evidence of the following facts:

(a) Having lived in Spain during at least three years as a holder of a stay permit, although this requirement may be reduced in certain cases, if not eliminated.[115] When appropriate, satisfying this requirement will be compulsory on the day that the foreigner's status is changed, i.e., from a stay to a residence status.
(b) Having completed their studies or successfully concluded their research work, training or internship.
(c) Not having been granted a scholarship or been subsidised by a public or private body within the framework of a cooperation or development programme, whether Spanish or from their country of origin.

168. The change of status, from stay to residence, has to be requested by the foreigners themselves, or, where appropriate, by the entrepreneur who provides the employment, in accordance with the administrative procedure established for each type of permit. If the permit is granted, it will be considered and treated as an initial permit, so that its effectiveness will be conditioned by the later inclusion of the worker in the corresponding Social Security regime – in the case that they are authorised to work. At the same time, i.e., also within a month from the granting of the permit, the foreigner will be obliged to apply for a foreign identity card with the competent immigration affairs office or police station (Article 199.3 of RD 557/2011). If the Spanish authorities establish that the foreigner does not meet the requirements necessary to obtain a residence and work permit, but that he does meet the requirements necessary to be granted an initial residence permit, then the competent Spanish administrative body is obliged to adopted a favourable decision in relation to the latter, even if its effectiveness is subject to the condition that the corresponding visa (Article 199.6 of RD 557/2011).

169. Finally, the legal treatment given the work that a foreign student is allowed to do for a family in Spain in exchange for their accommodation and subsistence while they improve their professional or language proficiency, an activity generally refer to as 'au pair placement', is quite peculiar. In relation to this activity, Article 33.5 of OL 4/2000 establishes that his kind of work 'is regulated according to the provisions in international agreements on the au pair status'. To date, Spain has only

---

115. Article 199.4 of RD 557/2011 provides for the possibility to reduce the above-mentioned three-year period if the Secretary of State of Immigration and Emigration issues a favourable report in this sense in the case of foreigners whose residence in Spain is deemed appropriate due to the exceptional relevance of their professional and scientific achievements, duly accredited by them.

In addition, Spanish law does not impose this requirement on: (a) foreigners who have exceeded the period of their internship and/or the complementary training period specified in the law regulating the conditions for the acknowledgement, for professional purposes, of the degree of specialist in Health Sciences, obtained in States that do not belong to the European Union; and (b) foreigners who are holders of an officially approved of degree in Medicine, as long as the activity to be developed after the change of status entails them entering the complementary Military Health Corps.

signed the European Agreement on Au Pair Placement, of 24 November 1969,[116] which is, therefore, the only international agreement to be considered on this matter.

170. This is a special agreement in the sense that it only links Spain to Italy, France, Norway, Denmark and Luxembourg, and that the rules established by it are only applicable to third-country nationals living in one of the above-mentioned States. In this sense, the agreement defines 'au pair placement' as 'the temporary reception by families, in exchange for certain services, of young foreigners who come to improve their linguistic and possibly professional knowledge as well as their general culture by acquiring a better knowledge of the country where they are received' (Article 2). The activity regulated is, nevertheless, defined in this agreement according to a series of parameters: (a) age: not being less than 17 or more than 30 years old – although national authorities are entitled to make exceptions to the maximum age limit; (b) health conditions: au pairs shall be in possession of a health certificate issued not more than three months before the beginning of their activity, in which the general health state of the person is specified; and (c) time limit of the activity: the activity cannot last more than one year, although it is possible to extend it to a maximum of two years.

171. The relationship between the au pair and the host family is regulated by a written agreement between the two parties, although the European Agreement acknowledges a series of rights for each party (*see* Article 8). The agreement is preferably signed before the au pair leaves his country of residence, although it is also possible to sign it during the first week of his stay with the host family. Once the placement is verified, the au pair has access to the benefits that Spain acknowledges for these persons, in accordance with the European Agreement, in matters related to sickness, maternity or accidents.

116. Ratified by Spain through an Instrument of ratification on 24 June 1988 (OSG 6 Sep. 1988, No. 214).

Chapter 3. Researchers and Teachers

172. The current special regime that authorises the entry, residence and work in Spain of researchers and teachers finds its origin in OL 2/2009, which was amended OL 4/2000 introducing two new concepts, one of them through Articles 38*bis*, which focuses on the status of researchers, and the other one through Articles 39*ter*, which regulates the situation of highly qualified professionals. This was a response to demands of the EU to modernise the procedure to enter Spain and access its labour market for certain groups hereby requiring a differentiated treatment in application of Union directives such as Directive 2005/71/EC or Directive 2009/50/EC. This legislative action was completed years later with the passing of the abovementioned Law 14/2013, which established a migration channel different than the one established by OL 4/2000 that will be analysed presently.

173. Even if there has been a legal regime for researchers adapted to Union law since 2009 (Articles 38*bis* of OL 4/2000), it was only in 2011 that the Spanish government updated the terms enabling differentiated treatment for teachers, with the passing of RD 557/2011, Title IX entitled 'procedure to authorise the entry, residence and work in Spain of foreigners whose professional activity is of economic, social or labour interest, or the object of which is the performance of research, development or teaching work requiring a high qualification, or entails the performance of artistic actions of special cultural interest'.[117] This procedure has been designed to also allow for the possibility that companies, established in Spain, hire foreign researchers from States that do not belong to the EU. It is time to analyse the regime of these two groups, starting with the researchers.

174. To start, the legal status of temporary residence and research work (Articles 38*bis* of OL 4/2000; Articles 73–84 and 163 of RD 557/2011) is acquired through the corresponding permit. According to the law the main purpose of this authorisation is to enable the realisation of a research project in the framework of a hosting agreement signed between the foreign researcher and a Spanish research centre. In this sense, a research centre is understood as 'any physical or legal person, be it public or private, with a main or secondary establishment in Spain, which develops research and technological development activities and has been authorised to sign hosting agreements'.[118] Obtaining a research visa is not required when the

---

117. The new regime established by Title IX of RD 557/2011 implements the third final disposition of OL 2/2009, which necessitated the adaptation of the Resolution of the Secretary of State of Immigration and Emigration, of 28 February 2007, on the agreement that approved the instructions for the procedure to authorise the entry, residence and work in Spain of foreigners whose professional activity has an economic, social or labour interest, is related to research, development or teaching work, requires a high qualification, or involves artistic actions of special cultural interest to comply with Union law.

118. Not all research activities are subject to this legal regime. The following examples are not included in this special regime: (a) foreign researchers who have been admitted by another EU Member State and need to continue their research in Spain during a period of at least three months (Arts 38.7*bis* of OL 4/2000 and Art. 84 of RD 557/2011); (b) research projects performed within the framework of training programmes or voluntary services (Art. 73.3 of RD 557/2011), which are subject to the

researcher exercises his right to mobility after having initiated his research in another EU Member State. In any case, Spanish law establishes that a research permit is valid for a period of no less than three months and no more than five years, and that its validity shall coincide with the duration of the research project in relation to which it is granted. For stays in Spain of less than three months, and according to Article 84 of RD 557/2011, it is not necessary to apply for any administrative permit.

175. The conditions to be met in order to obtain the corresponding permit are, as in previous cases, of two different types. On the one hand, the residence authorisation requires: (a) that the foreigner is not illegally in Spain; (b) that the foreigner does not have a criminal record, neither in Spain, nor in any of the countries where he has lived in the past five years, for offences and crimes laid down in Spanish law; (c) that the foreigner is not listed as 'rejectable' by the authorities of the countries with which Spain has signed an agreement in this regard; and (d) that the foreigner has paid the fee for the processing of the application to obtain a temporary residence permit. In addition, regarding the activity to be developed by the foreign researcher, Spanish law requires: (a) that the research centre where the foreign researcher will work is authorised to sign hosting agreements as those referred to in the law;[119] (b) that the research centre has formalised the inclusion of the foreign researcher in the corresponding regime of the Social Security system and that the research centre has complied with all its tax and Social Security obligations; (c) that the research centre has signed a hosting agreement with the foreign researcher that guarantees the latter a continuous activity during the period in which his permit is valid and that includes the corresponding labour contract;[120] (d) that the researcher has the professional training and qualifications that are legally required to exercise the profession for which he has been hired; and (e) that the fee for the proceedings to obtain the work permit has been paid.

---

regime established by Arts 37 ff. of RD 557/2011; (c) the activity of members of international scientific missions who enter Spain to perform work or conduct research and who have been authorised by the competent state or regional administration (Arts 41.1 ff. of OL 4/2000 and Art. 117 of RD 557/2011).

119. According to Arts 38.2*bis* of OL 4/2000, the research institutions, whether public or private, that meet the requirements established by law are authorised by the Spanish State or the autonomous regions to hire foreign researchers for periods of no less than five years, although these permits may, exceptionally, be granted for shorter periods.

Order CIN/1795/2011 of 28 June (OSG 30 Jun. 2011, No. 155) is the law that regulates the authorisation of research centres to sign the above-mentioned hosting agreements. This law establishes that the following institutions do not have to request an authorisation: (a) universities, both public and private, registered in the *Registro de Universidades, Centros y Títulos de España* (Spanish Registry of Universities, Centres and Degrees); (b) public bodies dependent on the State or the autonomous regions; and (c) technological centres registered in the *Registro de Centros Tecnológicos y Centros de Apoyo a la Innovación Tecnológica* (Registry of Technological Centres and Centres for the Support of Technological Innovation).

120. The signing of a hosting agreement is a fundamental requirement for the issuing of residence and work permits to researchers, to such extent that, should the agreement finally not be implemented, this will result in the denial of the permit (Art. 79 of RD 557/2011).

176. A foreign researcher has to obtain a research visa while resident outside the EU. Consequently, the residence and work permit that the researcher applies for is an initial authorisation (Article 80 of RD 557/2011). The issuing of a visa will be subject to compliance with the legal requirements to obtain a temporary residence and employment visa – as regulated by Article 70 of RD 557/2011.

177. The initial temporary residence and work permit shall, according to the law, is valid for a period of no less than three months and no more than five years. The period of validity, however, coincides with the duration of the research project that led to the issuing of the permit. A permit is exclusively limited to the research activity for which it was granted. The law defines two basic situations in which the above-mentioned permit is terminated (Article 163 of RD 557/2011): (a) termination without the issuing of an administrative decision, whenever the period for which the above-mentioned permit was granted has expired, or when the foreign resident is forced to renew the permit under extraordinary circumstances because the competent authorities have declared a state of emergency or siege; and (b) termination by decision of the competent body that issued the permit, when there is evidence that the permit was obtained by fraudulent means, when the circumstances that served as the basis for the issuing of the permit no longer exist or if it is established that those circumstances did not exist, or when its holder lives in Spain for a reason other than that for which he was authorised to temporarily reside and work in that country.

178. The administrative procedure to issue a permit starts with a request submitted to the competent administration by the research centre, which has signed the corresponding hosting agreement with the foreign researcher. The administration has forty-five days to issue a justified decision. A procedure for the renewal of the temporary residence and research work permit in annual periods is provided for, as long as the researcher proves compliance with the requirements that enabled the granting of the initial permit (Article 82 of RD 557/2011). A renewal application must be submitted within sixty days prior to the expiry date of the initial permit. The validity of this initial permit is then extended until the decision on the renewal is adopted. If three months should pass without an explicit decision by the administrative authorities, the application is deemed to be accepted and the renewal of the permit will be granted.

179. An interesting aspect of the special regime for foreign researchers, as established in Articles 38*bis* of OL 4/2000, concerns the compatibility, which is permitted by law, between a foreigner's main research activity and the possibility to teach, as a secondary activity, or to perform other activities than the research work. Whether these primary and secondary activities are legally compatibility, depends on the terms in which the researcher's hosting agreement has been drafted, since this is the reference document to be taken into account in these cases.

180. The special procedure in Title IX of RD 557/2011 (Articles 178–181), is designed to allow employers already established in Spain to apply for residence and work permits for non-EU foreign workers, in order to develop a labour relationship, in the following cases: (a) when the purpose is to bring to Spain highly qualified foreign technicians and scientists hired by the State, the AR, city councils or other bodies devoted to the promotion and development of research and supported by the former or in which the former have a major stake; and (b) when there is a need for highly qualified technicians or scientists to perform research work or to participate in development activities in universities, renown and prestigious R+D centres, or R+D departments in companies established in Spain.

181. The application for a permit, which has to be submitted by the employer and is decided on by the competent administration within a one-month period, has to be supplemented by a descriptive report of the project in which the foreigner will participate. This report must explicitly indicate the objective and justification of the research, as well as the human resources and budget available, together with a work plan and the tasks entrusted to the foreigner. This information may be included in the hosting agreement signed by the researcher, in which case it will be enough to submit the agreement. In addition, and depending on the case, it may also be necessary to submit documents proving that the objective of the institution hosting the foreign researcher is to promote and develop research activities and that it is supported or controlled in its management by a territorial public administration – those cases in which the territorial public administration is directly hiring the researcher are excluded from this documentary obligation. In some situations, it may be necessary to submit a favourable report of the competent State or regional body, as proof that the hosting institution satisfies the requirements of being a prestigious and renowned R+D centre or the R+D department of a company.

182. The regime established in Title IX of RD 557/2011 for teachers only applies to foreign professors hired by Spanish universities, whether public or private. As with researchers, the employer is obliged to submit the corresponding request and, in this case, the only additional document demanded is a certificate signed by the university rector or representative specifying the teaching tasks assigned to the professor.

183. In relation to the regime for the family members of researchers and teachers, Spanish law recognises the right of foreign non-EU researchers and teachers' family members to apply for a temporary residence permit without the right to work (Article 181.1 of RD 557/2011). There is the possibility of granting family members a residence and employment permit, if they meet the corresponding legal requirements and their application is submitted jointly with that of the researcher or professor or during the validity period of the latter's permit. In this case, RD 557/2011 explicitly provides for derogation to the rule to take into account the national employment situation in Spain when assessing the permit application. The permit issued to family members cannot exceed, in any case, the validity period of the main permit – i.e., the one granted to the researcher or teacher. These rights do not affect the foreigner's right to apply for the reunification of their family members, under the terms and conditions established by the current legislation (Articles 16–19 of OL 4/2000).

184. All family members mentioned in Article 17 of OL 4/2000 qualify for a permit under the above-mentioned rules (Article 181.2 of RD 557/2011) with the exception of ascendants over 65 years, who cannot obtain a residence and employment permit. This exclusion played an important role in the decision to raise the ordinary retirement age in Spain to 65 years and 5 months in 2017.

185. The permit application for a family member may either be submitted together with that of the foreign worker or separately at a later moment. In this last case, the application will be submitted to the Spanish diplomatic mission or consular office in the territory where the family home is located. If the application is made for a temporary residence and employment permit, it is the employer who is obliged to submit the application not to the diplomatic and consular mission, but to the registry of the General Directorate of Immigration or to the corresponding immigration affairs office in the province where the work activity will be developed. The administration has one month to decide on the application for a residence permit and, where appropriate, an employment permit. A decision on an application for a visa requests must be adopted and notified to the applicant within ten working days from submittal.

Chapter 4. Labour and Economic Migration

§1. Labour Employment

186. Spanish migration legislation provides in a differentiated way, i.e., five specific legal frameworks, for the admission of foreign employed workers. The legislative technique used is quite special, because three of those cases are regulated by OL 4/2000, while the other two are regulated by Law 14/2013, which, as mentioned at the beginning of this work, is an attempt of the Spanish legislator to provide a selective channel for economic migration which, in no way, is connected with the ordinary channels for labour migration in OL 4/2000.

I. Highly Qualified Professionals Who Are Holders of the EU Blue Card

187. The first framework is set out in Articles 38*ter* of OL 4/2000 and regulates temporary residence for the purpose of employment by highly qualified professionals who are holders of the EU blue card.[121] Highly qualified professionals are 'all foreign workers authorised to perform a labour activity for which it is required to have a higher education qualification, or who, exceptionally, can prove to have a minimum of five years of professional experience that can be considered equivalent to that qualification and that is related to the activity for the execution of which the permit is granted' (Article 85.1 of RD 557/2011).[122] In order to define the worker who qualifies as a highly qualified worker, two factors, each with their own nature, are indiscriminately relevant. On the one hand, the possession of a higher education qualification and, on the other, professional experience that can be considered

121. Regulated as well by Arts. 85–96 of RD 557/2011.

122. Article 85.2 of RD 557/2011 establishes that 'a higher education qualification is one derived from a higher education training, with a duration of at least three years and providing the level of qualification necessary to exercise a profession requiring a high proficiency level or to enter an advanced research programme'.

There are certain differences in the terminology used in Arts. 38*ter* of OL 4/2000 and Art. 85.1 of RD 557/2011 when describing this legal situation. Thus, while Arts 38.2*ter* seems to refer to professionals in general in terms that are quite vague – 'For the purpose of this article, it is considered that highly qualified professionals are those who can prove qualifications … ' – the regulatory norm establishes that 'The temporary residence and highly qualified professional work situation is that which affects the foreign worker who … '. The answer to the questions arising from this different use of terminology is that only workers who are employed by a third party can obtain this type of permit, and that self-employed persons and other professionals who wish to develop their professional activity in Spain have to use other legal procedures designed for them. In this sense, Art. 2 b) of Council Directive 2009/50/EC, of 25 May 2009, on the conditions of entry and residence of third-country nationals for the purposes of highly qualified employment (OJEU, L 155/17 of 18 Jun. 2009) defines 'highly qualified employment' as the 'employment of a person who: – in the Member States concerned, is protected as an employee under national employment law and/or in accordance with national practice, irrespective of the legal relationship, for the purpose of exercising genuine and effective work for, or under the direction, of someone else'.

equivalent to the above-mentioned qualification, so that when the workers can provide evidence of one or the other condition they can apply for the corresponding temporary residence and work permit.

188. In practice, it has proven very difficult to provide evidence of the existence of professional experience – which must be related to the professional activity for which the residence and work permit is granted – that may be considered equivalent to higher education qualification. Ironically, quite often, professional experience is actually more interesting than the fact that the applicant has a degree. Like the Union norm in Directive 2009/50/EC, the following persons are excluded from submitting an application for a residence and work permit under this preferential regime by third-country nationals in the following circumstances (Article 3.2. of Directive 2009/50/EC):

(a) When they have been authorised to reside in a Member State under a temporary protection regime or have applied for a permit to reside in that Member State on the basis of such a protection regime and are awaiting a decision on their status.
(b) When they are beneficiaries of international protection under Council Directive 2011/95/EU, of 13 December 2011, on standards for the qualification of third-country nationals or stateless persons as beneficiaries of international protection, for a uniform status for refuge or for persons eligible for subsidiary protection, and for the content of the protection granted (recast),[123] or have applied for international protection under that Directive and whose application has still not been decided on.
(c) When they are beneficiaries of protection in accordance with national law, international obligations or the practice of the Member State, or have applied for protection in accordance with national law, international obligations or the practice of the Member State and whose application has still not been decided on.
(d) When they have applied for residence permission in the Member State as researchers, in the sense of Directive 2005/71/EC, in order to carry out a research project.[124]
(e) When they are family members of EU citizens who have exercised or are exercising their right to free movement within the Community in conformity with Directive 2004/38/EC of the European Parliament and the Council, of 29 April 2004, on the right of citizens of the Union and their family members to move and reside freely within the territory of the Member States.[125]
(f) When they enjoy the EC long-term residence status in a Member State in accordance with Directive 2003/109/EC and exercise their right to reside in another Member State in order to carry out an economic activity as an employed or a self-employed person.[126]

---

123. OJEU, L 337/9 of 20 Dec. 2011.
124. OJEU, L 289/15 of 31 Nov. 2015.
125. OJEU, L 158/77 of 30 Apr. 2004.
126. OJEU, L 16/44 of 23 Jan. 2004.

(g) When they enter a Member State by virtue of the commitments in an international agreement facilitating the entry and temporary residence of certain categories of commerce and investment-related natural persons.
(h) When they are admitted to the territory of the Member State as seasonal workers.
(i) When their expulsion has been suspended by reasons of fact or law.
(j) When they benefit from Directive 96/71/EC of the European Parliament and the Council, of 16 December 1996, concerning the posting of workers in the framework of the provision of services,[127] as long as they are posted in the Member State concerned.
(k) When they or their family members, whatever their nationality and in accordance with the agreements signed by the Union and its Member States and those third countries, enjoy rights of free movement that are equivalent to those of Union citizens (Article 3.2, final paragraph, of Directive 2009/50/EC).

189. The initial permit granted to highly qualified workers is valid for one year (Article 86.2 of RD 557/2011). When considering an application for a residence and work permit as a highly qualified worker, the competent Spanish administration enjoys a large degree of discretion, so that there is no such thing as a right of admission as a highly qualified worker. In this sense, Article 6 of Directive 2009/50/EC acknowledges the right of every Member State 'to determine the volume of admission of third-country nationals entering its territory for the purposes of highly qualified employment', according to the needs of its national labour market and, in brief, its estimated hosting capacity. This is why Spanish law establishes (Articles 38.3*ter* of OL 4/2000) that, when granting these permits, 'the national employment situation may be taken into account, as well as the need to protect the availability of human resources in the foreigner's country of origin'.

190. The conditions that have to be satisfied to be granted an initial temporary residence and work permit for highly qualified professionals are the following:

(a) In relation to the residence of the highly qualified worker, the law requires that he:
   (i) is not living irregularly in Spain;
   (ii) does not have a criminal record in Spain or in the countries where he has lived during the past five years, for offences and crimes punishable according to Spanish law;
   (iii) is not listed as a person who has to be rejected when entering one of the countries with which Spain has signed an agreement in this regard; and.
   (iv) he has paid the fee for the processing of the temporary residence permit.
(b) In relation to the activity to be developed, it is required that:
   (i) the employer has submitted a labour contract that guarantees the worker a continuous activity during the period of validity of the temporary residence and work permit;

127. OJEU, L 018 of 21 Jan. 1997.

(ii) the conditions of the labour contract comply with those established by current regulations and the collective bargain agreement applicable to the specific activity, professional category and place, and that the annual gross salary specified in the labour contract is, at least, 1.5 the average annual gross salary;[128]
(iii) the employer has registered the highly qualified worker for the corresponding Social Security regime and has complied with all his tax and Social Security obligations;
(iv) the employer has sufficient economic, material and personal means to support the business project and to face his obligations towards the worker under the labour contract;
(v) the foreigner is trained and, where appropriate, has the professional qualifications legally required for the exercise of his profession;
(vi) the fee for the processing of the permit has been paid;
(vii) the national employment situation allows for the hiring a foreign worker according with the terms in Article 65 of the RD 557/2001.

II. Highly Qualified Professionals in the Sense of Law 14/2013

191. Second, as pointed out before, Law 14/2013 defines 'highly qualified professionals' as those persons benefitting from the selective migration channel established by this law, as granting these foreigners the right to enter and stay in Spanish territory is necessary 'for reasons of economic interest' (Article 61.1 of Law 14/2013). The label 'highly qualified professional' brings together three different types of professionals (Article 71 of Law 14/2013): (a) managers or highly qualified staff who aim at developing a labour or professional relationship with firms or groups of firms with certain characteristics; (b) professionals who wish to carry out training, development or innovation activities in Spain, whether in public or private institutions;[129] and (c) graduates and postgraduates of renown and prestigious universities and business schools. In all three cases, the professionals will be a staff member of a company located in Spain.

192. In the case of managers or highly qualified staff, Spanish law limits the admission of these professionals to a limited number of firms or groups of firms with a very specific profile. Therefore, this option is not option open for all kinds of

128. Exceptionally, Art. 87.2 b), second paragraph, of RD 557/2011 establishes that, as long as the contract complies with the current legal norm and the applicable collective bargain agreement, the salary threshold may be 1.2 the average annual gross salary for those professions in which there is 'a special need for third-country workers' and which belong to groups 1 and 2 of the International Standard Classification of Occupations (ISCO).

129. The following persons will be required to obtain a residence visa or permit for the purpose of training: (a) research staff, as specified in Art. 13 and the first additional disposition of Law 14/2011, of 1 June, on Science, Technology and Innovation; (b) scientific and technical staff involved in scientific, development or technological innovation projects in companies or R&D&I centres in Spain; (c) researchers hosted, within the framework of an agreement, by public or private research institutions; and (d) professors hired by universities, higher education institutions, research centres or business schools in Spain.

companies. For the purpose of this law, a firm or group of firms are those which satisfy the following conditions (Article 71.1 a) of Law 14/2013): (a) an average staff of more than 250 employees during the three months prior to the submission of the residence permit application; (b) an annual net turnover of over EUR 50 million, in Spain, or a net equity of over EUR 43 million, also in Spain; (c) an average annual foreign gross investment of no less than EUR 1 million during the three years immediately prior to the submission of the application; (d) a stock value or investment position of over EUR 3 million according to the last data of the *Registro de Inversiones Exteriores* (Registry of Foreign Investment) of the Spanish Ministry of Economy and Competitiveness; and (e) for small and medium-sized companies established in Spain, belonging to an industry considered to be strategic.

193. For the purpose of the law, the staff have to participate in a 'business project', which is considered and proven to be 'of general interest'. Companies or groups of companies are not mentioned. This conditions guarantees that one or more of the following objectives is achieved with the employment of a highly qualified worker: (a) a 'significant increment' in the creation of direct jobs by the firm requesting the professional's services; (b) the maintenance of employment; (c) a 'significant increment' in the creation of jobs in the activity sector or geographical area where the labour activity is to be developed; (d) an extraordinary investment with a 'relevant' socio-economic impact in the geographical area where the activity will be carried out; and (e) a relevant contribution to scientific and/or technological innovation.

194. As for the foreigners who intend to enter Spain, or who, being holders of stay and residence permits, wish to perform training, research, development or innovation activities in public or private institutions, Article 72 of Law 14/2013 provides that they can stay in Spain once they have obtained a visa or residence permit for training or research purposes, which will be valid for the whole national territory. This legal option is only open to the following extra-Union foreigners: (a) research staff, as defined within the meaning of Law 14/2011, of 1 June 2011, on Science, Technology and Innovation (Article 13 and first additional disposition); (b) scientific and technical staff performing scientific, development or technological innovation work in companies or R&D&I centres established in Spain; (c) researchers hosted, within the framework of an agreement, by public or private research bodies, under the conditions established by Royal Decree; or (d) professors hired by universities, higher education institutions, research centres or business schools established in Spain, according to the criteria defined by Royal Decree. This law still needs to be developed. Consequently, there are some substantial shortcomings in the law.

195. Besides the specific conditions to obtain the different visa or permit issued to 'highly qualified professionals', as defined in Law 14/2013, they also have to satisfy the following general requirements (Article 62), if they intend to benefit from the special regime of entry and residence in Spain on economic interest grounds, within the meaning of Articles 61ff. of Law 14/2013:

(a) For stays of no more than three months: the conditions of entry specified in 2016 Schengen Borders Code.
(b) For stay visa: the conditions in Regulation (EC) 810/2009, of 13 July 2009, establishing a Community Code on Visas (Visa Code).
(c) For residence visa as well as for residence permits, the following conditions in Regulation (EU) No. 265/2010, of 25 March 2010, amending the Convention Implementing the Schengen Agreement and Regulation (EC) No. 562/2006, of 15 March 2006, as regards movement of persons with a long-stay visa: (i) not staying irregularly in Spain; (ii) over the age of 18 years old; (iii) not having a criminal record in Spain or the countries where the applicant has lived during the past five years, for offences and crimes as defined by Spanish law; (iv) not being listed as a person who has to be refused entry permission by the countries with which Spain has signed an agreement in this regard; (v) in possession of a public or private health insurance with an insurance company authorised to operate in Spain; (vi) sufficient financial means for himself and accompanying family members during their time of residence in Spain; and (vii) having paid the fee for the processing of the permit or visa application.

196. The family members who can accompany or be reunited with highly qualified professionals are, as listed in Article 62.4 of Law 14/3013, are: the spouse or person in an equivalent relationship – i.e., the unmarried partner – their children under the legal age of majority or economically dependent on the highly qualified professional, who have not yet started their own family, and ascendants for whom the holder is responsible. These family members are entitled to apply for, jointly and simultaneously with the highly qualified professional or at a later stage, for a stay or residence permit and, when required, the necessary visa. For this purpose, family members have to comply with the general requirements specified before in relation to highly qualified professionals, as established by Article 62 of Law 14/2013.

III. The Transnational Service Provisions

197. Temporary residence and work within the framework of transnational service provision[130] is another situation regulated by OL 4/2000. Transnational service providers are foreign workers who are posted to a work centre in Spain and are employed by a company established in a State that is not a member of the EU or the European Economic Area.[131] The following situations are possible:

---

130. Regulated in Art. 42 of OL 4/2000 and Arts 110–116 of RD 557/2011.
131. This is a totally different situation to the previous one, because it does not require any temporary residence, is that of cross-border workers, which is, nevertheless regulated in the same article of OL 4/2000 and addresses the situation of workers who provide transnational services. Thus, Spanish law defines cross-border foreign workers as those who 'living in the border area, carry out their activity in Spain and return to their place of residence daily' (Art. 43.1 of OL 4/2000; Arts 182–184 of RD 557/2011). These workers must also apply for an administrative permit in order to work in Spain, although, for reasons of good neighbourliness there are groups, as for example among the cross-border workers living in Morocco and working in the Spanish cities of Ceuta and Melilla, who are exempted from the obligation to apply for this permit – see the Declaration on the cities

(a) temporary posting takes place on behalf and under the direction of a foreign company that has signed a contract with the recipient of the service to be provided by the foreign worker in Spain, as provided for by the fourth additional disposition of Law 45/1999, of 29 November 1999, on the posting of workers within the framework of transnational service provision;
(b) temporary posting at a work centre in Spain that belongs to the same company or another company within the group to which the former belongs;
(c) temporary posting of highly qualified workers who supervise or assess the work or services that companies established in Spain intend to perform abroad.

198. A residence and work permit is issued that is limited to a specific occupation and territory and is valid for the period that the worker will be posted in Spain, which is limited to one year (Article 119.3 of RD 557/2011). A residence and work permit is not issued if the posting concerns the development of training activities in cases identified as a) and c) in the previous paragraph, as well as for sailing staff employed by companies active in the merchant navy (Article 110.2 of RD 557/2011).

199. The conditions that apply to be issued a permit (Article 111 of RD 557/2011), concern both the person and the labour activity to be developed:

(a) Requirements related to the foreigner's residence:
  (i) Not to be irregularly in Spain.
  (ii) Not have a criminal record, neither in Spain nor in the countries where he has lived in the previous five years, for offences or crimes laid down in Spanish law.
  (iii) Not to be listed as a person who has to be refused entry permission by the countries with which Spain has signed an agreement in this regard.
  (iv) Not have returned to Spain before the period during which, in the framework of their voluntary return to their country of origin, the foreigner accepted not to do so has expired.
  (v) To be a stable and regular resident of the country or countries where the company that requires the posting is established.
  (vi) To have paid the fee for the processing of the temporary residence permit application.
(b) Requirements related to the labour activity:
  (i) the national employment situation allows the posting;[132]

---

of Ceuta and Melilla included in Annex III of the Agreement on the Accession of the Kingdom of Spain to the Convention implementing the Schengen Agreement (OJEU, L 239 of 22 Sep. 2000).

132. As specified in Art. 65 of RD 557/2011, the national employment situation is defined according to the 'Catalogue of occupations that are not easily covered' for each province or territorial demarcation, which is drawn up by the state administration or, when thus established, by the autonomous regions using data provided by the Public Employment Services of the autonomous regions, and which, in brief, allows identifying those jobs that the Spanish domestic labour market predictably will not be able to cover. The second paragraph of Art. 111.1 b) of RD 557/2011 waves consideration of this requirement when the employer proves that the activity to be developed by the

(ii) the foreign worker's professional activity in the country or countries where the company that requires his posting is established is considered normal, the foreign worker has performed the professional activity during at least one year and has been employed by the firm for at least nine months;
(iii) the firm to which the worker is posted is complied with all its tax and Social Security obligations in Spain;
(iv) the firm to which the worker is posted guarantees that the workers who are temporarily posted in Spain will enjoy the same labour conditions, as provided for by Spanish law;
(v) the fee for the processing of the work permit application has been paid.

200. A residence and work permit issued to a posted worker will allow the foreigner's entry into and residence in Spain for a maximum period of three months and for the purpose of starting, within three months from the date of entry into Spain, the labour activity in relation to which the foreigner has been granted permission to enter that country (Article 114 of RD 557/2011). The worker's registration in the corresponding Social Security regime is the moment that the residence and work permit take effect. If a residence and work permit is granted for more than six months, a foreigner is obliged to apply for a foreign identity card.

201. The law provides for possibility to issue seasonal work permits within the framework of transnational service provision (Article 116 of RD 557/2011), to foreign workers who are a member of the staff of a company developing its activity in a State that is not a Member State to the EU or the European Economic Area and who want to work temporarily in Spain for the same company or group of companies, as long as they comply with a series of conditions that are very similar to those discussed for the above-described type of permit.[133]

IV. Workers Involved in Intra-corporate Transfers Within the Same Company or Group of Companies

202. Fourth, Law 14/2013 establishes a special regime for 'workers involved in intra-corporate transfers within the same company or group of companies'.[134] In addition to the general requirements specified in Article 62 of Law 14/2013, Law

worker requires a direct and irrefutable knowledge of the firm and that the temporary posting will be at a work centre of the company or the group of companies to which the latter belongs.

133. The following conditions in Art. 116 of RD 557/2011 need to be satisfied: (a) the 'national employment situation', subject to the exceptions provided for by law, allows the transfer; (b) the professional activity to be developed by the foreign worker is his normal activity which he has performed during a period of t least one year and the foreign worker has been employed by the company that transfers him for at least nine months; (c) the company that transfers the foreigner must guarantee work conditions as set out in Law 45/1999; (d) the fee for the processing of the work authorisation has been paid; and (e) the residence of the foreign worker in the country or countries where the company, that is transferring him, is established, is considered stable and normal.

134. This regime is established by Arts 73 and 74 of Law 14/2013 and, through it and a later legal modification by Law 25/2015, the transposition of Directive 2014/66/EU of the European Parliament

14/2013 requires evidence that the following circumstances are satisfied: (a) the existence of a real business activity; (b) a higher education or equivalent degree or, when required, a minimum professional experience of three years; (c) the existence of a prior and continuous labour or professional relationship during at least three months with one or several of the companies in the group; and (d) the company's involvement in the transfer.

203. Spanish law provides for two different kinds of residence permits for intra-corporate transferees:

(a) The EU intra-corporate transfer residence permit that is issued in the case of a temporary posting as manager, specialist or trainee,[135] from a firm established outside the EU to an undertaking belonging to the same firm or group of firms established in Spain. The maximum duration of the transfer will be three years in the case of managers and specialists, and one in that of trainees. This permit, when issued by the Spanish authorities, will allow its holder to enter, reside and work in one or several EU Member States, if communicated to or applied for authorisation with the authorities of those States, as provided for by Directive 2014/66/EU of the European Parliament and of the Council, of 15 May 2014, on the conditions of entry and residence of third-country nationals in the framework of an intra-corporate transfer.[136]
(b) The national residence permit for intra-corporate transfers. This permit is granted in cases not covered by the first permit, and when the maximum duration of the transfer stipulated in the previous section has expired.

204. Authorised intra-corporate transfers may be either individual, or collectively managed. In this sense, Article 74.1 of Law 14/2013 provides that the companies or groups of companies that satisfy the above-mentioned conditions in Article 71.1 of that law may request for the joint processing of permit applications,

---

and of the Council, of 15 May 2014, on the conditions of entry and residence of third-country nationals in the framework of an intra-corporate transfer (OJEU, L 157/1 of 27 May 2014) was accomplished.

135. Article 73.3 a) of Law 14/2013 defines manager as 'a person who has, among his duties, the management of a firm or of a department or subdivision thereof', while a specialist is 'a person who has specialised knowledge relating to the activities, techniques or management of the company', and a trainee is 'a university graduate who is posted in order to obtain training in the techniques and methods of the firm and who is remunerated for it'.

136. Likewise, Art. 73.3 a) of Law 14/2013 states that the companies established in other EU Member States may post foreign workers holding an EU ICT intra-corporate transfer permit during the validity period of the said permit to Spain, provided that they have informed the *Unidad de Grandes Empresas y Colectivos Estratégicos* (Large Companies and Strategic Groups Unit). Within twenty days the Directorate General for Migration may refuse the transfer, by motivated decision, in the following cases: (a) when the legal conditions established in Art. 73 of Law 14/2013 are not fulfilled; (b) when the documents submitted have been acquired on a fraudulent basis or have been forged or manipulated; and (c) when the maximum duration of the transfer has expired. Additionally, Spanish law establishes that, in the event of a refusal by the Directorate General, the sending State will allow the foreign worker's re-entry without further formalities, if the posting has already taken place.

based on the planned management of a provisional quota of permits.[137] For the purpose of facilitating and speeding up the processing of a collective permit application, the company or group of companies may request their registration in the Large Companies and Strategic Groups Unit. This registration is valid for three years, on a renewable basis, if compliance with the requirements is ensured. Spanish law determines that registered companies will be exempted from providing evidence, at the time of application, of compliance with the conditions in Article 73.2 a), b) and c) of Law 14/2013.[138] However, the Spanish administration is entitled to check compliance with these requirements ex officio.

205. The general administrative procedure for the granting of a temporary residence and work permit, in fact, applies to all four options which have been discussed in this chapter and is regulated by Articles 75 and 76 of Law 14/2013. According to Spanish law stay and residence visa are issued by the Spanish diplomatic missions and consular offices according to Regulation (EC) No. 810/2009 of the European Parliament and of the Council, of 13 July 2009, establishing a Community Code on Visas (Visa Code), and Regulation (EU) No. 265/2010 of the European Parliament of the Council, of 25 March 2010, amending the Convention Implementing the Schengen Agreement and Regulation (EC) No. 562/2006 as regards the movement of persons with a long-stay visa. Visa requests are to be decided on and notified within ten labour days, unless an application requires an additional informative consultation, which is allowed by Article 22 of the EU Visa Code, in which case it is necessary to observe the deadlines in that code.

206. The so-called uniform visa can be issued for one, two or multiple entries and cannot be valid for more than five years. The duration of authorised stay is subject to an examination made in accordance with the conditions in Article 21 of the EU Visa Code. A 'visa of limited territorial validity', is issued when there are 'national interest circumstances', in conformity with the conditions in Article 25 of the Visa Code. A residence visa is valid for one year and authorises its holder to reside in Spain without having to apply for a foreign identity card.

207. The processing of an application for a residence permit is carried out by the Large Companies and Strategic Groups Unit, a body attached to the Directorate General for Migrations, which is actually the authority qualified to issue or refuse

137. Article 74.3 of Law 14/2013 excludes the application of this preferential treatment and, in brief, of the regime laid down in Art. 74 of that law in the case of companies or groups of companies that, in the three years immediately prior to the permit application: (a) have been sanctioned due to a serious or very serious infringement in matters related to migration affairs or immigration; or (b) have not provided evidence of compliance with the requirements in the case that ex officio verifications are made by the administration.

138. Therefore, they will not have to, every time, justify the existence of a real entrepreneurial activity, that the workers are graduates or have, when required, at least three years of professional experience, or the existence of a prior and continuous labour or professional relationship of at least three months with one or several companies in the group. The Spanish administration may verify ex officio compliance with these requirements and, consequently, they shall provide the corresponding documents to prove it.

to issue these permits. The period to decide on the application for a residence permit is twenty days from the moment the application is submitted to the abovementioned Unit. On expiry of this period, should the administration fail to adopt a decision, the application is deemed to be accepted. It is possible to apply for the renewal of these permits for periods of two years, as long as the conditions that justified the issuing of the permit in the first place are satisfied.

V. Foreign Workers Who, Residing in the Border Area, Develop Their Activities in Spain

208. Fifth and lastly, Article 43.1 of OL 4/2000 regulates the right of 'foreign workers who, residing in the border area, develop their activities in Spain and return to their place of residence daily', generally identified as cross-border workers. Section 2 of this provision refers to the regime of the so-called transnational provision of services, which is a different situation from the one just mentioned.

209. In the case of cross-border workers,[139] OL 4/2000 establishes that they need to obtain an administrative work permit, which is necessary to develop lucrative, labour or professional activities, whether through self-employment or wage employment (Article 182 of RD 557/2011). The law also establishes that these workers have to comply with the general requirements and conditions for the granting of work permits.[140] RD 557/2011 (Article 183.2) specifies the requirements that these foreigners must meet, depending on the type of activity that they intend to carry out, as follows:

(a) For an employment permit: (i) not having a criminal record in Spain or in any of the countries where they have resided during the past five years, for criminal offences considered as such by Spanish law; (ii) not being listed as a person to be refused entry permission in countries with which Spain as signed agreements in this regard; (iii) residing in a border area with Spain – the territories initially considered are Portugal, France, Andorra, Morocco and Gibraltar; (iv) the national employment situation allows the hiring of a foreign worker; (v) the employer has signed a labour contract with the cross-border worker, with a starting date coinciding with the issuing of the permit, and guarantees the worker a continuous activity for as long as the permits is valid; (vi) the employer has formalised the registration in the Social Security regime and has satisfied all outstanding tax and Social Security obligations; (vii) the conditions of the labour

139. According to Art. 182 of RD 557/2011 a situation of cross-border work is a situation in which the worker who has been authorised to develop gainful activities, labour or unsalaried employment, in Spain's border areas, resides in the border area of a neighbouring State to which he returns on a daily basis.

140. Note that the initial employment permit is not necessarily issued by the State because it may happen that the competent authority is an Autonomous region. In any case, once the decision has been notified, a foreign worker has a month to register with the Spanish Social Security service and join the insurance scheme. The worker is obliged to apply for the Foreigner Identity Card, even if the permit granted is valid for less than six months (Art. 183.3 of RD 557/2011).

contract meet those defined in the current law and the applicable collective bargaining agreement; (viii) the employer has sufficient economic, material or personal means to carry out the business project and face the obligations towards the worker; (ix) the worker is trained and, where applicable, has the professional qualifications which are legally required to exercise his profession.

(b) Self-employment permit: the above-mentioned conditions (i), (ii), (iii) and (iv), and, compulsory membership of a professional association, when required by Spanish law. Additionally, compliance with the following conditions may also be required: (i) evidence that the investment planned for the implementation of the project is sufficient and, where applicable, its impact on job creation and (ii) evidence that the activity produces, from the first year, enough revenues to at least cover the applicant's living expenses, after the costs involved with the activity have been deducted.

210. Article 184 of RD 557/2011 establishes that the duration of the initial work permit must coincide with that of the labour contract in relation to which it is granted, although there is a time limit fixed at no less than three months and no more than one year. This criterion also applies in the case of self-employment, in relation to the activity planned by the foreigner. In addition, the validity of the work permit is limited to the territory of the autonomous region or autonomous city – in the case of the Spanish cities of Ceuta and Melilla – in the border area of which the worker resides, and to the job or activity specified. Extensions of a permit are granted insofar as the labour relationship or self-employed activity continues and the circumstances that justified the issuing of the permit in the first place have not changed. Having said this, the validity of successive extensions is limited to a maximum period of one year. The holder of a work permit for cross-border workers does not have a right to obtain a residence and work permit, either for wage employment or self-employment. It is, however, possible to take the fact that the foreigner has worked as a cross-border worker in the past into consideration if, at some point in the future, he applies for a residence and work permit.

§2. Seasonal Workers and Temporary Workers

211. Temporary residence and employment is regulated by Article 38 of OL 4/2000; Articles 62–72 of RD 557/2011). A temporary residence and employment permit allows a foreigner to live and take up employment in Spain, if he has obtained a residence visa and has registered in the Social Security regime within three months after entering Spain. In principle, this initial temporary residence and employment permit only allows a foreigner to work in one specific province and profession[141] for a maximum period of one year.

212. Article 38 of OL 4/2000 recognises two different situations in which a temporary residence and employment permit can be applied for:

141. The condition 'national employment situation' does not apply in the following situations (Art. 63.1, second paragraph, of RD 557/2011): (a) positions of trust and management in companies; (b) highly

(1) The foreigner is already in Spain, in which case he must apply for and obtain a residence and employment permit.
(2) The entrepreneur or employer submits an application to cover a vacant position to the competent authorities together with a labour contract and the other documents required to offer the position to a foreign worker in a third country.

213. The initial granting of a residence and employment permit is subject to an assessment of the so-called national employment situation, a concept which ultimately refers to the 'Catalogue of occupations that are not easily covered', which is periodically updated by the National Employment Public Service and contains a list of jobs which foreign workers may perform (Article 38 of OL 4/2000).[142] An entrepreneur can apply for an initial temporary residence and employment permit for foreign workers if the application concerns a job vacancy if there is little chance of finding labour already available in Spain.

214. To be issued a visa for the purpose of temporary employment (Article 70 of RD 557/2011) the following conditions have to be satisfied:

(a) an initial temporary residence and employment permit has been issued;
(b) if over the age of criminal responsibility, the applicant may not have a criminal record in their country of origin or in the countries where they have lived in the past five years, for offences and crimes, as laid down in Spanish law;
(c) not suffer from a disease that may have serious public health implications in accordance with the provisions in the 2005 International Sanitary Regulation; and
(d) the fee for the processing of the application has been paid.

215. These conditions to obtain a residence permit are very similar to those already analysed.[143] A residence permit is only to be issued for the purpose of employment if the following conditions are met (Article 64.3 of RD 557/2011):

(a) the national employment situation allows for the hiring of the foreign worker (Article 65 of RD 557/2011);

---

qualified professionals, including technicians and scientists hired by public institutions, universities or research, development or innovation centres dependant on companies; (c) the staff of a company or a group of companies in another country wishing to develop their economic activity for the same company or group in Spain; and (d) renown and prestigious artists.

142. The so-called Catalogue of occupations that are not easily covered was introduced in 2004 by the later repealed RD 2393/2004, of 30 December 2004, approving the regulation of OL 4/2000, of 11 January 2000, on the rights and freedoms of foreigners in Spain and their social integration.

143. In particular: (i) not being irregularly present in Spain; (ii) not having a criminal record, neither in Spain nor in the countries of former residence during the past five years, for offences and crimes, as laid down in Spanish law; (iii) not being listed as a person to be refused entry permission in countries with which Spain has signed an agreement for this purpose; (iv) expiration of the period during which the foreigner has committed himself not to return to Spain, where the foreigner has voluntary returned to his country of origin; and (v) the fee for the processing of the temporary residence permit application has been paid (Art. 64.2 of RD 557/2011).

(b) the employer submits a labour contract signed by the worker that guarantees continuous employment during the entire validity period of the initial temporary residence and employment permit;
(c) the conditions of the labour contract comply with Spanish law and the collective bargaining agreement that apply to the labour activity to be carried out;
(d) the employer has registered the foreign worker in the Social Security regime and has complied with all his tax and Social Security obligations;
(e) the employer has sufficient economic, material or personal means to support the business project and to face the obligations assumed through the contract with the worker in accordance with Article 66 of this regulation;
(f) the worker has the necessary training and, when applicable, the professional qualifications legally required to exercise of his profession; and
(g) the fee for the processing of the employment permit application has been paid.

216. The temporary residence and employment of specific duration (Article 42 of OL 4/2000; Articles 97–102 of RD 557/2011) is, for its part, a legal case that affects every 'foreigner over 16 authorised to stay in Spain and participate in seasonal or campaign activities, whether as worker, service provider, trainee or professional intern' (Article 97 of RD 557/2011). For the performance of activities with a specific duration, Spanish law requires, in addition to an administrative permit, that a visa is obtained under the terms set out in Chapter III of RD 557/2011 (Article 101). In addition, seasonal employment offers are preferably to be directed to those countries with which Spain has signed agreements on the regulation of migration flows (Article 42 of OL 4/2000). In addition, Article 98.2 of RD 557/2011 limits the labour activities that these foreigners are allowed to perform to the following:

(a) Seasonal or campaign activities – for instance, in the agricultural, tourism or trade sectors.
(b) Work or services like: (i) assembling industrial or electrical plants; (ii) constructing infrastructures, buildings, or electrical, telephone, gas supply or railway networks; and (iii) installing starting-up, maintaining and repairing production equipment.
(c) Temporary activities carried out by senior or middle managers, professional sportsmen and women, artists and other groups, as determined by the Spanish Ministry of Employment.
(d) Training and professional internships.

217. The duration of the permit granted in these cases depends on the kind of activity to be developed in Spain. While for seasonal or campaign activities it is established that the duration of the permit must correspond with that of the labour contract – with a maximum of nine months within a period of twelve consecutive months – in the rest of cases the permit is issued for the same period as that of the labour contract. If the period of employment is not specified in the labour contract, then the permit is issued for a period that corresponds with 'the envisaged duration of the activity, as duly proved' – which is sometimes hard to determine. In relation to the present legal situation, Spanish law provides the possibility of initiating an administrative procedure for collective permit management, when the purpose is to hire ten or more workers for the same activity. This procedure is regulated through the so-called Order on the collective management of hiring processes in countries of origin.[144]

218. The conditions to obtain a temporary residence and employment permit of specific duration, which are set out in Article 99 of RD 557/2011,[145] are: compliance with the conditions to be issued an initial temporary residence and employment permit (Article 99.1 of RD 557/2011) and the foreigner's commitment to return to his country of origin once the labour relationship is over.[146] In addition, there are the following specific conditions which have to be satisfied, depending on the purpose for which a permit is applied for:

(a) For seasonal or campaign activities, work or services:
   (i) The employer shall provide the worker with suitable accommodation, as provided for by law. Exceptionally, compliance with this requirement may be waived if the conditions under which the labour activity is performed thus allow.
   (ii) The employer shall organise and pay for the journey to Spain and back to the country of origin, thus guaranteeing the worker's return to his country of origin.

(b) Temporary activities carried out by senior and middle managers, sportspeople, professionals, artists and others, as determined by the Spanish Government, in the sense specified above. They will need to be holders of an administrative permit required for the development of their professional activities.

---

144. The collective management of the hiring procedure in countries of origin is designed to cover the annual labour market prognosis which is periodically determined by the Spanish Ministry of Employment and Social Security. This is an administrative procedure that can also be used to process certain nominated job offers if the Ministry deems this appropriate. See for this purpose: the Public Employment Service Resolution, of 30 March 2016, which contains the 'Catalogue of occupations that are not easily covered' for the second three-month period of 2016, published in the OSG 2 May 2016, No. 105. The initial Ministerial Order ESS/1/2012, of 5 January 2012, regulating the collective management of the hiring procedure in countries of origin for 2012 (OSG 6 Jan. 2012, No. 5) established the non-advisability of hiring foreign workers for indefinite labour market positions. It is, therefore, a procedure to manage the hiring of temporary workers. The Ministerial Order does not provide for, for instance, the granting of visa for the purpose of seeking employment to children or grandchildren of native Spaniards or for certain occupations. Extended in its own terms to the whole of 2016 – by virtue of Order ESS/2811/2015, of 22 December 2015, extending the validity of Order ESS/1/2012, of 5 January 2012, regulating the collective management of hiring procedure in countries of origin for 2012 (OSG 28 Dec. 2015, No. 310) – the administrative procedure has, nevertheless, been limited to the hiring of workers for agricultural seasonal campaigns and from countries with which Spain has signed an agreement for the regulation of migration flows, in line with the reinforcement of circular migration and, in brief, of cooperation with certain border countries, like Morocco.
145. *See*: para. 108.
146. For the purpose of verifying the worker's effective return to his country of origin, Art. 99.2 of RD 557/2011 establishes that a worker must appear before the diplomatic mission or consular office that issued his visa in the first place within one month after the expiry date of his permit to stay in Spain. Non-compliance with this obligation may justify a denial of a future application for a permit to work in Spain in the three years following the expiry of the initial permit.

219. The condition to obtain a visa in Article 101 of RD 557/2011 also applies to these situations. The reference regime is the one established for the granting of temporary residence and employment permits. In the case of work or services, temporary activities carried out by managers, sportspeople, professionals, artists and other groups, as determined by the Government, training activities or professional internships, it is not necessary to apply for a Foreign Identity Card when the workers are hired for a period of no more than six months (Article 101 of RD 557/2011).[147]

§3. Independent Economic Activities

220. Temporary residence and self-employment, according to Article 37 of OL 4/2000; Articles 103–109 of RD 557/2011, concerns 'foreigners over 18 years of age, authorised to stay in Spain for a period of no less than 90 days and no more than five years for the purpose of developing a self-employed lucrative activity' (Article 103 of RD 557/2011). This initial permit is limited by law to the geographical area of an autonomous region. The administration may establish a smaller territorial area (Article 104 of RD 557/2011) or limit the permit to a specific activity sector. The granting of the initial work permit is a competence of that autonomous region, when thus specified in its Statute of Autonomy. For this reason, this administration must cooperate with the State, as the State is the competent administration for the granting of residence permits (Article 107 of RD 557/2011). In addition, the initial permit is limited in time, as it valid for at the most one year.

221. In relation to a visa application, Article 108 of RD 557/2011 establishes that an applicant must submit his application, using the official visa request form, to the Spanish diplomatic mission or consular office in their place of residence within one month from the date on which the decision to grant a temporary residence and self-employment permit is notified. The application shall be submitted with the following documents: passport or travel document, recognised as valid in Spain, with a minimum validity period of four months, and a criminal record and health certificate proving that the worker does not suffer from a disease that may have serious public health implications according to the 2005 International Sanitary Regulation. The diplomatic mission has one month to decide on the application.

222. As other visa applications, the initial temporary residence and self-employment permit becomes effective when the worker has registered with the Social Security Regime, which has to be completed within three months after their entry into Spain. If the worker fails to register, this will amount to a serious administrative breach of the law because he will be in Spain irregularly. The worker will

147. The Foreign Identity Card is a single and exclusive document granted to foreigners legally residing in Spain and providing evidence of their right to stay in Spanish territory for a period of more than six months.

have to leave the country (Article 108 of RD 557/2011). Within one month from the registration in the above-mentioned regime, the foreigner has to apply in person for a foreign identity card.

223. To be granted an initial temporary residence and self-employment permit compliance with a number of conditions of a different nature is required (Article 105 of RD 557/2011):

(a) On the matter of residence:
  (i) Not being in Spain irregularly.
  (ii) Not having a criminal record, neither in Spain nor in any of the countries where a self-employed person has lived during the past five years, for offences and crimes as provided for by Spanish law.
  (iii) Not being listed as a person to be refused entry permission by a country with which Spain has signed an agreement in this regard.
  (iv) Expiry of the period during which a foreigner has committed himself not to return to Spain, within the framework of a voluntary return programme with his country of origin.
  (v) Having paid the fee for the processing of the temporary residence permit application.
(b) On the matter of self-employment:
  (i) Satisfying the conditions, as provided for by law, which apply to Spanish nationals who start and carry out an economic activity.
  (ii) Having the legally required professional qualification or accredited experience in the exercise of his professional activity, as well as, when applicable, being a member of a professional association.
  (iii) Proving that the estimated investment for the setting up of the project is sufficient and, when required, that it creates employment for those already in Spain.
  (iv) Having sufficient economic means for his subsistence and accommodation.
  (v) Having paid the fee for the processing of the self-employment permit.

224. Finally, there are three situations in which Article 109 of RD 557/2011 allows for the renewal of a temporary residence and self-employment permit. Such a request must be made within sixty days prior to the expiry date of the initial permit:

(a) When there is sufficient evidence that the activity that justified the issuing of the permit in the first place can be continued and the tax and Social Security obligations have been complied with. The latter is verified ex officio. In the event of irregularities in the payment by the self-employed worker of his Social Security contribution, this will not stand in the way of the renewal of the permit, as long as the normal performance of the activity is guaranteed.
(b) When the spouse or person with whom the foreigner has a relationship – unmarried partner – complies with the economic conditions to apply for reunification with the worker.

(c) When the competent management body, according to the applicable law, has granted the foreign self-employed worker a benefit corresponding with the termination of their activity – in brief, the right to a Social Security allowance to compensate for the lack of activity of the self-employed person.

225. The renewed residence and self-employment permit is valid for two years, unless the situation allows for the granting of a long-term residence permit. Like the other applications discussed, a permit application is deemed to be granted if the administration has not adopted a decision within three months after its submission.

226. Regardless of the other situations commented on, there are rules facilitating international mobility in Law 14/2013 which ultimately aim to attract talent and investment to Spain. This is a special legal regime, favouring the mobility of foreigners identified as 'entrepreneurs'.[148] For this purpose, Article 70 of Law 14/2013 defines 'entrepreneurial activity' – entrepreneur will obviously be the person who develops the activity – as 'an innovative activity that is especially interesting for Spain from an economic point of view and that, for this reason, has received a favourable report from the competent body of the State administration'(). In relation to this specific case, an activity is labelled 'entrepreneurial' if its aim is 'especially and primarily, the creation of jobs in Spain'. When assessing the activity that justifies the permission to enter and reside in Spain as a reputed entrepreneur, the following issues are considered: (a) the applicant's professional profile; (b) the business plan, including a market, service, product and financing analysis; (c) the added value for the Spanish economy, innovation or investment opportunities.

227. In relation to these entrepreneurs, Article 68 of Law 14/2013 acknowledges their right to apply for a visa to enter and stay in Spain for a period of one year for a single or main purpose, i.e. to carry out the preliminary formalities necessary to develop their entrepreneurial activity. Additionally, the law recognises the right of holders of this visa to reside in Spain as an entrepreneur without a previous minimum period of stay and without having to apply for a visa, since they already have one, when the entrepreneurial activity for which the visa was requested has actually been started.

228. Article 69 of Law 14/2013 regulates the granting of a residence permit for entrepreneurial activities, which is valid for Spain as a whole and allows the entrepreneur, in the sense already specified, to start, develop and manage an economic activity in this country. Acquiring this status entails, in addition to meeting the above-mentioned legal requirements, compliance by non-Union foreigners with the general conditions to obtain a stay or residence permit, as established by Article 62 of Law 14/2013 as examined in paragraph 1 of Chapter IV4 in Part III of this work. In addition, the foreigner must satisfy the legal conditions that apply to the setting up of the envisaged activity in accordance with the applicable sector regulation.

148. Article 2 of Law 14/2013 states that 'entrepreneurs are those individuals who, independent of being a natural or legal person, develop an entrepreneurial or professional economic activity as provided for by this Law'.

§4. INVESTMENT ACTIVITIES

229. Like for entrepreneurs, Law 14/2013 provides a specific migration channel for foreign investors who wish to temporarily stay or reside in Spain. The purpose of this regime is to make the country an attractive territory for investors. Article 63.1 of Law 14/2013 provides that non-resident foreigners who intend to enter Spain with the objective of making a significant capital investment can apply for a stay visa or, when required, a residence visa for investors that will be valid for a period of one year. According to Spanish law, the status of investor can be acquired by every person who intends to make 'a significant capital investment', which is one in which the following factors occur (Article 63.2 of Law 14/2013):

(a) An initial investment of no less than EUR 2 million in Spanish public debt securities or of no less than EUR 1 million in participating or non-participating shares of Spanish companies or in bank deposits of Spanish financial entities. It may also be EUR 1 million in investment funds, closed investment funds or risk capital funds constituted in Spain, in accordance with Spanish legislation.[149]
(b) The acquisition of real estate in Spain through an investment of no less than EUR 500,000 per applicant.
(c) A business project to be developed in Spain of general interest, meaning that it either: (i) creates employment; (ii) has a relevant socio-economic impact in the geographical area where the activity will be developed; or (iii) has a relevant contribution to scientific and/or technological innovation.

230. According to Spanish law, the investor status also includes all foreigners having, directly or indirectly, the majority of the voting rights and the faculty to appoint or dismiss the majority of members of the board of directors of a company with a registered office in Spain that is not a tax haven according to Spanish law and that makes a significant investment in this country. Article 63.2 c) of Law 14/2013 even establishes that a residence visa for investors is granted to the 'investor's appointed representative' for the management of 'a project of general interest', provided that the project complies with the requirements in this provision.

231. Article 65 of Law 14/2013 provides that a residence visa for investors suffices to live and work in Spain during its validity period. Nevertheless, the Spanish law conditions the granting of this visa to compliance with a set of legal conditions meant to prove the effectiveness of the investment that vary depending on whether

149. If the investment is made by a married couple married with common ownership of property or a similar regime, Art. 63.4 of Law 14/2013 states that, when the amount does not at least double the threshold established in points a) and b) of s. 2, it will be considered that the investment is made by one of the partners. The other partner is entitled to apply for a residence visa as a family member in accordance with the terms established by Art. 62.4 of Law 14/2013.

the investment is in public debt, shares or investment funds,[150] the acquisition of real estate,[151] the development of a business project[152] or the participation in a company mostly controlled by a foreigner.[153]

---

150. In this case, evidence must be provided of the investment having been made with the minimum amount required, within a period of no more than one year after the submission of the visa application and as follows: (a) for investments in unquoted or participating shares, a copy of the investment statement made to the Registry of Foreign Investment of the Ministry of Economy and Competitiveness also has to be submitted; (b) for investments in quoted shares, a certificate of the financial intermediary, duly registered by the '*Comisión Nacional del Mercado de Valores*' (National Stock Market Commission) or the Bank of Spain and stating that the applicant has made an investment for the purposes established in this norm; (c) for investments in public debt, a certificate of the financial entity or the Bank of Spain indicating that the applicant is the sole holder of the investment for a period of no less than five years; (d) for investments in investment funds, closed investment funds or risk capital funds constituted in Spain, a certificate of the company managing the funds, founded in Spain, duly registered by the National Stock Market Commission and stating that the applicant has made an investment of at least EUR 1 million in a fund or funds managed by them; and (e) for investments in a bank deposit, a certificate of the financial entity indicating that the applicant is the sole holder of the bank deposit.
151. The person applying for the visa has to provide evidence of having invested in real estate by submitting a certificate of ownership and encumbrances issued by the '*Registro de la Propiedad*' (Land Registry) and corresponding to the property or properties. The certificate must be endorsed with an electronic verification code to be checked online. The certificate has to include the amount of the acquisition. If not, the corresponding public deed must be submitted. If the acquisition is registered with the Land Registry when the visa is applied for, it will suffice to submit the above-mentioned certificate including the registry date of the purchasing document, together with the documents proving the payment of the corresponding taxes.

    The applicant needs to prove having made an investment in real estate for EUR 500,000 that is free of all encumbrances or taxes. The part of the investment that exceeds the amount required may be the subject of encumbrances or taxes.

    If the foreigner has not formalised the acquisition of a property or properties but there is a pre-contract guaranteeing compliance through a deposit or other means as provided for by the law and formalised by a public deed, they must, in addition, satisfy the conditions in Art. 62.3 of Law 14/2013. They will thus have to submit the pre-contract with the guarantee clause together with a certificate of a financial entity registered in Spain indicating that the applicant has a non-available bank deposit with the amount necessary for the acquisition of the property or properties, including encumbrances and taxes – thus complying with the pre-contract terms. The sum in the bank deposit is only used for the acquisition of the property or properties specified in the pre-contract. In this case, the applicant will be granted a residence visa for investors with a six-month validity period.

    If the effective acquisition of the property or properties is established, the applicant may apply for a residence visa for investors with a one-year validity period or a residence permit for investors in conformity with Art. 66 of Law 14/2013.
152. In this case, a favourable report shall be submitted to prove that the business project has a reason of general interest. The report is issued by the '*Oficina Económica y Comercial*' (Spanish Economic and Commercial Office) in the geographical area where the visa application has been lodged.

    If the investor appoints a representative to manage the business project and intents to obtain a residence visa for investors for this representative, the report of the Spanish Economic and Commercial Office has to establish, compliance with the conditions in Art. 63.2 c) of Law 14/2013 and the actual need for this representative to participate in the adequate management of the business project. The representative has to provide evidence to the consular office that he satisfies the conditions in Art. 62.3 of Law 14/2013.
153. On this occasion, the law requires the submission of a favourable report in relation to the investment, drawn up by the Spanish Economic and Commercial Office of the geographical area where the visa application has been submitted.

232. Like all residence permits, Article 66 of Law 14/2013 provides that a residence permit for investors is valid for the whole Spanish territory. It is the Directorate General for Migration of the Ministry of Employment and Social Security that is competent to decide on the application for a residence permit for investor that is processed by the Large Companies and Strategic Groups Unit, in line with the idea that this is a special kind of migration movement. This permit is also peculiar in that it can be obtained by a representative appointed by the investor to manage the project, provided that the project actually meets the conditions established by Law 14/2013, particularly in Article 63.2 c.

233. Like the visa application, the procedure for applying for a residence permit not only requires that the non-Union foreigner satisfies the general requirements in Article 62 of Law 14/2013[154] but also a number of other specific conditions.[155] The specific conditions vary depending on whether: (a) the investment is in public debt, unquoted or participating shares or investment funds;[156] (b) concerns the acquisition of real estate;[157] (c) the development of a business project;[158] (d) or the participation in a company mostly controlled by a foreigner.[159]

---

154. In the case of an applicant who is the holder of a valid residence visa for investors or if the period of ninety days after the visa's expiry date has not yet expired.
155. Besides having fully complied and being up-to-date with all tax and Social Security obligations, according to Spanish legislation.
156. By submitting the following documents, the investor provides evidence of having maintained the investment to a value equal to or greater than the minimum amount required (Art. 66 of Law 14/2013): (a) for investments in unquoted or participating shares, a notarised certificate proving that the ownership of the unquoted or participating shares that justified the issuing of the visa for investors has been continued during the reference period. The certificate must be dated within thirty days prior to the submission of the application; (b) for investments in quoted shares, a certificate of a financial entity indicating that the applicant has had at least an average amount of EUR 1 million invested in shares from the date on which he obtained his residence visa for investors. The certificate must be dated within thirty days prior to the submission of the application; (c) for investments in public debt, a certificate of a financial entity or the Bank of Spain verifying that, from the date on which the residence visa for investors was granted, the number of public debt securities acquired by the investor at the moment of the initial investment was the same or higher. The certificate must be dated within thirty days prior to the submission of the application; (d) for investments in investment funds, closed investment funds or risk capital funds constituted in Spain, a certificate of the company managing the fund, duly registered with the National Stock Market Commission, indicating that, from the date on which he obtained a residence visa for investors, the applicant has, at the least, invested an average amount of EUR 1 million in the fund or funds managed by them. The certificate must be dated within thirty days prior to the submission of the application; (e) for investments in bank deposits, a certificate of the financial entity verifying that after the date on which the investor obtained a residence visa for investors has held or increased the deposit. The certificate must be dated within thirty days prior to the submission of the application.
157. The applicant must prove that the investor is the owner of property or properties with a value of at least the minimum amount required by Art. 64 of Law 14/2013. For that purpose, the applicant has to submit the certificate or certificates of ownership and encumbrances issued by the Land Registry and corresponding to the property or properties, which must be dated within ninety days prior to the submission of the application. If the applicant holds a six-month residence permit for investors, he has to prove that he has effectively acquired the property or properties by submitting the corresponding documents.

234. However, if the applicant of the residence permit for investors is already legally in Spain and does not hold a residence visa for investors, in addition to satisfying the above-mentioned general requirements in Article 62 of Law 14/2013, he must submit evidence, in person, of having made a significant capital investment in the terms already set out, which are defined in Article 64 of Law 14/2013.[160]

235. As for the duration of the initial residence permit for investors, Article 67.1 of Law 14/2013 establishes that it is two years. However, in the case of a non-formalised purchase of real estate, the permit will have a maximum duration of six months. Once this period has expired, should the foreign investor be interested in living in Spain for a longer period, he is entitled to apply for the renewal of the residence permit for successive five-year periods, as long as the conditions that justified the issuing of the permit in the first place are still satisfied. If, during the residence period, the investment is modified,[161] the investor will, in any case, have to satisfy some of the conditions in Article 63 of Law 14/2013 in order to maintain his right to reside in Spain.

236. Finally, the benefits of this special migration channel have been extended to the investor's family members, in the same way as has for all foreigners who are allowed to enter and stay in Spain by Article 62.4 of Law 14/2013. Therefore, the spouse and their minor children and those who have reached the legal age of majority, but who are economically dependent on the visa holder and have not yet established their own family, and the investor and the spouse's ascendants for whom they are responsible can join or accompany the investor. They can apply, whether jointly and simultaneously with the investor or separately at a later stage, for the necessary permits and, when required, a visa. For this purpose, family members have to provide evidence that they satisfy the general requirements in Article 62 of Law 14/2013.

---

158. A favourable report of the '*Dirección General de Comercio Internacional e Inversiones*' (Directorate General for International Commerce and Investment) of the Ministry of Economy and Competitiveness has to be submitted as evidence that the reasons of general interest initially proved have continued (Art. 66.2 c) of Law 14/2013).
159. A favourable report of the Directorate General for International Commerce and Investment of the Ministry of Economy and Competitiveness must also be submitted, as evidence that the conditions which applied when the visa was granted are still complied with (Art. 66.2 d) of Law 14/2013).
160. The variety of situations is, nevertheless, notable. Thus, for example, Art. 66.3, fifth paragraph, of Law 14/2013 establishes that, if the investor has not formalised the acquisition of property or properties but there is a pre-contract guaranteeing his compliance through a deposit or other means, as admitted by the law and formalised in a public deed. In addition, he has to satisfy the conditions in Art. 62.3 of Law 14/2013, submit the pre-contract with the guarantee clause together with a certificate of a financial entity established in Spain indicating that the applicant has a non-available bank deposit with the amount necessary for the acquisition of the property or properties including encumbrances and taxes – thus compliance with the pre-contract. The sum in the bank deposit is only used to finalise acquisition of the property or properties specified in the pre-contract. In this case, the applicant is granted a residence visa for investors with a six-month validity period.
161. The variation of the investment value due to market fluctuations is excluded.

Chapter 5. Humanitarian Reasons

§1. Humanitarian Grounds

237. Article 31.3 of OL 4/2000 states that the Spanish administration may grant a temporary residence permit on humanitarian grounds, to foreigners already settled in the country, who collaborate with the courts of law or find themselves in other exceptional circumstances, as determined by law. A visa is not required in these cases. This means that, in practice, it is possible to obtain a residence permit and, eventually, a work permit without leaving Spain.

238. The label 'exceptional circumstances' refers to a set of circumstances that are not specified in OL 4/2000, but which, according to the Spanish administration, merit protection and justify that those foreigners are granted a residence permit. In this sense, Title V of RD 557/2011, entitled 'Temporary residence under exceptional circumstances', not only regulates 'Temporary residence under exceptional circumstances on the grounds of integration, international protection, humanitarian reasons, collaboration with the authorities, national security or public interest' – Chapter I, Articles 123–130 – but also: 'Temporary residence and work under exceptional circumstances in the case of foreign women who are victims of gender-based violence' – Chapter II, Articles 131–134; 'Temporary residence and work under exceptional circumstances on the grounds of collaboration against organised networks' – Chapter III, Articles 135–139; and 'Temporary residence and work under exceptional circumstances in the case of foreigners who are victims of trafficking in human beings' – Chapter IV, Articles 140–146. These legal situations are also addressed in OL 4/2000, for instance in Articles 31*bis* (victims of gender-based violence), 59 (collaboration against organised networks trafficking in human beings) or 59 (victims of trafficking in human beings).

239. In relation to humanitarian reasons stricto sensu, the main rule is the one specified in Article 126 of RD 557/2011 that includes the granting of temporary residence permits on humanitarian grounds in the following cases:

(a) to foreigners who are victims of the criminal offences defined in Articles 311–315,[162] 511.1 and 512[163] of the Criminal Code, criminal offences with the aggravating circumstance of racist or an anti-Semitic motivation or any other kind of discrimination referred to in Article 22.4 of the Criminal Code, or criminal offences associated with violence within the family, as long as there is a court decision putting an end to the legal proceedings and establishing the person's condition as a victim of those criminal offences;

162. This article includes some of the so-called crimes against the rights of workers.
163. This article includes some of the 'crimes committed during the exercise of the fundamental rights and public freedoms guaranteed by the Constitution'.

(b) to foreigners who can prove that they are suffering a sudden serious disease that requires specialised medical care not available in their country of origin and that interrupting or not receiving the treatment involves a serious risk for their health or life;[164] and

(c) to foreigners who can prove that returning to their country of origin or to that from which they have arrived, for the purpose of applying for corresponding visa, entails a danger for their security or that of their family, as long as they satisfy the other conditions necessary to obtain a temporary residence or a residence and work permit.

240. Additionally, Article 34 of OL 4/2000 regulates, under the title 'Residence of stateless persons, undocumented persons and refugees', three completely different situations in which foreigners can find themselves and in which the recognition of a right of residence in Spain on humanitarian grounds is set out. This regime is limited because it does not include (probably intentionally) other situations where there are humanitarian reasons which would also deserve legal protection, as in the case of: asylum seekers, persons who were not granted refugee status, or those who, as a consequence of different disasters (wars, etc.), have left their countries in large groups for the purpose of saving their lives.[165]

241. With regard to stateless persons – defined in Article 34.1 of OL 4/2000 as foreigners 'who lack an identity' – OL 4/2000 does not regulate in detail the terms under which residence permission can be granted to them, but refers to their need to comply with the requirements established in the Convention relating to the Status of Stateless Persons, signed in New York on 28 September 1954.[166] When a foreigner who declares not to have a nationality satisfies those requirements, the Spanish Ministry of the Interior will issue the documents as provide for in Article 27 of the aforementioned Convention, i.e. an identity document. In addition RD 865/2001, of 20 July 2001, approving the regulation of recognition of the status of stateless person,[167] provides, among other aspects and in accordance with international law, that this status will not be granted to those persons who find themselves in one of the situations considered in Article 1.2 of that Convention[168] and who will,

164. Exceptionally, a disease will not have to be sudden if the need to temporarily extend the stay of a foreign minor in Spain in order to receive medical treatment, as provided for by Art. 187 of RD 557/2011 has been established, if the possibility to extend the stay has been exhausted and as long as the stay is indispensable to continue the treatment. The renewal of this type of permit will correspond with the minimum time necessary to complete the treatment.

165. On these groups, see the considerations made on Law 12/2009, regulating the right to asylum and subsidiary protection, in Chapter 6 of Part III in this work.

166. Spain acceded to the Convention on 24 April 1997 (OSG 4 Jul. 1997, No. 159).

167. OSG 21 Jul. 2001, No. 174.

168. This article in the Convention states that the status will not be applied to: (a) persons who are presently being protected or assisted by a United Nations body or organisation different from the United Nations High Commissioner for Refugees, while they are receiving that protection or assistance; (b) persons to whom the competent authorities in the country where they have settled their residence acknowledge the rights and obligations associated to the possession of that country's nationality; (c) persons who, as duly proved, can be considered: (i) to have committed a crime against peace, a war crime or a crime against humanity, as defined by international instruments referring to

therefore, not be considered stateless persons. In any case, Spanish legislation protects both the stateless persons who are considered as such from the beginning and those who, due to various circumstances, only are eventually acknowledged as such.[169]

242. In relation to undocumented persons, they are not necessarily stateless persons, as is clearly specified in Article 34.1 of OL 4/2000 that provides that they are different from stateless persons, although in certain cases the two conditions may coincide in one and the same person. In this sense, Spanish law identifies an undocumented person as a foreigner who, due to any 'insuperable cause' other than statelessness, cannot be furnished with documents in any country and wishes to be so by Spain. For this purpose, it may be considered that the lack of documents – whether loss, theft or expiry – is insuperable if the foreigner has unsuccessfully tried to obtain the corresponding documents.

243. In order to obtain identity documents, a specific application in writing has to be made with the competent immigration affairs office or police station. This application will trigger an investigation, to be carried out by Spanish authorities. If the foreigner wishes to stay in Spain while the necessary inquiries are made, the Spanish authorities may issue a provisional identity document that will enable the foreigner to stay in Spain during three months once the first verifications in relation to the application submitted have been completed, allowing them to draw the first conclusions on the veracity of the facts detailed in that application.[170] An identity document will not be granted if it is established that the applicant has been banned from entering Spain, as provided for by Article 26 of OL 4/2000.[171] Namely, when the foreigner a) has been expelled, for as long as the entry ban is valid; and b) is not allowed to enter Spain for any other legally justified reason or by virtue of an international agreement to which Spain is a party.[172] If, eventually, the Spanish authorities refuse to grant the requested documents, the undocumented foreigner is

those crimes; (ii) to have committed a grave non-political crime outside their country of residence, before they were admitted into that country; (iii) to be guilty of acts against the purposes and principles of the United Nations.

169. It has thus been established by the Spanish Supreme Court through two judgments of the Contentious-Administrative Division, of 19 November 1986, in relation to Syrian citizens who had lost their passports, but presumably had been issued a French residence permit.

170. If, during the period in which the administrative file is being assessed, the foreigner wishes to travel out of Spain, Spanish law allows for the granting of a travel document to leave Spain, indicating the country or countries of destination and specifying the return to Spain (Art. 212 of RD 557/2011). The issuance of this travel document is regulated by Order INT/3321/2011, of 21 November 2011, on the issuance of travel documents for foreigners (OSG 5 Dec. 2011, No. 292).

171. Article 26.2 of OL 4/2000 states that foreigners who do not comply with the conditions to enter the country will be refused entry permission through a motivated decision. This decision must include information on the tight to appeal that may be lodged against it, the time frame to lodge an appeal and the authority before which this must be done. Likewise, they must be informed on their right to be assisted by a lawyer, who may be a public defender, and by an interpreter. This is a right that the foreigner has from the very moment that they are checked at the border control point.

172. Article 11 of RD 557/2011 includes two additional situations, the legal nature of which has been highly discussed in the past, especially where they did not imply an infringement of Art. 26 of OL 4/2000, given that regulation goes beyond the provisions of the law. In particular, Art. 11 RD 557/

expelled and returned to their country of origin. The problem here is that the current law does not specify what to do if the foreigner's country of origin is, in fact, unknown.

244. OL 4/2000 does not, at any time, acknowledge the right of the undocumented foreigner to be furnished with documents by Spanish authorities and this has been confirmed by the SSC.[173] An in-depth reading of Articles 4 and 34 of OL 4/2000 clarifies that foreigners are, in fact, obliged to be in possession of documents to support their right to remain in Spain.[174] According to Article 34 of OL 4/2000, once a foreigner is granted the documents establishing their legal status in Spain, they can apply for a residence permit under exceptional circumstances (Article 211.9 of RD 557/2011).

245. As far as refugees are concerned, OL 4/2000 is merely testimonial to their situation, because it only refers to the then current legislation on asylum, which at that moment is the Convention relating to the Status of Refugees, signed in Geneva on 28 July 1951, and Law 12/2009, of 30 October 2009, regulating the right to asylum and subsidiary protection,[175] and RD 203/1995, of 10 February 1995.[176] The

---

2011 includes as causes for exclusion: (a) being informed – though a diplomatic conduct, Interpol or any other international cooperation instrument, whether judicial or police – that they are wanted, in relation to criminal cases arising from serious common offences, by the judicial or police authorities of other countries, as long as the events for which they are being searched are considered a criminal offence in Spain, notwithstanding their detention, where necessary; (b) they have been expressly banned from entering Spain by a decision of the head of the Ministry of the Interior, for developing activities that are contrary to Spanish interests or to human rights, or due to their obvious connections with criminal organisations, whether Spanish or foreign, or other judicial or administrative reasons that justify the adoption of such measure, notwithstanding their detention, where necessary. However, the Spanish Supreme Court, through judgments issued by the Contentious-Administrative Division on 10 January 2007, established that the regulation complies in this respect with the law, and reiterated that foreigners have no constitutional right to enter Spanish territory, because there is not a subjective right to enter a country other than one's own, amongst other reasons. Entry is only possible to the extent that it is provided for in treaties and by international laws.

173. *See* the Supreme Court judgment (Contentious-Administrative Division) of 17 June 2007.

174. This legal obligation is explicitly included in Art. 13 of OL 4/2015, of 30 March 2015, on the protection of public security (OSG 31 Mar. 2015, No. 77), which establishes that foreigners in Spain have the right and are obliged to keep and carry with them the documents that prove their identity issued by the competent authorities of their country of origin or origin, as well as those that prove their right to remain in Spain. This law also establishes that foreigners may not be deprived of these documents except in the course of a criminal investigation. It also establishes that foreigners are obliged to show those documents in order to prove their identity and their right to remain in Spain and to allow the verification of said documentation, when they are required by the authorities or their agents in consonance with the provisions of the law and for the time necessary for such verification. However, they may prove their identity by any other means in case they were not carrying their documents.

175. Article 34.3 of OL 4/2000 literally refers, in the case of Spain, to Law 5/1984, of 26 March 1984, regulating the right to asylum and the status of refugee, as amended by Law 9/1994, of 19 May 1994, and the regulations adopted to develop this law. The 1984 law was, in fact, repealed by the current law, Law 12/2009.

176. In this case, in what does not infringe Law 12/2009 and in the absence of the further regulation, RD 203/1995, of 10 February 1995, approving the regulation implementing Law 5/1984, of 26

refugee status is granted to 'every person who, due to justified fear of being persecuted for reasons of race, religion, nationality, political opinions, belonging to a specific social group, gender or sexual orientation,[177] are outside their country of nationality and cannot or, because of that fear, do not want to accept the protection of that country, or to those stateless persons who, lacking a nationality and being outside the country where they previously had their usual residence, for the same reasons cannot or, due to that fear, do not want to return to it, as long as they do not find themselves in a situation that corresponds to any of the causes of exclusion[178] or refusal foreseen in Spanish legislation'.[179]

246. The procedure to obtain refugee status is examined in the next chapter – more specifically, in §1.1– because it is exclusively regulated by Law 12/2009. For now, it is only necessary to underline that Article 34.3 of OL 4/2000 specifies the effects of a favourable decision on an asylum application: an acknowledgement of the refugee status of the applicant, who has the right to reside in Spain and to develop labour, professional and mercantile activities in the terms established by Law 12/2009. This article also establishes that, because of their legal status, refugees cannot be removed or expelled as provided for by Article 33 of the aforementioned Geneva Convention, that enshrines the international law principle of 'non-refoulement' – the prohibition of removal or expulsion. This is too essential to refugee protection to hide in a footnote. According to this principle, no State having signed the Convention will be able to, through removal or expulsion, put by any means the refugee in the border with territories where their life or freedom may be

---

March 1984, regulating the right to asylum and the status of refugee, as amended by Law 9/1994, of 19 May 1994 (OSG 5 Mar. 1995, No. 52), is still applicable.

177. The fact that the Spanish law considers gender or sexual orientation-related motives is a relevant improvement of the Geneva Convention on the Status of Refugees, given that this international instrument did not include this legal case.

178. Article 8 of Law 12/2009 specifies that the following persons are excluded from refugee status: (a) those who are protected by virtue of s. D of Art. 1 of the Geneva Convention in all that concerns the protection or assistance of a United Nations body or institutions other than the United Nations High Commissioner for Refugees, because, when this protection ends for any reason and their situation is yet unresolved according to the resolutions adopted on this matter by the General Assembly of the United Nations, they will immediately be granted the right to the benefits of asylum as established in this law; (b) those to whom the competent authorities of the country where they have fixed their residence have recognised the rights and obligations that come together with being a national of that country, or other equivalent rights and obligations. Foreigners will also be excluded from this status when there is evidence to believe that: (a) they have committed a crime against peace, a war crime or a crime against humanity, as defined in the corresponding dispositions of international instruments; (b) they have committed a serious offence in the country of refuge before they were admitted as refugees, i.e., before the issuing of a residence permit based on the recognition of the refugee status – serious offences being those included in the Spanish Criminal Code and affecting the life, freedom, sexual inviolability, freedom, or integrity of a person or the heritage, in the terms in which this legal concept is reflected in Spanish legislation, and as long as these acts were carried out with force in the case of objects, or violence or intimidation in the case of persons, as well as in cases of organised crime.

179. Article 9 of Law 12/2009 states that the following persons will be refused the right to asylum: (a) those who, for well-founded reasons, pose a danger to the security of Spain; (b) those who, having been subject to a final judgment for a serious offence, constitute a threat to the community – meaning society.

in danger for reasons of race, religion, nationality, belonging to a specific social group, or political opinions. Nevertheless, this benefit will not be applied to refugees who, for well-founded reasons, pose a danger for the security of the country where they are, or who, having been subject to final judgment for a particularly serious offence, constitute a threat to the community of this country.

§2. Unaccompanied Minor Children

247. Article 189 of RD 557/2011 defines the concept of 'unaccompanied foreign minor' as a minor under 18 years of age arriving in Spain without the company of an adult who is responsible for him, whether legally or according to custom, when there is risk of lack of protection and while this adult is not effectively in charge of them. The concept also includes any foreign minor who, once in Spain, finds himself in this situation. The legal regime established by Article 35 of OL 4/2000 and the corresponding regulation does not apply in all cases,[180] because, depending on the specific situation of the minor, it may be possible for them to benefit from the family reunification regime or from international protection by applying for asylum and subsidiary protection.

248. The legal logic used in this regard, is that the minor's repatriation as to be considered the first priority. This means that only if repatriation is not possible, a residence permit is granted to an unaccompanied minor. For this reason, one of the objectives of Spanish law is that both the Spanish government and the AR – i.e.,, their respective regional governments – can sign collaboration agreements with those countries from which unaccompanied foreign minors are more likely to arrive governing a child's social care and integration. These inter-State collaboration agreements aim at integrally managing the prevention of irregular immigration and the protection and return of unaccompanied minors to their home countries. The agreements signed by the AR aim at supporting social care and integration in a minor's country of origin, guaranteeing the protection of the minor's interests and monitoring, through the appropriate means and instruments, the minor's situation in those countries.

249. In the event of the minor finally being allowed to reside in Spain, Article 35.11 of OL 4/2000 establishes that both the central State administration and the AR are entitled to sign agreements with non-governmental organisations (NGOs), foundations and institutions devoted to child protection with the purpose of assigning to them the guardianship of unaccompanied foreign minors.[181] The decision to assign guardianship is not taken by the Spanish administration – its role being that of carry out the required procedure – but by the court of the place where the minor will reside. Spanish law expressly states that the guardianship regime is the one defined

180. The regulatory norms in this case are found in Arts. 185–198 of RD 557/2011.
181. The agreement shall specify the number of minors whose guardianship an institution is willing to assume, the minor's place of residence and the material resources devoted to taking care of them.

in the Spanish Civil Code and the corresponding legislation, and that the general legal provisions on minor protection in Spanish law also applies to these minors.

250. In the event that the Spanish administration decides to issue a residence permit to a foreign unaccompanied minor, Spanish law provides that this permit will be of a normal nature, although its legal effects will be retroactive, i.e., take effect from the moment in which the minor was placed under the custody of the child protection services. Nevertheless, and for the purpose of guaranteeing the legal protection of unaccompanied minors, the law explicitly affirms that the absence of a residence permit – as a result, for instance, of its being processed – will not prevent the recognition and enjoyment of the minor's rights as such (Article 35.7 of OL 4/2000).

251. The issuing of a residence permit does not stand in the way of a later decision adopted by the Spanish authorities to repatriate the minor, as long as this decision is considered to be in favour of the minor's higher interest. In any case, the Spanish law recognises the right of the minor who has been issued a residence permit to apply, once he has reached the legal age of majority, for both a renewal of this permit and a residence and work permit (Article 35.9 of OL 4/2000). In both cases, all positive reports submitted by competent public institutions on the minor's effort to integrate, continue training, studies, and incorporation, whether effective or potential, into the labour market will be taken into account. In relation to the latter aspect, the AR have to develop the necessary policies to facilitate a minor's integration into the labour market when they become of age.

252. The decision on the unaccompanied minor's repatriation or, where applicable, their residence in Spain is adopted, in either case, within the framework of a repatriation administrative procedure initiated by the central State administration.[182] The report on the minor's family circumstances, to be requested by the Spanish administration prior to the commencement of the procedure, from the diplomatic representation of the minor's country of origin in Spain will play a key role in that procedure. Therefore, the minor's nationality has to be known, which is not always easy to establish. It may be equally difficult to determine the minor's age and to ultimately establish with absolute certainty whether they are actually minors or not. In this sense, Spanish law, apart from defining the protocol to determine a minor's age,[183] provides that, when an undocumented foreigner is found whose

182. Article 35.6 of OL 4/2000 acknowledges the capacity of minors between 16 and 18 years old to act in the repatriation procedure, as well as before the court that is competent on this procedure. Their action may be direct or through a representative appointed for this purpose. In the case of minors under 16 endowed with enough judgment, the Spanish law expressly states that, should their will be contrary to that of the person or institution holding their guardianship or representation, the referred administrative procedure will be suspended until a legal defender is appointed to represent the minor.

183. This aspect is regulated by Art. 180 of RD 557/2011. The performance of radiographic tests on minors in order to determine their age has traditionally generated considerable controversy among lawyers in Spain. In any case, and taking into account the doctrine of the Spanish Constitutional Court established in judgments such as No. 207/1996, on the protection of the fundamental right to

minority of age is not known with absolute certainty, he will immediately be assisted by the competent child protection services, in accordance with the Spanish legislation on child protection, and the Public Prosecutor's Office will be informed immediately so that the procedure to determine the minor's age can be started in collaboration with the competent healthcare institutions, which will give priority to the performance of the necessary tests.

253. Notwithstanding the above-mentioned in the case of unaccompanied minors, Spanish law not only regulates their right of residence in Spain but also their temporary movement to Spain on humanitarian grounds (Article 187 of RD 557/2011), including, therefore, the possibility of short-term stays. More specifically, the law considers the movement of foreign minors to Spain for periods of no more than ninety days in the framework of humanitarian programmes promoted by public administrations, non-profit associations or foundations, or other organisations having no relation to those holding parental authority or guardianship over them, for the purpose of undergoing medical treatment or enjoying a vacation. In these cases, an express authorisation from the person or institution holding parental authority or guardianship over the minor will be required in order to allow their travelling and temporary stay, together with a favourable report from the Government Delegate's or sub-Delegate's Office in the autonomous region where the minor will be staying. This report is the document actually supporting the granting of the necessary visa. In any case, it is necessary to verify the existence of a written commitment to facilitate the minor's return to his country of origin, whether the minor is travelling for the purpose of adoption and whether the minor's return will entail any costs for the Spanish administration, unless these costs have previously and expressly been assumed by a competent body. If the minor is hosted by family or individuals during their stay, these must express in writing their knowledge that the minor's movement is not for the purpose of adoption, as well as their commitment to favour the minor's return to his country of origin or residence. The Ministry of the Interior of the Spanish government is the body that is responsible to guarantee the minor's return to his country of origin or residence.

254. Article 188 of RD 557/2011 also covers the temporary movement of foreign minors to Spain for the purpose of being educated. Their stay, as specified in that provision, is classed as a stay for study purposes. The procedure to be followed is identical to the one described in the previous situation, with the additional requirement that a document proving that the minor has been admitted to an officially recognised teaching centre in Spain also has to be submitted. The right to temporary stay expires at the end of the school year, when the minor, unless prevented

---

physical integrity (acknowledged in Art. 15 of the Spanish Constitution), there seems to be some consensus on the fact that, should a foreigner refuse to be subjected to the corresponding medical test, the Spanish Public Prosecutor's Office will not be able to act as authority that can substitute the consent that is required. Effectively, this will mean that the test cannot be performed and the minor's age will be established using the information derived from data obtained by other means. In summary, the minor will not be forced to undergo a radiographic test to determine with greater certainty his biological age.

by exceptional circumstances, must return to his country of origin. If the minor wishes to continue his study beyond that first year, he will need to be enrolled in a new academic programme.

§3. Victims of Trafficking in Human Beings

255. The reception of foreigners – usually foreign women – in Spain due to their status of victims of human trafficking is regulated in two different provisions in OL 4/2000,[184] more specifically in Articles 59 – 'Collaboration against networks'[185] – and 59*bis* – 'Victims of trafficking in human beings'.[186] This legislative regime takes into account the international instruments and EU laws on this matter.[187] An important reform to the Spanish law occurred twice; in 2009 and 2010. The first was achieved through the amendment of OL 4/2000, implemented by OL 2/2009,[188] which oriented Spanish legislation towards a more detailed consideration of the victim's rights. The second through changes to the classification as a criminal offence of trafficking in human beings, for the purpose of which OL 5/2010, of 22 June 2010, amending OL 10/1997, of 23 November 1997, on the Criminal Code, amended the Spanish Criminal Code.

256. In the case of Article 59 of OL 4/2000 that provision clearly aims at encouraging the collaboration of victims in human trafficking with the Spanish authorities, for the purpose of contributing towards the persecution and criminalisation of this illegal trafficking. In this sense, foreigners who are irregularly in Spain – whether this is the original or a later supervening circumstance, i.e., after having legally

184. In the sense defined by Directive 2011/36/EU (Art. 2), including 'the recruitment, transportation, transfer, harbouring or reception of persons, including the exchange or transfer of control over those persons, by means of the threat or use of force or other forms of coercion, of abduction, of fraud, of deception, of the abuse of power or of a position of vulnerability or of the giving or receiving of payments or benefits to achieve the consent of a person having control over another person, for the purpose of exploitation'.
185. Regulated in Arts. 135–139 of RD 557/2011.
186. Regulated in Arts. 140–146 of RD 557/2011.
187. At the international level, the following instruments are relevant: the Protocol to prevent, suppress and punish trafficking in persons, especially women and children, supplementing the United Nations Convention against transnational organised crime (OSG 11 Nov. 2003, No. 296), and the Protocol against the smuggling of migrants by land, sea and air, supplementing the United Nations Convention against transnational organised crime (OSG 10 Dec. 2003, No. 295), as well as the Council of Europe Convention on action against trafficking in human beings (No. 197), of 16 May 2005 (OSG 10 Sep. 2009, No. 219). For the European Union: Council Directive 2002/90/EC, of 28 November 2002, defining the facilitation of unauthorised entry, transit and residence (OJEU, L 328, 5 Dec. 2002), Council Directive 2004/81/EC, of 29 April 2004, on the residence permit issued to third-country nationals who are victims of trafficking in human beings or who have been the subject of an act to facilitate illegal immigration, who cooperate with the competent authorities (OJEU, L 261/19, 29 Apr. 2004), and Directive 2011/36/EU, of the European Parliament and of the Council, of 5 April 2011, on preventing and combating trafficking in human beings and protecting its victims, and replacing Council Framework Decision 2002/629/JHA (OJEU, L 101/1, 15 Apr. 2011).
188. Article 59*bis* of OL 4/2000 was also the object of a legislative reform in 2011 (OL 10/2011) and 2015 (OL 8/2015).

entered Spanish territory – and are victims, aggrieved by or witnesses of an act of illicit trafficking in human beings, irregular immigration, labour exploitation, trafficking in forced labour, or exploitation through prostitution, they may be exempted from any administrative responsibility, in addition to being guaranteed that they will not be expelled if they testify against the actors or those cooperating with the actors trafficking, or if they cooperate and collaborate with the competent authorities by providing essential information or testifying, where appropriate, in the corresponding criminal proceedings against those actors.[189] For the purpose of contributing towards improving the knowledge of the protection offered by Spanish law to its potential beneficiaries, the competent administrative bodies in charge of conducting procedures against criminal networks – the penal responsibility of these illegal networks being a different issue – must inform the victims of its existence so that they can decide whether or not to avail themselves of protection and collaborate with the authorities.

257. Should a victim decide to benefit from the legal protection provided to victims of trafficking by Article 59.1 of OL 4/2000, then Spanish law establishes that the above-mentioned administrative bodies should draw up an appropriate proposition which they submit to the Spanish authorities which can then decide whether the victim should be granted a residence and work permit for exceptional circumstances, as defined in RD 557/2011.[190] Alternatively, a victim is given the possibility to opt for assisted return to his country of residence, rather than being granted a residence and work permit. Assisted return programmes basically entail the assessment, before departure, of the risks that the victim may run when returning to his country of origin; his security, means of transportation and the authorities' assistance at the point of departure, transit and destination (Article 138.2 of RD 557/2011). The possibility of returning may not be an if option the Spanish authorities decide that they need the victim to remain in the country, as a result of an ongoing investigation concerning an organised network of traffickers in human beings.

258. As far as residence and work permits are concerned, Spanish law differentiates between collaboration with non-police administrative authorities and collaboration with police, fiscal or judicial authorities. The legal effects are similar in both cases. If a definitive residence and work permit is granted – a provisional permit may also be obtained until a final decision on the corresponding administrative file has been taken – it will be valid for five years and will allow the foreigner to take up employment, whether employed or self-employed, in any occupation, activity sector or part of the country. The law also foresees the foreigner's timely access to a long-term residence permit, insofar as he meets the legal conditions subject to which a long-term residence permit is issued.

189. Article 59.5 of OL 4/2000 includes the application of this condition to foreign minors, even if the Spanish law establishes in this case the need to take into account the minor's age and maturity, as well as the a minor's higher interest. *See*: Arts 59*bis* of OL 4/2000 for the obligation take the minor's interests into account which also applies to these minors.

190. The Spanish law states that the Spanish authorities must specify the conditions for the collaboration with non-profit non-governmental organisations to receive and protect victims of crimes related to trafficking in human beings.

259. To a large extent, Articles 59*bis* of OL 4/2000 complements the above legal regime, which is, notably, influenced by the Council of Europe Convention on action against trafficking in human beings, which is a much more complete instrument than Directive 2004/81/EC. The approach adopted is still somewhat peculiar. The first problem to be solved in this kind of situation is the identification as a victim of human trafficking, which is not always easy. This is why Spanish law establishes, in the first place, the legal obligation of the Spanish authorities to adopt the necessary measures to identify victims of human trafficking according to the conditions in Article 10 of the Council of Europe Convention.

260. Spanish law recognises the right of foreign persons in an irregular situation, when there is reasonable evidence that they may have been victims of human trafficking, to be informed by the Spanish authorities of their rights, as specified in the above-mentioned Articles 59*bis* of OL 4/2000. At the same time, the law indicates that these authorities may propose to the competent body to grant, where applicable, a so-called period of re-establishment and reflection. This period of, initially, no less than ninety days, may, however, be extended by the authorities, its main purpose being to give the victim time to reflect whether they wish to cooperate with Spanish authorities in the investigation of the possible crime of trafficking in human beings and, where applicable, the criminal procedure. If the victim decides to collaborate, he immediately becomes a potential beneficiary of the already discussed legal protection, as specified in Article 59 of OL 4/2000.

261. Additionally, the law provides that during the period of re-establishment and reflection, the victim is authorised to stay in Spain temporarily, and that the authorities take care of the livelihood, security and protection of both the victim of trafficking in human beings and their children under the legal age of majority or with a disability, who are in Spain while the victim is being identified as such. These children under the legal age of majority or with a disability benefit from an extension of both the residence and work permit granted to their parent – for the work permit, they need to be over 16 years old – and the possible assisted return, as appropriate.[191] Finally, Spanish law provides for the denial or revocation of the period of re-establishment and reflection if indicated by reasons related to public order, or when there is knowledge that the status of victim has been unlawfully obtained (Article 59.3 of OL 4/2000).

191. The law also provides that the public administration has to ensure the security and protection of those persons in Spain with whom the victim is related, through family ties or any other kind of relationship, when there is evidence that the situation of vulnerability in which the victim may find himself in relation to the suspected human trafficker could be an insuperable obstacle for the victim to cooperate.

§4. Others

262. Gender-based violence is one of the curses of our time. The Council of Europe has promoted the drafting of the Council of Europe Convention on preventing and combating violence against women and domestic violence, which has been ratified by Spain[192] amongst other countries. In the case of Spain, and from the perspective of gender-based violence against foreign women, Articles 31*bis* of OL 4/2000 is the key provision in the fight against this blight on society.[193]

263. For this purpose, Spanish legislation acknowledges in general terms the rights of foreign women who are victims of gender-based violence. More specifically, Article 31.1 bis of OL 4/2000 states that these women's rights, as acknowledged by OL 1/2004, of 28 December 2004, on comprehensive protection measures against gender-based violence,[194] are guaranteed by law, just as the protection and security measures established in the current legislation. There is thus a legal mandate that establishes the equal status of Spanish and foreign women who are victims of gender-based violence.

264. The specific regime established for the protection of foreign women who are irregularly in Spain applies from the moment that gender-based violence is reported to the Spanish authorities and it is established that it concerns a foreign woman in an irregular situation. The first consequence of this report is that the administrative sanctioning procedure regarding the woman's irregular situation is not started. Where appropriate, the execution of an expulsion or removal order is suspended.

265. If a protection order has been issued by Spanish authorities in favour of the foreign woman, or a report of the Spanish Public Prosecutor's Office establishing the existence of evidence of gender-based violence, that woman can apply for a residence and work permit under exceptional circumstances, even if this application will not be decided upon until the corresponding criminal procedure in relation to the suspected crime of gender violence is completed. Having said this, for the purpose of avoiding the continuation of a woman's irregular situation, Spanish law includes the possibility of issuing, while the procedures are being conducted, a provisional residence and work permit in her favour. If the criminal procedure is completed with a sentence finding the perpetrator guilty of the offence or with a court decision that states that the woman has, indeed, been a victim of gender-based violence, the Spanish immigration authorities will grant her a residence and work permit. If she has not yet submitted an application, she will be informed of the possibility of doing so and she will be given some time to do it. When criminal proceedings are completed without establishing the existence of gender-based violence, Spanish law provides for the opening or continuation of the administrative

192. Through the corresponding instrument of ratification published on the OSG 6 Jun. 2014, No. 137.
193. *See also*: Arts 131–134 of RD 557/2011.
194. OSG 29 Dec. 2004, No. 313.

sanctioning procedure for the infringement of Spanish migration legislation – particularly of Article 53.1 a) of OL 4/2000.

266. Finally, when a foreign woman has children under the legal age of majority or with a disability, who are objectively not able to provide for their own needs, Spanish law provides that she may be granted a residence permit, whether provisional or definitive, for exceptional circumstances. Likewise, if the woman has children older than 16 years and they are in Spain at the time when the gender-based violence was reported, it will be possible for her to apply for a residence and work permit for their benefit.

267. According to Article 127 of RD 557/2011 it is also possible to issue a temporary residence permit under exceptional circumstances for the purpose of collaborating with the public authorities, reasons of national security or in the public interest. This temporary permit is designed to preserve the foreigner's integrity in very specific situations: (a) when they have collaborated with police, fiscal or judicial authorities in relation to issues not specifically related to the fight against organised networks – because, if they were related, the applicable regime would be the one described in Article 59 of OL 4/2000 – but in any case connected with the fight against crime; and (b) when public interest or national security measures justify the need to authorise their residence in Spain. The possibility of a woman applying for this temporary residence permit is not considered. The law states that it is up to the Spanish authorities to make an application with the competent bodies if they deem this appropriate, for the aforementioned residence permit.

268. Integration is probably the way most frequently used to obtain a permit to reside in Spain under exceptional circumstances. According to the SSC, integration, as a legal term, identifies 'the bonds that link the applicant with the place where they reside, whether these bonds are economic, social, family-connected, labour-connected, academic or of any other kind, as long as they are relevant to appreciate the applicant's interest in residing in this country'.[195] From a normative point of view, however, RD 557/2011 only includes the granting of a temporary residence permit when there is evidence of: (a) labour integration; (b) social integration; or (c) family integration. In all three situations the foreigner may not have a criminal record, a requirement that has become more restrictive over the years. By now the foreigner must prove that he does not have a criminal record in Spain, nor in his country of origin and in the countries where he has resided during the past five years.

269. Thus, foreigners can apply for temporary residence permits on grounds of labour integration by providing evidence of their continuous stay in Spain during a period of at least two years, the absence of a criminal record in the above-specified sense and the existence of a labour relationship during no less than six months (Article 124.1 of RD 557/2011). Residence in Spain requires that the foreigner has

195. Supreme Court judgment (Contentious-Administrative Division) of 20 September 2007 (Appeal No. 7780/2003).

not left Spain for more than ninety days within a two-year period. Although Spanish law initially stated that in these cases evidence of the foreigner's labour relationship and its duration entails the submission of a court decision confirming this relationship, or an administrative decision confirming an infringement notice issued by the Labour and Social Security Inspection Service, which certainly proves the relationship but also places the person in a situation of total irregularity. However, it is also possible that the foreigner's situation becomes irregular situation at a later stage, because, for instance, he is unable to renew his work permit.

270. Social integration legally justifies the issuing of a temporary residence permit if the foreigner can prove his continuous stay in Spain during a minimum period of three years (Article 124.2 of RD 557/2011). This means that the foreigner shall have to: (a) have a labour contract that is valid for no less than one year;[196] (b) have family ties with other foreign residents; or (c) submit an integration report providing evidence of their degree of social inclusion, drawn up by the autonomous region where the foreigner has his habitual residence. In relation to this integration report, Spanish law establishes that it must provide the following information: the duration of residence of the person concerned at his current address, as registered with the competent municipal authorities; and the foreigner's economic situation, the relationship with relatives who are resident in Spain and all efforts to participate in social, labour and cultural integration programmes. In relation to significant family ties that may facilitate the foreigner's integration, Spanish law is categorical where it states that 'family ties will refer exclusively to the spouse or registered unmarried partner, as well as the direct first-degree ascendants and descendants'. In any case, Spanish law establishes that, should the Ministry of the Presidency of the Spanish government deem it appropriate the national employment situation test will be applied in the assessment of the temporary residence permit application to be issued for reasons of integration (Article 124.4 of RD 557/2011).

271. Regarding family integration, the issuing of a temporary residence permit is possible in the following two situations: (a) the foreigner is the parent of a minor holding Spanish nationality, as long as the applicant is in charge of the minor and lives with him or her, or complies with his/her paternal/maternal obligations towards the child;[197] (b) the foreigner is the child of a father or mother who was originally Spanish.

196. The law includes the following exceptions: (a) in the agricultural sector, it will be possible to submit two labour contracts, related and signed by different employers, but each of them valid for no less than six months; (b) in the case of activities developed within the same occupation, working part-time and simultaneously for more than one employer, it will be possible to submit various contracts, all of which will be valid for no less than one year and will account taken together for a working week of no less than thirty hours.

197. This was a novelty in Spain when RD 557/2011 was passed and, through it, Spain adjusted its legal regime to the doctrine of the European Court of Justice, which, in its judgment of 8 March 2011 (*Ruiz Zambrano,* case, C-34/90, ECLI:EU:CC:2011:124), considered that Art. 20 of the Treaty on the Functioning of the European Union precluded a Member State from refusing a residence or work permit to a third-country national parent who supports a minor who is a citizen of the Union.

272. RD 557/2011 (Article 125) also provides for the issuing of temporary residence permits for the purpose of what is identified as international protection reasons. In particular, it is established that these temporary residence permits may be granted following a proposal made by the '*Comisión Interministerial de Asilo y Refugio*' (Inter-ministry Asylum and Refuge Commission): (a) to persons whom the Ministry of the Interior has authorised to stay in Spain, in accordance with Articles 37 b) and 46.3 of Law 12/2009, regulating the right to asylum and subsidiary protection;[198] (b) to foreigners displaced within the meaning of the rules on temporary protection in the case of mass influx of displaced persons;[199] (c) in the cases foreseen by the law developing Law 12/2009, regulating the right to asylum and subsidiary protection.[200]

273. In relation to the procedure to request the above-mentioned temporary residence permit under exceptional circumstances, and recalling that it is not necessary to obtain a visa in these cases, Spanish law provides that the application must be submitted in person by the foreigner to the competent body. In the case of minors or disabled persons, the application may be submitted by their legal representative.[201] In any case, a temporary residence permit on the grounds of integration is always combined with a work permit, which will be valid for as long as the residence permit is. A work permit is also issued to those who obtain a temporary residence permit for the purpose of international protection (Article 129 of RD 557/2011). In all of the other cases a work permit has to be applied for separately. Due to their exceptional nature, these residence permits are valid for one year. If the circumstances under which they were initially issued remain unchanged and if the temporary permit was granted for reasons of collaboration with police, fiscal or judicial authorities it can be extended (Article 130.2 of RD 557/2011). In the other cases, neither the renewal, nor the extension of the residence permit is possible. Therefore, should the foreigner wish to prolong his legal stay in the country, he will have to satisfy the conditions to be issued a residence permit under the general residence regime.

274. A temporary residence permit under exceptional circumstances can be issued in more situations than those listed in Articles 123–130 of RD 557/2011. The First Additional Disposition of RD 557/2011 includes in its fourth section the possibility that 'when economic, social or labour circumstances thus require, and in non-regulated cases of special relevance, the Spanish Council of Ministers may

198. In particular, the norm identifies those foreign people who do not meet the requirements to be recognised as refugees, to be granted asylum or to receive subsidiary protection, but who can return to their country of origin according to the principle of non-refoulement in the Geneva Convention on the Status of Refugees, of 28 July 1951 (Art. 33.1).

199. RD 1325/2005, of 24 October 20005, passing the Regulation on the temporary protection regime in the case of mass influx of displaced persons (OSG 25 Oct. 2003, No. 256) applies in these situations.

200. Currently, Law 12/2009 is not developed by its own regulation. To date it is not anticipated that this will happen.

201. Article 128 of RD 557/2011 specifies the documents that must be submitted together with the application.

issue instructions that regulate the issuing of temporary residence or work permits, or stay permits, specifying when the conditions and periods within which these permits may be granted'.

Chapter 6. Asylum

§1. Conditions

I. Refugee Status

275. In Article 13.4 of the SC there is a very brief recognition of the right of third-country nationals and stateless persons to enjoy asylum in Spain, as provided for by the law. As in many other cases regarding immigration, the Spanish asylum regime is conditioned by the commitments undertaken by the country as a member of the EU, and particularly in the framework of the so-called Common European Asylum System, which has started to develop after the adoption of a set of Directives and Regulations, such as: (a) Directive 2013/32/EU of the European Parliament and of the Council, of 26 June 2013, on common procedures for granting and withdrawing international protection (recast);[202] (b) Directive 2013/33/EU of the European Parliament and of the Council, of 26 June 2013, laying down standards for the reception of applicants for international protection (recast);[203] (c) Directive 2011/95/EU of the European Parliament and of the Council, of 13 December 2011 on standards for the qualification of third-country nationals or stateless persons as beneficiaries of international protection, for a uniform status for refugees or for persons eligible for subsidiary protection, and for the content of the protection granted (recast);[204] (d) Regulation (EU) No. 604/2013 of the European Parliament and of the Council, of 26 June 2013, establishing the criteria and mechanisms for determining the Member State responsible for examining an application for international protection lodged in one of the Member States by a third-country national or a stateless person (recast);[205] (e) Regulation (EU) No. 603/2013, of the European Parliament and of the Council of 26 June 2013, on the establishment of 'Eurodac' for the comparison of fingerprints for the effective application of Regulation (EU) No. 604/2013 establishing the criteria and mechanisms for determining the Member State responsible for examining an application for international protection lodged in one of the Member States by a third-country national or a stateless person and on requests for the comparison with Eurodac data by Member States' law enforcement authorities and Europol for law enforcement purposes, and amending Regulation (EU) No. 1077/2011 establishing a European Agency for the operational management of large-scale IT systems in the area of freedom, security and justice (recast).[206] The legal regime discussed in the following paragraphs also reflects the standards set by the Geneva Convention relating to the Status of Refugees, of 28 July 1951 and the Protocol relating to the Status of Refugees, of 4 October 1967, is the sense that the definition of the concept of refugee in Spanish law is derived directly from this Convention.

202. OJEU, L 180/60, 29 Jun. 2013.
203. OJEU, L 180/96, 29 Jun. 2013.
204. OJEU, L 337/9, 20 Dec. 2011.
205. OJEU, L 180/31, 29 Jun. 2013.
206. OJEU, L 180/1, 29 Jun. 2013.

276. Law 12/2009 that currently regulates the right to asylum and subsidiary protection reflects the idea of joint consideration of both forms of international protection which befits the current international situation, although, undisputedly, this is not reflected in the Geneva Convention.[207] According to Article 2 the law 'aims at establishing the terms in which nationals from non-EU countries and stateless persons may enjoy in Spain the international protection implied in the right to asylum and subsidiary protection, as well as the contents of such protection'.

277. Taking into account the above said, Law 12/2009 (Article 3) grants refugee status to every person who, due to a well-founded fear to be persecuted for reasons of race, religion, nationality, political opinions, belonging to a certain social group, gender or sexual orientation, is out of their country of origin and cannot, or due to the above-mentioned fear, wishes not to avail of the protection of that country. Stateless persons who, lacking a nationality and being out of the country where their habitual residence is, who for the same reasons cannot or, due to the above-referred to fear, do not wish to return to that country can also be granted refugee status. In either case, the person must not be in a situation justifying that person's exclusion from the refugee status, as provided for in Article 8 of Law 12/2009, or a refusal to recognise the right to asylum, as detailed in Article 9 of that law.[208]

278. For the purpose of avoiding an excessive discretionary power on the part of the administration, Spanish law specifies what is to be understood as 'acts of persecution' or 'reasons for persecution'. In relation to the first concept, Article 6 of Law 12/2009 establishes that the acts on which the person's well-founded fear of being persecuted is based, should meet the following requirements:[209] (a) to be sufficiently grave by their own or recurrent nature to be considered a serious violation of the person's fundamental rights, in particular of those rights that cannot be an exception according to Article 15 section 2 of the European Convention on the protection of human rights and fundamental freedoms; or (b) to be a sufficiently grave accumulation of various acts, including violations of human rights, as to affect a person in a similar way to that which is indicated in the previous case. The law requires that these acts of persecution are related to the above-mentioned reasons for persecution and that the following elements are taken into account (Article 7 of Law 12/2009): race, religion, nationality, political opinion and belonging to a certain

207. Article 34 of OL 4/2000 also addresses the issue of a refugee's right of residence, mostly by making reference to the current legislation on the matter, i.e., Law 12/2009 and other international law. *See*, in this respect, § 1 of Chapter 5 in Part III of this work.

208. The causes for exclusion or refusal specified in Arts. 8 and 9 of Law 12/2009 are analysed in § 1 of Chapter 5 in Part III of this monograph, more specifically in para. 245 and notes 178 and 179.

209. Additionally, Art. 6.2 of Law 12/2009 establishes that the acts of persecution may be of the following kinds, among others: (a) acts of physical or psychological violence, including sexual violence; (b) legislative, administrative, police or judicial measures that are discriminatory by themselves or applied in a discriminatory manner; (c) criminal procedures that are disproportionate or discriminatory; (d) a refusal of legal guardianship resulting in disproportionate or discriminatory penalties; (e) prosecution or penalties following a refusal to perform military service during a conflict in which complying with such service would entail committing crimes or acts included as part of the causes of exclusion established in Art. 8 of Law 12/2009; and (f) acts of a sexual nature affecting adults or children.

social group. Law 12/2009 expressly provides that the occurrence of any of these elements is an indifferent factor if it is established that there is an agent of persecution and that, consequently, persecution exists.[210]

II. Subsidiary Protection Status

279. In relation to subsidiary protection, Law 12/2009 defines it as a right (Article 4), to be enjoyed by third-country nationals and stateless persons who do not meet the requirements to be granted asylum or to be acknowledged as refugees. Subsidiary protection is thus legally differentiated from that provided to refugees. To be eligible for subsidiary protection, there must be well-founded reasons to believe that, should that person return to his country of origin, in the case of third-country nationals, or to the country of habitual residence, in the case of stateless persons, that person would risk suffering serious harm, as set out in Article 10 of Law 12/2009, and, therefore, cannot or, because of that risk, does not wish to be placed under the protection of that country. A right to subsidiary protection is recognised as long as none of the situations mentioned in Article 11 (causes of exclusion) or 12 (causes of refusal) of Law 12/2009 exists.

280. According to Article 10 of Law 12/2009 the following situations amount to serious harm, justifying the implementation of the subsidiary protection regime to the foreigner concerned: (a) the death sentence or the risk of it being executed; (b) torture and inhuman or degrading treatment in the applicant's country of origin; (c) serious threats against the life or integrity of civilians motivated by indiscriminate violence in international or civil conflicts.

281. A foreigner cannot benefit from subsidiary protection, according to Spanish law if it is established that that 'there are well-founded reasons' to consider that the person concerned encouraged or participated in the commissioning of one of the following crimes or acts: (a) crimes against peace, war crimes or crimes against humanity as established by international law; (b) serious crimes, as defined by the Spanish Criminal Code that affect the life, freedom, sexual integrity or freedom, or integrity of persons or the heritage, if perpetrated outside the country of protection, before being admitted to Spain as a beneficiary of subsidiary protection – i.e., before

210. Law 12/2009 (Art. 15) includes the possibility of observing the need of international protection on site. In this sense, the well-founded fear of being persecuted or the actual risk of suffering serious damage referred to in Arts 6 and 7 of the law may be based on events or acts in which the applicant may have participated while leaving his country of origin or, in the case of stateless persons, the country where their habitual residence is, especially if it is established that these events or acts are the expression of convictions or orientations that are normal in the country of origin or habitual residence. Spanish law indicates that, for the purpose of acknowledging refugee status in these cases, the fact that the risk of persecution is based on circumstances that were expressly created by the applicant after leaving his country of origin or, for stateless persons, that of habitual residence will be taken into consideration and assessed.

the issuing of the residence permit identifying the person as a beneficiary of subsidiary protection – and when this involved the use of force against objects or violence against or the intimidation of a person, as well as in cases of an organised criminal networks,[211] as provided for in Articles 282*bis* of the Law on the Criminal Procedure; (c) acts that are contrary to the objectives and principles of the United Nations as established in the Preamble and Articles 1 and 2 of the Charter of the United Nations; and (d) acts that represent a danger to the internal or external security of Spain, or to its public order.

282. The grounds justifying a refusal to provide subsidiary protection in Article 12 of Law 12/2009 are: (a) being a person who, for well-founded reasons, it is believed to represent a danger to the security of the country; and (b) being a person who has been convicted of one or more serious offences by a final judgment and who are a present threat to Spanish society.

III. Temporary Protection Status

283. The implementation of the temporary protection regime has be realised, in Spain with the adoption of RD 1325/2003, of 24 October 2003, approving the regulation on the temporary protection regime in case of mass influx of displaced people.[212] This is the RD that transposed Council Directive 2001/55/EC, of 20 July 2001, on minimum standards for giving temporary protection in the event of a mass influx of displaced persons and on measures promoting a balance of efforts between Member States in receiving such persons and bearing the consequences thereof into the Spanish legal framework.[213] Article 1 of this royal decree states that its objective is to provide a temporary protection regime in the case of a mass influx of displaced persons coming from third countries that are not members of the EU, who

211. Articles 282.4*bis* of the Spanish Law on the Criminal Procedure – approved by Royal Decree of 14 September 1882– establishes that an organised criminal network is the association of three or more persons that permanently or repeatedly performs acts that aim at committing one or several of the following criminal offences: (a) crimes to illegally obtain, trade and transplant human organs (Arts. 156*bis* of the Criminal Code); (b) kidnapping persons (Arts. 164–166 of the Criminal Code); (c) trafficking in human beings (Art. 77 of the Criminal Code); (d) crimes related to prostitution (Arts 187–189 of the Criminal Code); (e) crimes against the heritage and against the socio-economic order (Arts. 237, 243, 244, 248 and 301 of the Criminal Code); (f) crimes against intellectual or industrial property (Arts. 270–277 of the Criminal Code); (g) crimes against the rights of workers (Arts 312 and 313 of the Criminal Code); (h) crimes against the rights of foreign citizens (Arts 318*bis* of the Criminal Code); (i) trafficking in endangered flora or fauna species (Arts. 332 and 334 of the Criminal Code); (j) trafficking in nuclear or radioactive materials (Art. 345 of the Criminal Code); (k) crimes against the public health (Arts. 368–373 of the Criminal Code); (l) crimes related to the counterfeiting of currency (Art. 386 of the Criminal Code) or credit or debit cards or traveller's cheques (Art. 399*bis* of the Criminal Code); (m) crimes related to the trafficking and deposit of arms, ammunition or explosives (Arts. 566–568 of the Criminal Code); (n) crimes related to terrorism (Arts. 572–578 of the Criminal Code); and (o) crimes against the historical heritage (Art. 21.e of Organic Law 12/1995, of 12 December, on the repression of smuggling).

212. OSG 25 Oct. 2003, No. 256. This royal decree additionally amended certain provisions in RD 203/1995.

213. OJEU, L 212/12, 7 Aug. 2001.

are not able to return to those countries as the conditions there are neither safe nor durable due to the situation in those countries. This means that the situation in these countries make its residents liable to eventually qualify for protection within the meaning of Article 1.A of the Geneva Convention on the Status of Refugee, of 28 July 1951, or any other international or national instrument for international protection.

284. For the purpose of this royal decree, Spanish law considers as 'displaced' those citizens of third countries that are not members of the EU or stateless persons who have been forced to leave their country or region of origin or who have been evacuated, in particular: (a) persons who have escaped from armed conflicts or permanently violent regions; and (b) persons who have been or are in serious danger of being exposed to a systematic or generalised violation of human rights. In any case, the implementation of this legal regime requires that the groups of displaced persons qualify under a general temporary protection decision adopted as specified in this royal decree.

§2. Procedures

I. Asylum Procedure

285. The right to asylum is defined in Spanish law as 'the protection given to non-EU citizens or stateless persons who are granted refugee status in the terms established in Article 3 of this law and in the Convention on the Status of Refugees, signed in Geneva on 28 July 1951, and its Protocol, adopted in New York on 31 January 1967'. The Spanish asylum legal framework is, until this day, provided by Law 12/2009, and RD 203/1995, of 10 February 1995, approving the regulation implementing Law 5/1984, of 26 March 1984, regulating the right to asylum and the status of refugee, as amended by Law 9/1994, of 19 May.[214] The fact that RD 203/1995 is still in force is somehow atypical because, as revealed by its title, it is the regulation developing the repealed law on the right to asylum in Spain: Law 5/1984. The issue is that there is still no regulation developing Law 12/2009, and, for this reason, RD 203/1995, which has not yet been repealed, applies to the extent that it is in line with Law 12/2009.

A. International Protection

286. The procedure to obtain international protection, i.e., the right to asylum or subsidiary protection, is regulated in such a way that submitting an application when not in Spain is not possible. This is one of the novelties of Law 12/2009 that put an end to possibility to apply for international protection at consular offices and diplomatic missions. At the very best, applications can be made at the Spanish border

214. OSG 2 Mar. 1995, No. 52.

control points (Article 21 of Law 12/2009). Considering the transfer of border controls to points in third countries in certain cases, this notably limits, in practice, the possibilities of submitting an application for asylum at the Spanish border.[215] An application for international protection must be submitted within one month from the person's entry into Spain or, where applicable, after the events that justify the already mentioned 'well-founded fear of persecution' or 'serious damage' took place (Article 17 of Law 12/2009). Irregular entry into Spain cannot, by law, be penalised if that person meets the requirements to be considered a beneficiary of international protection, as defined by law.

287. There are two administrative procedures which can be followed to assess an application for international protection: the ordinary procedure (Article 24 of Law 12/2009) and the emergency procedure (Article 25 of Law 12/2009).[216] In the first case, the *Oficina de Asilo y Refugio* (Asylum and Refuge Office), an administrative body attached to the Ministry of the Interior, is competent to conduct the procedure, and the Inter-ministry Asylum and Refuge Commission, also part of the same Ministry, is in charge of deciding on the application; either granting or denying international protection. Should a period of six months pass after the submission of the application without the person being notified by the administration of its decision, it is assumed that the application has been rejected. With regard to the emergency procedure, the differentiating element is that the administrative procedure is reduced by 50% to three months. The emergency procedure is adopted by

215. Law 12/2009 (Art. 38) exceptionally includes the possibility that Spanish ambassadors facilitate the transfer of asylum seekers to Spain, in order to allow them to submit an application whilst in Spain. The degree of discretionary power is very high. For this purpose, the applicant's nationality may not be that of the country where the Spanish diplomatic representation is located and his physical integrity must be in danger. The application may also be submitted by the applicant's representative, although the applicant will have to sign the application once the physical or legal circumstances preventing the direct submission of the application have disappeared (Art. 17.1).

In 2017 the European Court of Justice, in its judgment of 7 March 2017 (Case C-638/16 PPU), concluded that the application for a visa with limited territorial validity submitted by a third-country national on humanitarian grounds and in accordance with the EU's Visa Code, at the diplomatic office of an EU Member State in the territory of a third country, with the intention of submitting, once in the territory of the Union, an application for international protection and to remain therefore in that Member State for more than 90 days within a period of 180 days, is not covered by the Visa Code – which only regulates the issuing of visa for transit or stays of no more than 90 days within each period of 180 days in the territory of the Member States of the Union. For this reason, according to EU law, this issue is considered to be regulated by national law.

216. Generally speaking, and in relation to the Spanish administrative procedure, the role that Spanish legislation assigns to the United Nations High Commissioner for Refugees (UNHCR) is set out in Arts. 34 and 35 of Law 12/2009. Spanish law establishes that applications for international protection must be communicated to the UNHCR, a body that has been granted the right to be informed on the situation of those applications, to be present during the hearings of the applicant, to submit reports to be included in the administrative file corresponding to the application, and to have access to the applicant, including those who are in border control offices or in immigration detention centres or prisons. In addition, the UNHCR can attend the meetings of the Inter-ministry Asylum and Refuge Commission, should be informed immediately on the submission of applications at border control points and be heard prior to the publication of the decision on the application.

the Spanish Ministry of the Interior in one or several of the following circumstances: (a) the application is clearly well founded; (b) the application has been submitted by applicants with specific needs, particularly unaccompanied minors; (c) the applicant is a national of a country that is considered to be safe – as provided for by Article 27 of Directive 2005/85/EC –,or, in the case of stateless persons, they have their habitual residence in that country; (d) the applicant, without any justified reason, has submitted an application after the one-month period provided for by law has expired; (e) the applicant's situation is on that may justify an exclusion or refusal of the application, or has made a request that is not related to the recognition of refugee status or the granting of subsidiary protection. Likewise, the emergency procedure applies to an application for international protection that is submitted in an Immigration Detention Centre and declared admissible.

B. Temporary Protection

288. The implementation of the exceptional temporary protection regimes in Article 4 of RD 1325/2003 starts with a decision of both the Council of the EU – on proposal of the European Commission – and the Spanish government. In this second case, the Spanish regulation (Article 4 b) of RD 1325/2003) specifically establishes that the Spanish government may declare the application of the temporary protection regime, by agreement of the Council of Ministers, and on proposal of the Minister of Foreign Affairs in cases necessitating a mass evacuation of people, and the Ministry of the Interior when dealing with emergency situations. Authorisation by the Spanish government is necessary when Article 7(1) of Council Directive 2001/55 /EC applies: 'Member States may extend temporary protection as provided for in this Directive to additional categories of displaced persons over and above those to whom the Council Decision provided for in Article 5 applies, where they are displaced for the same reasons and from the same country or region of origin. They shall notify the Council and the Commission immediately'.

289. This decision is an indispensable requirement for the activation of this administrative procedure, allowing the Member States to grant temporary protection. The Council's decision identifies the specific groups of persons to who qualify for temporary protection, as well as the needs of the Spanish government to cope with the situation. If the decision is adopted by the Spanish government, the reasoned agreement of the Council of Ministers will include a detailed description of the groups of persons to whom this temporary protection will be applicable, the date on which this protection will be implemented and an estimate of the influx of displaced persons.

290. Once the general temporary protection decision has been adopted, the Spanish Ministry of the Interior is the competent body in charge of issuing, individually and in a reasoned manner, a decision on an application submitted by a person seeking temporary protection as provided for by OL 4/2000 and other related legislation. According to Spanish law, the Ministry of the Interior can extend, on the same grounds, the benefits of this regime to other displaced persons coming from the same country or region of origin as the ones covered by the general decision (Article 11.2 of RD 1325/2003). In any case, the law provides that the benefits of the temporary protection regime are to be refused when (Article 12 of RD 1325/2003): (a) there are well-founded reasons to believe that the applicant has committed a crime against peace, a war crime or a crime against humanity – in the terms established by international instruments – or has committed a serious common crime outside Spain before being admitted into Spain as a beneficiary of temporary protection, or is guilty of acts committed against the objectives and principles of the United Nations; (b) there are well-founded reasons to believe that the person concerned represents a danger for national security or, due to having been convicted of a serious offence by a final judgment, are a threat to public order. In any case, Spanish law includes the creation, within the Asylum and Refuge Office of the Spanish government, of a register including the data of all those persons who, after completing the appropriate administrative procedure, benefit from the temporary protection regime in Spain (Article 13 of RD 1325/2003).

II. Review of the Decision Rejecting the Application for Asylum

291. The review of a decision on an application for international protection as provided for by Law 12/2009 is legally configured on the basis of the principle established in Article 29 of Law 12/2009, which requires the exhaustion of the administrative remedies as provided for by that law. The review procedure is a procedure before a court of law and starts when an appeal is lodged with the contentious-administrative jurisdiction. This general rule has one exception, the petition to re-examine the decision dismissing or rejecting an application for international protection submitted at a border control point. A petition to re-examine a decision exhausts all administrative remedies, which means that it is only possible to lodge a contentious-administrative jurisdictional appeal against this petition to re-examine a decision.

292. The lodging of a judicial appeal allows the appellant to request for the suspension of the appealed act, which is treated, as provided for by Spanish procedural law urgent request. Spanish law also states that, after the application for international protection has been rejected, it is possible to request review by the Spanish administration if there are new facts. Spanish law guarantees the right of a person applying for international protection to remain in the country during the processing of (Article 22 of Law 12/2009): (a) the request to re-examine the application submitted; (b) the appeal for reversal, as provided for in Article 21.5 of Law 12/2009; and (c) the contentious-administrative appeal lodged by the applicant before the Spanish judicial bodies.

III. Unaccompanied Minor Asylum Seekers and Other Vulnerable People

293. The Spanish regime for the processing of applications for international protection includes special treatment for persons considered to be vulnerable. In particular, Article 46 of Law 12/2009 establishes that 'the specific situation of people applying for or benefiting from international protection in a situation of vulnerability' will be taken into account, and identifies, as such, the following groups: minors,[217] unaccompanied minors, disabled people, elderly people, pregnant women, single-parent families with children under the legal age of majority, victims of torture, rape or other serious forms of psychological, physical or sexual violence, and victims of trafficking in human beings.

294. In relation to these especially vulnerable people, Spanish law establishes that the necessary measures will be taken in order to provide, where applicable, a differentiated treatment to their applications for international protection (Article 46.2 of Law 12/2009). This differentiated treatment is also foreseen in the case of persons who, because of their personal characteristics, may have been persecuted for reasons considered by the same law (Article 46.2 of Law 12/2009). The issue is that the law does not specify what this differentiated treatment should be,[218] as it merely refers to the RD that has not yet been adopted, meaning that the RD developing the law that has been replaced by Law 12/2009 which is still in force.

295. However, in the case of unaccompanied minors, Law 12/2009 does provide some specifications that concern: (a) the children protection services that are competent with regard to these minors, and the Spanish Public Prosecutor's Office, that has to be informed of their existence; (b) the notification of the Public Prosecutor's Office if the minor's age cannot be determined with certainty, so that they can act as required to obtain this information; (c) a minor's refusal to be subjected to a medical examination which may not preclude the adoption of a decision on the application for international protection; (d) the necessary measures to be taken immediately in order to guarantee that the minor's representative, appointed in accordance with Spanish law on child protection, can act on his behalf and assist him in relation to his application for international protection.

§3. Legal Position

296. The submission of an application for international protection has certain legal effects that are best summarised as follows: the applicant will not be the object of a return, removal or expulsion decision until his application has been granted or

217. In the case of minors, Art. 47 of Law 12/2009 recognises their right to receive appropriate health and psychological assistance, as well as all the qualified help they may require, when they have been subjected to any kind of abuse, neglect, exploitation, torture, or cruel, inhuman or degrading treatment or are victims in an armed conflict.

218. The only reference is found in Art. 46.3 of Law 12/2009, which states that, on humanitarian grounds other than the ones specified in the statute of subsidiary protection, it is possible to authorise the applicant's stay in Spain in the terms foreseen by the current immigration laws.

dismissed (Article 19 of Law 12/2009), and he will not be the object of an extradition measure – i.e., the execution of the extradition process will be suspended. Additionally, the applicant enjoys the following rights (Article 18.1 of Law 12/2009): (a) free legal aid and interpreting services; (b) the United Nations High Commissioner for Refugees (UNHCR) will be informed on his case; (c) informed on the contents of his administrative file at any moment; (d) healthcare as provided for by Spanish law; (e) certain social benefits as provided for by Spanish law. The Spanish law also identifies the applicant as subject of the following obligations (Article 18.2 of Law 12/2009): (a) to cooperate with the Spanish authorities during the procedure for the granting of international protection; (b) to submit, as soon as possible, all the information that, together with the applicant's own statement, substantiate the application; (c) to provide their fingerprints, to allow to be photographed and, where applicable, to consent to have their statement recorded, as long as they have been previously informed on such action; (d) to inform the authorities of his place of residence in Spain and any subsequent changes; and (e) to inform the competent authorities or to appear before them when required in relation to his application.

297. Law 12/2009 (Articles 30–33) also regulates the so-called conditions of reception of applicants for international protection, which are basically the following: (a) they have the right to benefit from the necessary reception and social services in order to ensure that their basic needs are taken care of, if they lack the economic resources to provide for them themselves – the difficulty here is that these measures depend on the regulatory development that has not yet been adopted; (b) they have the right to maintain their family unity where family members are already present in Spain as long as they meet the requirements established in Law 12/2009; (c) the authorisation to work in Spain, in such a way that the temporary residence authorisation for reasons of international protection entails the granting of work authorisation in Spain during the term of the first one (Article 129 of RD 557/2011); and finally (d), when the reception regime can be reduced or withdrawn. If a person no longer benefits from the reception regime, this means that he can no longer use the services, aid or benefits of the different reception programmes. A reduction in the level of reception facilities or the withdrawal of all rights to reception facilities is possible if the applicant has left the assigned place of residence without informing the competent authorities or without their permission; has access to economic resources of his own and, nevertheless, still enjoys the benefits of the reception facilities which are free of charge; has been notified of the decision regarding his application for international protection – unless there are special circumstances that make it advisable to maintain the above-referred facilities in an individual case; violates, by action or omission, the rights of other residents or of the staff in charge of the centre where he lives, or seriously challenges the coexistence of residents in a centre; and the termination of the authorised benefit or programme.

298. For the purpose of adopting measures that allow the re-establishment of the family unit Article 40 of Law 12/2009 allows for the granting of the right of asylum or subsidiary protection by extension when the members of the family unit are:[219]

(a) Direct ascendants who accredited the dependency and their descendants in first grade who were minors. The right to extension is excepted when these people have different nationality. The family relationships of ascendants and descendants must be established through scientific tests that are necessary, in cases where this relationship of kinship cannot be determined without doubt.
(b) The spouse or person bound by an analogous relationship of affectivity and coexistence, except in the cases of divorce, legal separation, de facto separation, different nationality or granting of refugee status on grounds of gender, when in the application file it is proven that the person has suffered or had well-founded fears of suffering persecution singled out by gender violence by his spouse or partner.
(c) An adult who is responsible of the beneficiary of international protection, when said beneficiary is an unmarried child.
(d) Asylum or subsidiary protection may also be granted by extension to other members of the family of the refugee or beneficiary of subsidiary protection, provided that the dependence on such persons and the existence of prior cohabitation in the country of origin is sufficiently established.

299. Once refugee status or subsidiary protection has been granted and notified, the applicant enjoys the rights as specified in the Geneva Convention on the Status of Refugees, the EU standards of protection as well as those set out in Spanish immigration law. Article 36 of Law 12/2009 explicitly recognises the right of these persons to: (a) protection against removal in the terms established by the international treaties to which Spain is a party; (b) access to information on the rights and obligations associated with the international protection granted, in a language they can understand; (c) a permanent residence and work permit as provided for by OL 4/2000; (d) identity and travel documents for those who have been granted refugee status and, where applicable, for those benefitting from subsidiary protection; (e) access to the public employment services; (f) access to education, healthcare, housing, social assistance and services, all rights recognised to persons who have been victims of gender-based violence, social security where applicable, and integration programmes under the same conditions as Spaniards; (g) access, under the same conditions as Spaniards, to continuous or vocational training, and to internships, as well as to the procedure of recognition of their academic and professional diplomas and certificates; (h) freedom of movement; (i) access to general or specific integration programmes; (j) access to voluntary return programmes; and (k) the preservation of family unity as provided for by the law, and access to family support programmes.

---

219. From a procedural point of view, the Asylum and Refugee Office is the institution that processes the extension applications, as they are presented. In any case, it is in the Inter-ministerial Commission of Asylum and Refuge where they are studied, to subsequently submit a proposal to the Minister of the Interior, who will decide on the extension or not of the legal regime referred to.

300. Law 12/2009 includes the possibility of cessation of refugee status when (Article 42 of Law 12/2009): (a) the refugee thus requests; (b) a refugee has voluntarily accepted the protection of his country of nationality; (c) a refugee has voluntarily recovered his nationality, after having lost it; (d) a refugee has acquired a new nationality and can now enjoy the protection of his new country of nationality; (e) a refugee has voluntarily re-settled in the country he has left or from which he had fled for fear of being persecuted; (f) the refugee has left Spanish territory and settled in another country; (g) there is no longer a justified reason to continue refusing the protection of the country of nationality as the circumstances that led to him being acknowledged as a refugee have disappeared; and (h) a refugee who did not have a nationality can return to the country where he previously resided because the circumstances that led to him being recognised as a refugee have disappeared. Article 42.2 of Law 12/2009 states that the cessation of refugee status does not prevent the continuation of residence in Spain, where this is possible according to immigration law.

301. Cessation of subsidiary protection is possible according to Article 43 of Law 12/2009 under the following circumstances: (a) when the beneficiary requests it; (b) when the beneficiary has left Spanish territory and has settled in another country; and (c) when the situation that led to the granting of subsidiary protection has disappeared or has changed in a way that makes subsidiary protection unnecessary. As with the cessation of refugee status, the cessation of subsidiary protection will not prevent the continuation of residence in Spain, as long as this is possible according to the immigration law.

302. The revocation of both the refugee and subsidiary protection status is possible according to Spanish law (Article 44 of Law 12/2009) if: (a) the beneficiary's situation corresponds to any of the situations in Articles 8, 9, 11 and 12 of Law 12/2009); (b) the beneficiary has distorted or omitted facts in his application – including the use of fake documents – that were decisive for the granting of the status of refugee or subsidiary protection; or (c) there are well-founded reasons to believe that the beneficiary represents a danger for the security in Spain, or when, having been convicted of a serious offence by a final judgment, he is to be considered a threat to society. Where applicable, revocation will entail an administrative sanctioning procedure leading to expulsion from Spain of the person concerned. It will not, however, be possible to send this person back to a country where his life or freedom may be at risk, where he may be exposed to torture or inhuman or degrading treatment, or where they may lack effective protection against being deported to the persecuting or the country where the person runs the risk of suffering serious harm (Article 44.4 of Law 12/2009).

303. As regards the temporary protection status which is granted in the case of a mass influx of displaced persons, RD 1325/2003 lists the rights of the beneficiaries of such protection, which basically involves: (a) the right to free movement within and to free residence in Spain – although the Ministry of the Interior may take some interim measures in relation to these freedoms; (b) the right to be informed in writing on the rights and obligations associated with the status of a displaced person in a language that the beneficiary can understand – this document must be given to the applicant when he submits his application; (c) the right to obtain, as provided for by Spanish law, a residence permit that can be annually renewed; (d) the right to be provided with a travel document in the case that he needs to travel outside Spain and he does not have a passport or travel document, or they are not valid; (e) the right to be readmitted to Spain if he has not be authorised to reside on the territory of another EU Member State; (f) the right to be granted a work permit as provided for by Spanish immigration law; (g) the right to have access to social support if he lacks sufficient economic means to survive; and (h) the right to family reunification, as defined by Article 21 of RD 1325/2003. Likewise, a beneficiary of temporary protection can apply for refugee status, as provided for by Spanish law. An application for refugee status by a beneficiary of temporary protection can never enjoy the rights granted to asylum seekers in addition to the rights which are granted to that person by virtue of their status of temporary protection, according to Spanish that law while their application is being processed (Article 22 of RD 1325/2003).

304. The duration of temporary protection is limited by RD 1325/2003 (Article 7) to one year, which can be automatically extended for another year and, exceptionally, when the reasons for granting temporary protection prevail, for a third, the last year. RD 1325/2003 (Articles 23–26) also regulates when the temporary protection status can be withdrawn. In general, this is realised through an agreement of the Council of Ministers of the Spanish government when the conflict that motivated it has ended and the conditions for return are favourable (Article 7 of RD 1325/2003). Law 5/1984, of 26 March 1984, regulating the right to asylum and the status of refugee does, exceptionally, allow the issuing of a permanent residence permit if the circumstances that motivated the temporary protection decision persist. Likewise, the continuation of residence in Spain is allowed when the foreigner presents a reasonable justification for their permanent residence in Spain.

305. Automatic cessation of the benefits derived from the temporary protection regime in RD 1325/2003 is possible in the following situations (Article 24): (a) the end of the period established for temporary protection; (b) the beneficiary of temporary protection is granted Spanish nationality; (c) the beneficiary's voluntary decision return to his country of origin, which he has expressly communicated to the competent governmental authority; (d) the express waiver by the beneficiary to temporary protection; (e) the transfer of the beneficiary to the territory of another EU Member State by virtue of the right to family reunification; and (f) the tacit waiver of the temporary protection beneficiary takes place, by not appearing before the competent authority within a period of forty-five days to carry out an essential procedure.[220] Unless there is a justified reason for non-appearance, not appearing before the competent authorities – the Ministry of the Interior – after being

220. The tacit waiver must be assessed by the Minister of the Interior, although the allegation of justified cause for the aforementioned non-appearance is possible.

requested to do so, is treated as a tacit waiver by the beneficiary if more than forty-five days have passed since that request. Like the refugee and subsidiary protection status, temporary protection can be revoked according to Article 25 of RD 1325/2003, by the Spanish Ministry of the Interior, if temporary protection was granted because the applicant provided false data, documents or gave an incorrect statement that, if known by the authorities, would not have led to the granting of the status in the first place. Temporary protection can also be revoked if any of the grounds in Article 12 of RD 1325/2003 occurs.

306. Protection, according to the First Additional Disposition of Law 12/2009, also covers those who are admitted into Spain by virtue of a resettlement programme developed by the Spanish government in collaboration with the United Nations High Commissioner for Refugees and, where applicable, another international organisation. In this case, refugees who are subject of a resettlement programme enjoy the same protection as those who were granted it by virtue of the temporary protection regime defined by Law 12/2009. It is the competence of the Council of Ministers of the Spanish government to annually agree on the number of people who may be subject of resettlement in Spain according to the above-mentioned programmes.

§4. Position of Family Members

307. In the case of refugees and beneficiaries of subsidiary protection, the principle of guaranteeing family unity applies as provide for by Article 39 of Law 12/2009. This principle goes so far as to include a provisional residence permit for relatives of a foreigner who has applied for international protection, while this application is being assessed. This principle still needs to be developed through an RD.

308. In order to ensure family unity, Article 40 of Law 12/2009 includes the extension of the right to asylum or subsidiary protection to the family members of an asylum seeker in the following cases (): (a) when they are first-degree ascendants who can prove to be dependent on the foreigner, or first-degree descendants under the legal age of majority, unless their nationality is different than the applicant's; (b) when they are the foreigner's spouse or person in an equivalent affectionate relationship and cohabit, with the exception of cases of divorce, legal separation, de facto separation, different nationality or if refugee status is granted for reasons of gender, when the application file includes evidence of the person having suffered or having a well-founded fear of suffering persecution due to gender-based violence inflicted by their spouse or partner; and (c) when the family member is responsible for the beneficiary of international protection, the beneficiary being an unmarried minor; (d) when they are other family members, as long as their dependence on the beneficiary and the cohabitation in their country of origin are clearly established. The granting of the right to refugee or subsidiary protection on the grounds of family extension will require, in any case, a favourable decision adopted by the Ministry of the Interior. Spanish law does not allow for the granting of international protection on the grounds of family extension if the beneficiary's situation is one that would justify a refusal or exclusion from refugee status or subsidiary protection as provided for by law.

309. In any case, an extension of refugee status or subsidiary protection to family members depends on the refugee or beneficiary of subsidiary protection. Not without reason does Article 41 of Law 12/2009 include the possibility not to apply for the above-mentioned extension; something that does not prevent an application for family reunification. An application for extension of protection to family members may only be submitted once – it is expressly forbidden to submit several applications for this purpose – if the family members have a different nationality than that of the refugee or beneficiary of subsidiary protection. Again a complicating factor is that further rules still need to be adopted. If family reunification is granted, as administrative decision to this avail will entail the issuing of a residence permit and, where applicable, a work permit to the family members with the same period of validity as those issued to the applicant.

Chapter 7. Other Grounds

§1. Elective Residence

310. There are two different situations that need to be discussed here. The first is non-lucrative temporary residence (Article 31 of OL 4/2000; Articles 46–51 of RD 557/2011), a legal situation that Spanish law included after the amendment by OL 2/2009 which made it possible for a foreigner to reside in Spain without pursuing an economic activity, as long as he had sufficient financial means to cover the cost of his subsistence. In order to obtain non-lucrative temporary residence permission, the following conditions need to be satisfied: the foreigner:

(a) may not be staying irregularly in Spain;
(b) has reached the age of legal majority (18 years old in Spain), does not have a criminal record in Spain or in any of the countries where he has resided during the past five years for criminal offences as provided for by Spanish law;
(c) is not listed as a person to be refused entry permission in a country with which Spain has signed an agreement in this sense;[221]
(d) has sufficient financial means to pay for all costs of living, including, where applicable, those of his family, during the period in which he wishes to reside in Spain, without having to take up employment or pursue a professional activity, within the meaning of Article 47 of RD 557/2011;
(e) has taken out a public or private health insurance with an insurance agency that is authorised to operate in Spain;
(f) is not the subject of decision that is still in force that he cannot return to Spain after having voluntarily left that country to return his country of origin;
(g) does not suffer from a disease that may have serious public health implications, as provided for by the 2005 International Health Regulations;
(h) has paid the fee for the processing of the temporary residence application.

311. The second situation is temporary residence without a work permit (Article 41 of OL 4/2000; Articles 117–119 of RD 557/2011). Temporary residence without a work permit is possible in a range of situations in which foreigners may reside in Spain and develop a lucrative, labour or professional activity without having to obtain a work permit. In particular, Article 117 of RD 557/2011 exempts the following categories of foreigners from the obligation of obtaining a work permit:

(a) Foreign technicians and scientists, who have been invited or hired by Spanish administrations or institutions that promote and develop research – in the case of institutions, they must be supported by the public administration or that administration must participate in the institution.

221. Although the Spanish rule is phrased in very general terms, it basically refers to the foreigner not reported in the Schengen Information System as 'non-admissible' (or 'persons to be refused entry permission').

(b) Foreign professors, who have been invited or hired by Spanish universities and, in general, teachers and professors who have been invited or hired by institutions to carry out teaching, research or academic activities.
(c) Management or teaching staff of renowned and prestigious cultural or teaching institutions, dependant on another State or privately own, but officially recognised in Spain, developing cultural or teaching programmes on their respective countries, as long as they restrict their activities to the execution of those programmes.
(d) Civil or military officers of foreign administrations who come to Spain to carry out certain activities according to cooperation agreements signed with the Spanish administration.
(e) Foreign media correspondents.[222]
(f) Members of international scientific missions carrying out work and research in Spain with the authorisation of the competent State or regional administration.
(g) Artists coming to Spain for specific performances that do not entail an ongoing activity, which does not last more than five consecutive acting days or twenty acting days within a period of no more than six months.
(h) Religious ministers of different churches, denominations and religious communities, as well as members of religious orders.
(i) The staff of representative bodies, governments and the management board of internationally recognised labour unions and business organisations, insofar as their activity is strictly limited to the performance of the duties inherent to their position.
(j) Minors who have reached the working age and who have been placed under the guardianship of a competent child protection service, for those activities that, according to the above-mentioned institution and as long as they remain in that situation, may favour their social integration.

312. Being exempted from applying for a work permit in these cases does not mean being exempted from applying for a residence visa, when the foreigner is not a resident in Spain and the foreseen duration of their activity is more than ninety days. If the non-resident foreigner intends to develop his activity in Spain for less than ninety days, a visa has to be applied for. This application will be processed as a short-term stay visa (Article 118.1 of RD 557/2011). If the foreigner is a resident in Spain, he must request the immigration office to grant him the above-mentioned legal exemption. Article 118.2 of RD 557/2011 establishes that the validity of this exemption will depend on the activity or programme to be developed, with a maximum duration of one year for the initial recognition, two years for the first extension and another two years for the second extension, insofar as the circumstances that justified the exemption persist.

222. *See also*: RD 3882/1982, of 29 December 1982, on the authorisation of foreign media correspondents (OSG 31 Dec. 1982, No. 314).

§2. VOLUNTEERS

313. Historically, in Spanish immigration law there us a broad reading of the concept of 'student'. This changed when the legal regime applicable to students was extended to other foreigners by OL 2/2009, amending OL 4/2000, implementing Directive 2004/114/EC, of 13 December 2004, on the conditions of admission of third-country nationals for the purposes of studies, pupil exchange, unremunerated training or voluntary service. For the purposes that are relevant to this section, this legal reform extended the special regime for students to new categories of foreigners, including those providing voluntary services (Article 33.1 d) of OL 4/2000).[223] The reader is referred to the observations made in Chapter 2 of Part III in this work on that legal regime.

§3. PROFESSIONAL TRAINING

314. Law 14/2013 contains two regimes that apply to the right of residence accorded to foreigners interested in being professionally trained in Spain. Both regimes were discussed in §1 of Chapter 4, Part III of this work, which analysed the aforementioned law and to which the reader is now referred. The two regimes concern:

(a) Highly qualified professionals, within the meaning of Article 71 of Law 14/2013, wishing to carry out training, development or innovation activities in public or private institutions.
(b) Workers posted within the framework of intra-company transfers and moving from a non-EU Member State to Spain for the purpose of improving their skills (Articles 73 and 74 of Law 14/2013).

§4. RETURNED TO THEIR COUNTRIES

315. The foreigner who has voluntarily returned to his country of origin and wishes to reside in Spain temporarily (Articles 120–122 of RD 557/2011) is one of the situations, as provided for by Article 40.1 section 1) OL 4/2000 in which the above-mentioned 'national employment situation' is not to be taken into consideration when a temporary residence permit is issued. This provision establishes that the national employment situation will not be considered in the case of foreigners who have waived their right to a residence and work permit by participating in a voluntary return programme. This situation was introduced when, at the peak of the economic crisis, the Spanish government decided to foster returns to their country of origin of foreigners who were entitled to an unemployment benefit, allowing them to receive that benefit in two payments: 40% in Spain, 60% once they had

223. Directive 2004/114/EC (Art. 2 f) defines 'volunteer' as a foreigner participating in a 'voluntary service scheme', understood as a 'programme of activities of practical solidarity, based on a State or a Community scheme, pursuing objectives of general interest'.

returned to their respective countries of origin.[224] In exchange for this payment in two instalments, which differs from the monthly payment typical of the unemployment benefit in Spain and was designed to encourage a foreigner to start his life in his country of origin given the lack of employment prospects in Spain, a foreigner had to who agree to return to his country of origin within thirty days from the date on which the first payment was made and not to return to Spain within a period of three years. In accordance with this legal approach, Article 36.7 of OL 4/2000 establishes that foreigners who, within the framework of a voluntary return programme, committed themselves not to return to Spain within a specific period of time, will not be granted a residence permit or a permit to carry out a lucrative, labour or professional activity until that period has expired.

316. The right to temporary residence in Spain after having voluntarily returned to their country of origin, regardless of the legal framework for this return, is nowadays not only enjoyed by those who left Spain within the framework of a voluntary return programme fostered by the Spanish administration, but also those who returned to their country of origin independent of those programmes (Article 120.1 of RD 557/2011). In this sense, the law allows a foreigner to apply exclusively for a temporary residence permit, or for a temporary residence and work permit, although it specifies that, whether or not the foreigner has participated in an official return programme, the application shall not be submitted before three years have passed from the date of return to his countries of origin. In every case, a foreigner is requested to waive his residence permit when he leaves Spain to return to his country of origin and is obliged to appear before the competent diplomatic mission or consular office for the purpose of verifying that he has, indeed, returned.

224. According to RLD 4/2008, of 19 September 2008, on the accumulated and advance payment of the unemployment contributory benefit to non-EU foreign workers who voluntarily return to their countries of origin (OSG 20 Sep. 2008, No. 228), developed by RD 1800/2008, of 3 November 2008 (OSG 11 Nov. 2008, No. 272).

Part IV. Loss of the Right of Residence

Chapter 1. Conditions under Which the Right of Residence Might Be Lost

317. Loss of the right of residence, whether temporary or permanent, is regulated in Title VII of RD 557/2011, entitled 'Loss of the residence or residence and work permits' (Articles 162–166). In the case of temporary residence permits, the law distinguishes four different situations.

318. First of all, Article 162 of RD 557/2011 establishes that, except in those cases mentioned in subsequent paragraphs, temporary residence permits are lost without an administrative decision being issued, if: (a) the validity period has expired; (b) the foreign resident is obliged to exceptionally renew his permit, when the Spanish authorities invoke a state of exception or siege; or (c) a foreigner finds himself in a situation that justifies the adoption of an entry ban, according to Article 11 of RD 557/2011.[225] Likewise, a temporary residence permit is lost by decision of the competent body that granted it under any of the following circumstances: (a) the foreigner has changed or lost his nationality, notwithstanding his right to obtain another residence permit as a result of this change in circumstances; (b) the circumstances that justified the issuing of the permit no longer exist; (c) after it has been established that the statements made or the documents submitted by the holder of the residence permit in order to obtain it are seriously inaccurate or false; (d) the foreigner stops being the holder of a valid passport or similar document, or, where

225. Foreigners are not permitted to enter Spain and their access to Spanish territory will be prevented, even though they meet all legal conditions, when: (a) they have been previously expelled from Spain and the entry ban period has not yet expired or when an expulsion order has been issued, except when the procedure has expired or the infringement or sanction can no longer be imposed on the foreigner; (b) they have been the object of a removal decision and they are still within the entry ban period, as determined in the removal agreement; (c) it is known that they have been claimed in relation to criminal proceedings for serious common offences by the judicial or police authorities of another country, as long as the events for which they are sought are considered a criminal offence in Spain and notwithstanding their detention, where applicable; (d) they have been the object of an express entry ban, according to a decision adopted by the head of the Ministry of the Interior, due to activities against Spanish interests or human rights or due to their notorious connection with a criminal organisation, whether national or international, or due to other judicial or administrative reasons that justify the adoption of this measure, notwithstanding their detention, where applicable; (e) they are banned from entering Spain according to an international agreement, to which Spain is a party or according to EU law, unless it is considered necessary to make an exception on humanitarian or national interest grounds.

applicable, a valid registration card, unless he can prove having completed the necessary procedure to renew or recover his passport or similar document; or (e) the foreigner remains outside Spain for more than six month within one year.[226]

319. A temporary residence and work permit issued for the purpose of research is lost without an administrative decision (Article 163 of RD 557/2011), either because the validity period has expired or because the foreign resident is exceptionally obliged to renew their permit because the Spanish authorities have invoked the state of exception or siege. In addition, it is also lost following a decision of the authority that granted it when: (a) the permit was obtained by fraudulent means; (b) the circumstances that justified it being granted have changed or it is established that they never existed; (c) the holder resides in Spain on different grounds than the ones that justified the issuing of the permit. In the case temporary residence permits for highly qualified professionals, Article 164 of RD 557/2011 provides that they are lost for the same reasons.

320. A temporary residence and work permits for victims of trafficking in human beings is lost without an administrative decision as provided for by Article 165 of RD 557/2011. It is also be lost by decision of the competent authority that issued it when: (a) a judicial decision determines that the report on the alleged crime of trafficking in human beings was fraudulent or not well-founded, or appreciate fraud in the cooperation of the victim in the investigation of the crime of trafficking in human beings; (b) the circumstances that justified the issuing of the permit no longer exist; (c) the holder actively, voluntarily and on his own initiative resumes his relationship with the suspected criminals; or (d) the holder stops cooperating with the authorities.

321. In relation to the loss of long-term residence permits and EU long-term residence permits (Article 166 of RD 557/2011), this will occur when: (a) the permit has been obtained fraudulently; (b) an expulsion order is issued in those cases provided for by the law; (c) the holder is absent from the territory of the EU for twelve consecutive months; (d) the holder obtains an EU long-term residence permit in another Member State;[227] (e) having obtained the permit after being granted international protection by another EU Member State, the authorities of that other Member State decide to cease, terminate, refuse the renewal, or revoke the abovementioned status. In the case of EU long-term residence permits, their loss is also considered if the foreigner has been absent from Spanish territory for more than six

226. This does not apply to holders of a temporary residence and work permit who are by employed a non-governmental organisation, foundation or association registered in the corresponding general registry and officially recognised as being of common interest, as aid workers performing research, cooperation for development or humanitarian aid projects abroad. It, likewise, does not apply to holders of a residence permit who remain in the territory of another EU Member State in order to attend a temporary study programme promoted by the European Union.

227. This does not apply to holders of a temporary residence and work permit who are employed by a non-governmental organisation, foundation or association registered in the general registry and officially recognised as being of common use, as aid workers performing research, cooperation for development or humanitarian aid projects abroad.

years. In the latter case it is possible to negotiate an agreement with the Directorate General for Migrations so as not to implement the loss of the residence permit if exceptional reasons thus require. In deciding on this issue, the Spanish authorities enjoy considerable discretionary powers.

322. Finally, in the case of foreigners who have obtained a residence permit and a work permit if required by Law 14/2013, that law provides for the loss, of both their visa and their permit, if the Spanish administration establishes that they do not satisfy the conditions that justified these permits being issued in the first place (Seventh Additional Disposition of Law 14/2013).

Chapter 2. Legal and Administrative Procedures

323. In general terms, residence and work permits issued by virtue of OL 4/2000 are lost following a decision of the competent authority that issued them, and according to the procedures on the modification and loss of permits.

324. As discussed in the previous chapter, loss is sometimes automatic. See the previous chapter.

325. As far as the permits issued by virtue of Law 14/2013 are concerned, its Seventh Additional Disposition recognises the right of the competent authorities of the general State administration to perform the necessary checks to prove compliance with the current law in the first place and that these conditions are still satisfied. Should it be established that the conditions are no longer satisfied, the competent authority may adopt a motivated decision after hearing the interested party, which entails the loss of the visa or permit.

Part V. Sanctions

Chapter 1. Sanctions

§1. Administrative Sanctions

326. The competence to sanction immigration offences accorded to the Spanish administration belongs to the common administrative law on sanctions for non-compliance with Spanish administrative law. This is reflected in the fact that both Article 50 of OL 4/2000 and Article 216 of RD 557/2011 refer to the Law 39/2015, of 1 October 2015, on the common administrative procedure of public administrations as the applicable law if there is no special sanction for immigration offences.[228] The administrative sanction procedure underwent a significant reform by OL 2/2009, amending OL 4/2000, which affected, among other aspects, the definition of the infringements and higher sanctions.

327. In what can be considered a classical approach to administrative sanction law, OL 4/2000 defines three categories of infringements: minor, serious and very serious. In the case of minor infringements, Article 52 of OL 4/2000 lists the following five infringements:

(1) An omission or delay to inform the Spanish authorities on changes of nationality, civil status or residence, as well as all other, relevant circumstances regarding the foreigner's labour situation as required by law.
(2) A delay of up to three months in submitting an application for the renewal of permits once they have expired.
(3) Working in Spain without having applied for an administrative permit to be self-employed, while holding a temporary residence permit.
(4) Working in profession, activity sector or geographical area that are not included in the foreigner's residence and work permit.
(5) Hiring workers whose permit does not allow them to work in that specific occupation or geographical area. The law establishes that there will be as many infringements as foreign workers hired under these conditions.

328. As for serious infringements, it is possible to distinguish the following ones (Article 53 of OL 4/2000):

228. OSG 2 Oct. 2015, No. 236.

(a) Infringements that only the foreigner can commit: (i) staying irregularly in Spain, because an extension of their stay permit has not been obtained, a residence permit has not been issued, or that permit expired more than three months without having applied for its renewal as provided for by law; (ii) working in Spain without having obtained a work permit or a previous administrative permit to work, while not holding a valid residence permit; (iii) being guilty of fraudulent concealment or a serious misrepresentation of the facts when complying with the obligation to inform the authorities of changes in certain personal data or their registration in the municipal registry; (iv) leaving Spain using unauthorised border points, without showing their documents or in breach of a legal ban; (v) not complying with measures imposed on the foreigner for reasons of public security, regular reporting, or restraining orders (i.e., to keep away from borders or specific population centres); (vi) having committed a third minor infringement within one year; (vii) being engaged in serious activities contrary to public order as defined by Spanish law; and (viii) not complying with the obligation to obtain a foreign identity card.
(b) Infringements that can be committed by any person, independent of their nationality: (i) in the case of employers, not registering a foreign worker in the corresponding Social Security regime having applied for a residence and employment permit for that worker, or not registering the labour contract that was the reason to apply for those permits; (ii) getting married, simulating a comparable affective relationship or becoming the legal representative of a minor for the purpose of profit or to unlawfully obtain the right of residence, as long as those acts do not constitute a criminal offence – if they do, the applicable sanction would be of a penal nature; (iii) fostering a foreigner's irregular residence in Spain; (iv) in the case of owners, allowing a foreigner to register in the municipal registry when the address is not the foreigner's actual place of residence.

329. Finally, Article 54 of OL 4/2000 defines the following as very serious infringements:

(a) Being engaged in activities contrary to national security or that may damage Spain's relations with other countries, or being involved in very serious activities contrary to public order as provided for by Spanish law.
(b) Introducing, promoting, favouring or facilitating, whether individually or as a member of an organisation, illegal immigration for the purpose of profit, as long as these acts do not constitute a criminal offence.
(c) Discriminatory behaviour for reasons of race, belonging to an ethnic group, nationality or religion, as provided for by law and as long as this behaviour does not constitute a criminal offence.
(d) Hiring foreign workers without the required residence and work permit, as long as this act does not constitute a criminal offence.
(e) Registering a foreigner in the municipal registry for the purpose of profit, at an address that is not the foreigner's actual place of residence.

(f) Simulating a labour relationship with a foreigner for the purpose of profit or unlawfully obtaining the labour o social security rights recognised by the law, as long as these acts do not constitute a criminal offence.
(g) Committing a third serious infringement within one year.
(h) In the case of carriers: not complying with the legal obligations laid down in OL 4/2000.

330. In general terms, the sanctions for the above-described infringements are a financial penalty ranging from EUR 500, in the case of minor infringements, to EUR 100,000, for certain very serious infringements. Additionally, an expulsion measure can be adopted for certain administrative infringements, a possibility that will be discussed in §4 of this chapter. In any case, as the SSC held, 'the main sanction is the financial penalty […] as a more serious and secondary sanction, expulsion requires a specific motivation, which can be different or complementary […] should it decide on expulsion, the administration shall specify the reasons of proportionality, the degree of subjectivity, damage or risk derived from the infringement and, in general, let us add, the judicial or factual circumstances leading to the expulsion and the entry ban, a more severe sanction than a financial penalty'.[229] This legal criterion was, in fact, inserted into OL 4/2000 years later.

331. As far as the sanctioning procedure is concerned, there are currently four procedures, which apply depending on the type of infringement and the form of sanction that is deemed to be appropriate (financial penalty or expulsion).[230] The so-called simplified procedure is used in the case of minor infringements. The ordinary procedure is applied in the case of serious or very serious infringements and, in certain cases, when an expulsion measure can be adopted. For all other cases when an expulsion measure may be adopted, the preferential procedure is must be followed. Finally, the procedure that has to be followed in the case of breaches of the social order is the one in Articles 52 c), d) and e); 53.1 b); 53.2 a); and 54.1 d) and f). The sanction that is determined using these administrative procedures is either a minimum, medium or maximum one, depending on the degree of guilt of the offender, the seriousness of the offence and the damage caused or the risk emanating from it (Article 254 of RD 557/2011).

332. With regard to the limitation period of infringements and sanctions, very serious infringements expire after three years, while serious infringements do after two years and minor ones after six months. Sanctions imposed for very serious infringements expire after five years, those for serious infringements after two years and the ones which apply in the case of minor infringements expire after one year. In the event of expulsion from Spanish territory, the sanction does not expire until the period of entry ban period determined in the administrative decision has expired, with a maximum of ten years.

229. Supreme Court judgment (Contentious-Administrative Division), of 18 January 2007 (Appeal No. 8602/2003).
230. *See* Arts. 226 ff. of RD 557/2011.

§2. Penal Sanctions

333. The connection between criminal law and administrative sanctions law in immigration affairs needs to be taken into account when the penal regime is analysed. Often, the foreigner's penal situation determines his administrative situation. Likewise, the foreigner's administrative situation sometimes determines the applicable penal regime.

334. There is a close connection between very serious administrative infringements and conduct that is considered to be an offence. This is why the Spanish legislator – as mentioned in the previous section of this work – often specifies that the administrative sanction can only be imposed when the act or conduct concerned does not constitute a crime. Along the same line, the existence of a criminal record, or the commissioning of a crime, will condition the foreigner's right to enter Spain. The foreigner's presence in or departure from Spain can also justify the administration's refusal to grant a residence permit or an extension of that permit according to Article 64 of RD 557/2011.

335. Regarding the definition of criminal offences related to migration activities, the relevant law is Organic Law 10/1995, of 23 November 1995, on the Criminal Code,[231] in particular the crimes and offences defined in Articles 177*bis* – trafficking in human beings; Articles 312–314 – crimes against the right of workers; Article Articles 318*bis* – crimes against the rights of foreign citizens; and Articles 511 and 512 of the Criminal Code – crimes committed against the exercise of the fundamental rights and public freedoms guaranteed by the SC.

336. Starting with the crimes against the rights of workers, Article 312.2 of the Criminal Code imposes a sentence of imprisonment of two to five years and a financial penalty of six to twelve months on those who employ foreign subjects not having a work permit under conditions that harm, suppress or restrict the rights acknowledged to them by law, collective bargaining agreements and individual labour contracts. The same sentence is imposed on those deciding on or favouring a person's emigration to another country by simulating a contract or a job offer or any other similar form of deception (Article 313 of the Criminal Code).

337. The sentence will be a six months to two years of imprisonment and a fine payable over a period of between twelve and twenty-four months for those persons who gravely discriminate against a person in employment, whether public or private, for reasons of belonging to an ethnic group, race or nationality, amongst others, and who do not reinstall equality before the law after a request or administrative sanction and repairing any economic damage that has been suffered through this conduct (Article 314 of the Criminal Code). Discrimination that is relevant is that which takes place in employment, from the moment the person is hired and for the entire labour relationship while it exists.

231. The original Code, which was the object of several amendments over the years, was published in the OSG 24 Nov. 1995, No. 281.

338. With regard to criminal offences committed where fundamental rights and public freedoms as guaranteed by the SC are concerned, Article 511 of the Criminal Code establishes that a sentence of imprisonment of six months to two years and a fine payable over a period of between twelve and twenty-four months can be imposed on the offender. Disqualification for service in public office, a profession or calling during a period of one to three years can be imposed on any person working in public service who denies a benefit to anyone entitled to it on, amongst others, their ethnicity, race or nationality. The same sentence can be imposed where the above-mentioned acts are committed against an association, foundation, undertaking or corporation, or against their members, for reasons related to, amongst others ethnicity, race or nationality. Should a person accused of committing such an offence or crimes be a Spanish public servant, section 3 of Article 511 of the Criminal Code establishes that the sentence must be in the upper half of the range. Disqualification for public office, a profession or calling will be for a period of two to four years. Additionally, in all cases, it is possible to disqualify the person who has committed such a criminal act or offence from working in the education sector or taking on a position in teaching, sports or leisure time sectors during a period that is one to three years longer than the corresponding term of imprisonment. Disqualification must be proportional to the seriousness of the criminal offence and the criminal's circumstances.

339. A different but, at the same time, complementary sanction is provided for in Article 512 of the Criminal Code. According to this provision, a person who, in the exercise of his professional or entrepreneurial activities, has denied someone a benefit due to their belonging to a specific group, race or nationality, can be subject of the sentence of special disqualification to exercise a profession, occupation or work in industry or commerce for a period of one to four years. In addition, the same sentence can be imposed with respect to access to professions or educational positions in the education, sports and leisure sectors.

340. Crimes against the rights of foreign citizens are the subject of Article 318*bis* of the Criminal Code. This provision establishes that intentionally helping a non-Spaniard or a non-EU citizen to enter Spain or travel through the country, acts in breach of Spanish law on entry and transit of third-country nationals. Violation of this provision can be sanctioned with a fine payable over a period of between three and twelve months or imprisonment of three months to one year. If committed for the purpose of profit, the sentence to be applied must be in the upper half of the range. However, these acts do not amount to a criminal offence if the objective pursued is to provide humanitarian aid to the person concerned. There have been convictions of people who have been accused of committing a crime in in which the existence of humanitarian reasons was unclear or under discussion.

341. The aforementioned offence is punishable with a sentence of imprisonment of four to eight years in any of the following circumstances:

(a) The act was committed by an organisation dedicated to providing humanitarian aid. The sentence to be imposed must be in the upper half of the range, with the possibility of an even higher sanction, if a chief, manager or person in charge of the organisation or association is involved.

(b) The life of the people affected by the infringement has been put at risk, or there was a danger of causing serious injuries.

342. The above-mentioned sentence, plus absolute disqualification during a period of six to twelve years, is also foreseen for those who have committed the facts described in Article 318*bis* of the Criminal Code and in doing so have exploited their position as competent authorities, authorised officers or public servant (Article 318.4*bis* of the Criminal Code). If it is established that a legal person is responsible for committing the criminal offences defined in Article 318*bis* of the Criminal Code, the sanction is a fine payable over periods of between two and five years, or the triple to quintuple of the benefit obtained, should this be higher.[232]

343. Intentionally assisting, for the purpose of profit, a non-Spaniard or non-EU citizen to stay in Spain, thus violating Spanish law on the stay of foreigners is also classed as a crime (Article 318.2*bis* of the Criminal Code). In this case, the sentence that can be imposed is identical to that in Article 318.1*bis* of the Criminal Code: a financial penalty that can be paid over a period of three to twelve months or imprisonment for a period of three months to one year.

344. A variety of the crimes are defined in Article 318*bis* of the Criminal Code. Trafficking in human beings is, however, penalised in Article 177*bis* of the Criminal Code. According to this provision, a sentence of five to eight years of imprisonment can be imposed if the act was committed using violence, intimidation or deceit, or abusing a situation of superiority, need or vulnerability of a victim, be it a national or foreigner. A sentence can be imposed for any one of the following purposes:[233] (a) forcing the victim to perform forced labour or to provide services, slavery or practices similar to slavery, servitude or begging; (b) sexual exploitation, including pornography; (c) exploitation for criminal activities; (d) extraction of organs; and (e) performing forced marriages. Likewise a sentence can be imposed on a person receiving payments or benefits to obtain the consent of a person in control of the victim; to recruit, transport, transfer, receive, receipt or house such a victim, including the exchange or transfer of control over those persons, within Spain, from Spain, in transit or travelling to a destination in Spain if that person has acted to realise one of the aforementioned purposes.

345. In any case, the law establishes that victims of trafficking in human beings are exempted from punishment for criminal offences committed in situations of

---

232. In the case of a legal person, Art. 318.5 of the Criminal Code also includes the possibility of dissolution of the legal person or its temporary forfeiture in order to safeguard the rights of its workers or creditors.

233. According to the law, there is a situation of need or vulnerability when the person concerned has no real or acceptable alternative but to submit to the abuse involved. Provocation, conspiracy and a proposal to commit the crime of trafficking in human beings is also a criminal offence, although the sentence of imprisonment will, in this case, be lower than that imposed on the ones who actually commit the crime.

exploitation, as long as their participation was the direct consequence of the violence, intimidation, deceit or abuse to which they were subjected and there is an appropriate proportionality between the situation and the criminal act (Article 177.11*bis* of the Criminal Code).

346. The highest possible sentence, in the case of Article 177*bis* of the Criminal Code, can be imposed when: (a) the life or physical or psychological integrity of the victims has been put at risk; (b) the victim is especially vulnerable due to a disease, pregnancy, disability or his personal situation, or is under the legal age majority.[234] Additionally, as already underlined, the person who commits those acts, abusing their position of superiority as a competent authority, authorised officer or public servant can be sentenced to an absolute disqualification during a period of six to twelve years. Should the offender belong to an organisation or association of more than two people, even if temporary, dedicated to the above-mentioned activities, they can also be the subject of a special disqualification for any profession, occupation, industry or trade during their term.[235] Should the act be committed by a legal person, the sanction is a financial penalty that may range between the triple and the quintuple of its profits. The dissolution or, where applicable, the temporary forfeiture of the legal person in order to safeguard the rights of its workers or creditors is also possible.

§3. Detention and Imprisonment

347. The detention and imprisonment of foreigners are precautionary measures that are regulated within the framework of expulsion procedures (Article 61.1 d) and e) of Law 4/2000), and can be imposed to ensure the execution of expulsion orders (Article 64.1 of OL 4/2000).[236] These measures can also be imposed if a foreigner who wishes to enter Spain is refused permission to enter according to Article 26 of OL 4/2000. This provision establishes that the refusal of entry permission by the Spanish authorities to foreigners who have been expelled, as long as their entry ban remains valid, and to those who have been banned for other legally established reasons.

---

234. Sentences of foreign judges or courts for crimes of the same nature as those in Art. 177*bis* of the Criminal Code are taken into account in Spain for the purpose of assessing a possible recidivism of criminal behaviour in the event that a judgment is handed down under the aforementioned provision in the Spanish Penal Code. This legal consequence will have no effect if the criminal record that gave rise to the conviction by the foreign judges or courts was cancelled or could be in accordance with Spanish law (Art. 117.10*bis* of the Criminal Code).

235. A sentence imposed on the chiefs, managers or persons in charge of those organisations or associations will be in the upper half of the range and may even be higher.

236. Article 61 of OL 4/2000 gives the examining judge in the sanctioning procedure who issues an expulsion measures may be ordered the possibility to order amongst others the following precautionary measures to guarantee the execution of the final decision: (a) periodical appearance before the competent authorities; (b) obligatory residence in a specific place; (c) withdrawal of the passport or document proving their nationality; and (d) any other measure that the judge may deem appropriate and sufficient.

348. Detention and imprisonment decisions have a dual function in immigration Spanish law: (a) as precautionary measures that ensure the appropriate execution and completion of the sanctioning procedure; and (b) as measures to execute the mandatory departure from Spain resulting from an administrative sanctioning procedure or from an expulsion order not connected with a sanctioning procedure – for instance, when entry permission is denied at the border.

349. The legal framework for detention and imprisonment of foreigners has always been the object of controversy in Spain, because, despite the SCC's recognition that the right to personal freedom and security is a fundamental right, integral to human dignity (CCJ 107/1984) and applicable to both Spaniards and foreigners, the right is not mentioned in Title I of OL 4/2000, which specifies the rights and freedoms of foreigners. In contrast, Title III of that law, which establishes the sanctioning regime in immigration affairs, includes the most evident limitation to those rights: the person's detention and imprisonment. This choice, made by the Spanish legislator, although not necessarily shared, may be explained by the SCC's doctrine, according to which the right of foreigners to freedom and security may be restricted (judgment 115/1987). In this sense, the Spanish court held that the instigation of an expulsion procedure justifies that foreigner's loss or temporary restriction of his freedom. Article 5.1 f) of the European Convention on Human Rights expressly includes a person's detention or deprivation of liberty as an exception to the right to freedom and security, according to the law, for the purpose of preventing their illegal entry into the territory or when there is an effective expulsion or removal procedure underway against them.

350. In the case of detention, Article 61 d) of OL 4/2000 establishes that it shall not last more than seventy-two hours, expressly underlining its precautionary nature. It also specifies that, in all other cases, a committal for trial must take place within the above-mentioned period of seventy-two hours. The constitutional guarantee defined in Article 17.2 of the SC also applies. That article specifies that the deprivation of liberty cannot last longer than is strictly necessary in each case, and this cannot be changed unless a judge decides to extend the deprivation of liberty by confining the foreigner in a *Centro de Internamiento de Extranjeros* (CIE, Foreigners Internment Centre) as provided for by OL 4/2000. Likewise, and taking into account the guarantees established in the above-mentioned Article 17 of the Constitution, detained foreigners have the right to be informed of their rights and the reasons for their detention, as well as their right to remain silent and to be legally assisted by a lawyer during the procedure.[237]

351. With regard to imprisonment, it can only be considered in those cases in which a proceeding is launched that may lead to the foreigner's expulsion through the implementation of the so-called priority procedure (Article 63 of OL 4/2000). This will not be the case when the procedure is an ordinary one (Articles 63*bis* of OL 4/2000). Exceptionally, imprisonment may ultimately take place when it is

237. In fact, Art. 22 of OL 4/2000 acknowledges foreigners in Spain the right to free legal assistance under the same conditions as Spanish citizens.

established that the priority procedure has not been completed with the foreigner's voluntary departure from the country after the prescribed time limit is exhausted.[238] The following paragraph will explain the development of these two procedures.

352. The foreigner's imprisonment depends on whether a judge deems it appropriate. An application submitted by the governmental authority that opened the administrative file is the starting point of the procedure which can be either of the two above-mentioned administrative procedures. For this purpose, the judge hears the person concerned and the public prosecutor and subsequently decides on the issue handing down the decision as a motivated writ, which, according to the principle of proportionality, will take into account the concurring circumstances and, particularly, the foreigner's risk of failure to appear due to lack of residence or identity documents, any act to hinder or avoid expulsion, and the existence of a previous sentence or administrative sanction, or of other pending penal or administrative sanctioning procedures. If the foreigner suffers from a serious disease, the judge must assess the risk whether or not imprisonment could represent a threat to public health or the foreigner's own health.

353. As for its duration, the law establishes that imprisonment will last as long as it is necessary to fulfil the objectives of the administrative procedure, with a maximum of sixty days. A second period of imprisonment is not possible as long as this procedure lasts. As soon as the conditions that justified the foreigner's imprisonment disappear, the foreigner must be released by the competent administrative authority and the presiding judge is informed of this change in circumstances. The end of a period of imprisonment may be ordered by the judge, either ex officio or, at the initiative of the foreigner or the public prosecutor.

354. The imprisonment of foreigners in foreigners imprisonment centres (CIEs) is expressly forbidden in the case of minors;[239] i.e., in Spain, under the age of 18 years old. The law states that under no circumstances these centres can be penitentiary nature, and that they have to provide social, legal, cultural and health services (Article 60.2 of OL 4/2000).[240] Nevertheless, there is a longstanding controversy regarding the functioning of the CIEs not only in relation to an interned foreigner's rights but also regarding the living conditions in the centre. In this context, the right granted to foreigners interned in CIEs to contact non-governmental organisations

238. The length of the period for voluntary departure granted to the foreigner to leave Spain ranges from seven to thirty days, although it may be extended for a reasonable period of time according to circumstances such as: the length of stay in Spain, the responsibility for children attending school or the existence of other family and social ties.
239. Article 62*bis* of OL 4/2000 recognises the right of interned foreigners to have their children with them, when they are under the legal age of majority, as long as the Public Prosecutor's Office reports favourably on this measure and there are modules within the centre where family unity and privacy is guaranteed.
240. In relation to the functioning of the CIEs, the relevant rules are not only found in OL 4/2000, but also in RD 162/2014, of 14 March 2014, approving the regulation on the functioning and internal regime of foreigners imprisonment centres (OSG 15 Mar. 2014, No. 64).

and national, international and non-governmental institutions dedicated to the protection of immigrants is especially relevant (Article 62.1 j) bis of OL 4/2000).

§4. Expulsion and Removal Measures

355. There are two concepts that must be clearly distinguished when analysing the issue of a foreigner's forced departure from Spain. On the one hand, there is removal and on the other, there is expulsion. When it comes to establishing the difference between them, the first difficulty arises from the confusing treatment given to both concepts in OL 4/2000. This is why the differentiation made by the CCJ in decision 17/2013, of 31 January 2013 is very useful.

356. Thus, for the Constitutional Court 'removal' is 'the administrative decision regarding the departure from Spain of those persons who attempted to enter the country in violation of the law on immigration affairs. It is not an expression of the State's *ius puniendi*, but a measure of restoration of the rightful situation which resulted from the lack of compliance with the legal conditions for entry into the national territory (Articles 25–27 of OL 4/2000). This lack of compliance with the entry conditions justifies the obligatory departure from national territory in accordance with the legal mandate in Article 28.3 b) of OL 4/2000'. In this sense, the Court noted that 'as compared to expulsion, removal aims at avoiding the contravention of the legal system on immigration affairs, and it is, therefore, not a sanction, but the government's immediate reaction against a disruption of the legal order, issued through a flexible and rapid channel (…). In summary, removal is a measure available to the Spanish authorities within the framework of its immigration policy, which takes into consideration both the necessary control over the migration flows having Spain as destination and the establishment of requirements and conditions that foreigners are obliged to meet in order to enter and reside in Spain'.

357. It thus seems clear that removal implies that a foreigner has not been able to enter Spanish territory, while in the case of expulsion a foreigner's entry has, indeed, taken place. Consequently, Article 58.3 b) of OL 4/2000 establishes that it is not necessary to issue an expulsion order for the removal of foreigners when they have tried to enter the country illegally and they have been apprehended. However, Article 58.3 a) of OL 4/2000 indicates that foreigners are to be removed when, having been expelled, they violate an entry ban. In this case, removal is understood as a specific measure of expulsion. The connection between removal and expulsion actually goes beyond this as Article 58.6 of OL 4/2000 establishes that, when removal is not executed within seventy-two hours, the judicial authority is requested to order the foreigner's interment as a measure prior to the issuing of an expulsion order.

358. Article 58.4 of OL 4/2000 provides two legal exceptions to the implementation by the competent governmental authority – which is the authority that is also competent to decide on expulsion (Article 58.5 of OL 4/2000)– of the administrative measure of removal: (a) when the foreigners who are subject of a removal order apply for international protection. In this case the law establishes that removal is not possible until the application is officially dismissed; (b) in the case of pregnant women, when removal poses a risk to the foetus or the mother's health.

359. As for expulsion, it is a measure that, involves an order to leave Spain territory that may be issued both by the competent administrative authority – and, from this perspective, it is considered an administrative sanction – or by a criminal court judge in the course of a judicial procedure, in which case it will be considered an alternative measure to a sentence depriving the foreigner of his liberty. Expulsion as an administrative sanction can be applied in the case of the serious or very serious infringements listed in Article 53.1 a), b), c), d) and f) of OL 4/2000,[241] as an alternative to financial penalties.[242]

360. Spanish law excludes the implementation of this administrative sanction in the case of foreigners who find themselves in any one of the following circumstances (Article 57.5 of OL 4/2000): (a) they are born in Spain and have legally resided in the country during the last fifteen years; (b) they are long-term residents; (c) they were originally Spaniards and have lost their Spanish nationality; (d) they are beneficiaries of a permanent disability benefit as a consequence of an accident at work or an occupational disease which occurred in Spain, or a public Social Security benefit that is intended to facilitate their social integration or employability. Exceptions to this legal exclusion apply to foreigners who have committed any of the infringements described in Article 54.1 a) of OL 4/2000 – being in Spain irregularly; not having obtained an extension of their permit; not having a residence permit or having one that expired at least three months ago, without having applied for

241. The infringements specified in these ss are: (i) being irregularly in Spain, due to not having obtained an extension of the stay permit, not having a residence permit or having a permit that expired more than three months ago without having applied for its renewal as provided for by law; (ii) working in Spain without a work permit or a previous administrative authorisation to work, whilst not having a valid residence permit; (iii) being guilty of fraudulent concealment or a serious misrepresentation of the facts when obliged to inform the authorities on any change regarding certain personal data or their registration in the municipal registry; (iv) not complying with measures imposed for reasons of public security, regular reporting, or restraining orders (to keep away from borders or specific population centres); (v) committing a third minor infringement within one year; and (vi) being engaged in serious activities contrary to the public order according to Spanish law.

242. When the expulsion measure concerns a long-term resident of another EU Member State who is residing in Spain, the foreigner will only be expelled from the territory of the Union if the infringement committed is amongst those listed in Arts. 53.1 d) and f), and 54.1 a) and b) of OL 4/2000. In all cases, the competent authorities of the Member State that granted the long-term resident status is in relation to this sanctioning measure before it is imposed. If it is legally impossible to carry out the expulsion order to a country outside the European Union, the foreigner is expelled to the Member State that issued the long-term residence permit (Art. 51.10 of OL 4/2000).

Should Spain decide to expel a long-term resident who is a beneficiary of international protection granted by another EU Member State (Art. 57.11 of OL 4/2000), the Spanish authorities have to request this State to provide information clarifying that the foreigner is still a beneficiary of such protection. If the foreigner still enjoys international protection he will be expelled to that EU Member State. However, Spanish law recognises the right of Spain to expel these foreigners to a country other than the Member State that granted them international protection if there are reasonable grounds to consider that they represent a danger for the security of Spain or when, having been convicted of a serious crime by a final judgment, they constitute a threat to this country.

its renewal in the terms established by the law – and in those cases where an infringement of the same nature, that can be punished with expulsion measures, is again committed within a period of one year. Expulsion is also not possible if it entails a violation of the principle of non-refoulement,[243] or it affects pregnant women and could pose a risk to the foetus or the mother's health.

361. With regard to its effects, in addition to departure from Spanish territory, expulsion also entails the end of any authorisation to remain legally in Spain, as well as the filing of any procedure aimed at being granted a residence or work permit to the expelled foreigner. In the case that the foreigner, whether resident or not, is serving a prison sentence, the expulsion measure will be executed once that term of imprisonment has been served.[244] In any case, the decision on expulsion also entails a prohibition to enter Spain (Article 254.2 of RD 557/2011). The duration of this so-called entry ban is determined by the authority that issued the decision on expulsion, that must take into account the specific circumstances of every case, but can never exceed a period of five years, unless the foreigner is considered to pose a serious threat to public order, public security, national security or public health. If this is the case, the ban may be issued for up to ten years.

362. In relation to the administrative procedure required to issue, where applicable, an administrative decision of expulsion, as already pointed out, when the issue of in the sections on administrative sanctions, the law distinguishes two different types of procedures. First of all, there is the so-called priority procedure (Article 63 of OL 4/2000),[245] which is the one followed to effectuate the expulsion of foreigners who are deemed to: (a) have participated in activities against the public order, according to Spanish law; (b) have participated in against national security, or activities which may harm Spain's relationship with other countries, according to Spanish law; (c) have induced, promoted, favoured or facilitated, for the purpose of profit-making, whether individually or as part of an organisation, the irregular immigration of persons in transit or heading towards Spanish territory, or their stay in Spain, as long as the fact is not considered to be a crime; (d) have been sentenced, when inside or outside Spain, for a wilful misconduct that, in Spain, is considered to be a crime and is sanctioned with a term of imprisonment of more than one year – unless the criminal record is cleared; (e) have been in Spain irregularly because they have not obtained an extension of their permit, do not have a residence permit or their residence permit has expired more than three months ago and they have not applied for its renewal within the period provided for by law. This administrative procedure also applies when a foreigner has committed any of the

243. This principle was established in Art. 33 of the Geneva Convention, of 28 July 1951, on the Status of Refugees.
244. In particular, Art. 57.8 of OL 4/2000 establishes that this will be so when the foreigner has committed any of the criminal offences described in Arts. 312.1, 313.1 and 318*bis* of the Criminal Code.
245. The regulatory development is in Arts. 234–237 of RD 557/2011.

infringements listed in Article 53.1 a) of OL 4/2000,[246] insofar as any of the following circumstances occur: (a) there is a risk of non-appearance; (b) the foreigner avoids or hinders his expulsion; and (c) the foreigner constitutes a risk to public order, public security or national security.[247]

363. The ordinary procedure (Article 63*bis* of OL 4/2000)[248] is considered to be the standard procedure for every expulsion measure that cannot be processed by the above-mentioned priority procedure. In this case, the law provides a voluntary period for compliance with the expulsion order, which may be of seven to thirty days, starting from the moment when the administrative expulsion order is notified – in the priority procedure, the execution of the expulsion order is immediate. This period may be extended for a reasonable period – the law does not establish a maximum duration – depending on circumstances such as the length of the foreigner's stay in Spain, whether or not he is in charge of children attending school, or the existence of other family and social ties.

364. The use of one or the other procedure is a controversial issue in Spain due to the lack of precision in the legislation that sets out when either of these procedures should be followed.[249] The priority procedure is the one foreseen for the most cases and it is the one most often used to issue expulsion orders. However, from a foreigner's point of view, this procedure is certainly the one most feared, because OL 4/2000 clearly specifies that it will be accompanied by a series of precautionary measures to be implemented while the case is being settled (Articles 61 and 62 of OL 4/2000), amongst which the person's internment, without the possibility – which does exist in the ordinary procedure – of a voluntary period to leave Spain.

365. At the beginning of the analysis of the legal framework for expulsion it was stated that, within the Spanish system, this concept has a dual nature, being an administrative sanction and a criminal sanction simultaneously.[250] The focus is now

---

246. In particular, lack of compliance with the measures imposed for reasons of public security, regular reporting to the authorities or restraining orders to keep away from borders or specific population centres.
247. The law allows for the suspension of this procedure in certain cases – Art. 31.3 read in connection with Art. 53.1 a) and b) of OL 4/2000– when the foreigner can prove having applied, prior to the procedure, for a temporary residence permit, so that the administrative sanctioning procedure will only be resumed if the application is dismissed.
248. *See* for its regulatory development: Arts. 226–233 of RD 557/2011.
249. In fact, the security forces of the Spanish State follow, on these matters, the specifications in Memorandum 1/2010, of 25 January 2010, issued by the Directorate General for the Police and the Guardia Civil, which aim at clarifying certain aspects related to these procedures. The Memorandum has also been subject to criticism because it is deemed to provide a questionable interpretation of the current law.
250. Article 89 of the Criminal Code has been traditionally considered difficult to implement – amongst other reasons, because of occasional coordination problems between the Spanish public administrations and Spanish courts. It was immediately put into question due to the wide margin of discretion granted to the judge in charge of deciding, where applicable, on the foreigner's expulsion from Spanish territory. This is why OL 11/2003, of 29 September 2003, on specific measures in the matter of public security, domestic violence and social integration of foreigners (OSG 30 Sep. 2003, No. 234), which amended the Criminal Code, removed those elements of discretionary power in

on the latter. Even though it is not listed in Article 33 of the Criminal Code in the general catalogue of sentences – which is certainly an anomaly – Article 89 of the same code regulates the expulsion of foreigners who are in an irregular administrative situation specifically as an alternative measure to compliance with certain prison sentences.[251] The following situations are also dealt with within the framework of the Spanish penal jurisdictional order: the foreigner's administrative expulsion while the criminal procedure is in progress (Article 57.7 of OL 4/2000),[252] and the foreigner's expulsion from Spanish territory when he has been sentenced, either in Spain by the Spanish judiciary or outside Spain by judges of another State, for wilful misconduct considered to be a crime according to Spanish law with a term of imprisonment of more than one year, unless the criminal record has been removed (Article 57.2 of OL 4/2000).

366. As far as the expulsion measures, described in Article 89 of the Criminal Code, are concerned, they are an alternative measure to sentences issued by criminal judges or courts. Thus, Article 89.1 of the Criminal Code establishes that terms of imprisonment of more than one year imposed on foreign citizens are substituted by that foreigner's expulsion from Spanish territory, without any margin of appreciation. Nevertheless, the law includes one exception to this legal obligation, which is almost automatically implemented in the following circumstances: it is necessary to protect the legal order and to re-establish trust in the legal system that was infringed by the person committing the crime. If these circumstances occur the judge or court will agree on the execution of one part of the sentence – no more than two-thirds of its duration – and the substitution of the rest by expulsion from Spanish territory. The expulsion, therefore, takes place when the convicted foreigner has served sentenced and has been granted open-prison status – i.e., he only needs to go back to prison to sleep – or conditional release. According to the law,

---

favour of greater automaticity, when there is a legal basis to decide on the expulsion. The technical improvement of this provision was also one of the objectives of the last reform of Art. 89 of the Criminal Code carried out by OL 1/2015, of 30 March 2015, amending OL 10/1995, of 23 November 1995, on the Criminal Code (OSG 24 Nov. 1995, No. 281).

251. Article 96.3 second of the Criminal Code qualifies the expulsion from Spanish territory of foreigners who are not lawfully residing in Spain as a measure of security that does not entail deprivation of liberty and that may be adopted by a judge or a court. Likewise, Art. 108.1 of the Criminal Code establishes that a judge or court may rule that a foreigner not lawfully resident in Spain can be expelled rather than subject of a security measure.

252. In particular, OL 4/2000 provides that, when in a legal procedure the foreigner is being prosecuted for or is accused of a criminal offence for which the law foresees a sentence of imprisonment of less than six years, or a sentence of a different nature, and this fact is proved during the administrative proceeding, within the shortest possible time and in no case later than three days, the judge, after hearing the public prosecutor, must authorise the expulsion of a foreigner, unless the judge acknowledges the existence of circumstances that justify the dismissal of this measure. If there are several criminal procedures underway in different courts against a foreigner, the governmental authority has to obtain the authorisation from each one of them. Spanish law includes the possibility that the judge can authorise, at the request of the foreigner concerned and after hearing the public prosecutor, the foreigner's departure from Spanish territory. Art. 57.8 of OL 4/2000 does not apply when the crimes to be judged affect the rights of workers (Arts. 321.1 and 313.1 of the Criminal Code) or the rights of foreign citizens (Art. 318*bis* of the Criminal Code).

substitution is not possible if, considering the foreigner's personal and de facto circumstances, in particular their social integration in Spain, expulsion is to be considered a disproportionate measure. Substitution is also not possible for sentences imposed for crimes related to trafficking in human beings (Articles 177*bis* of the Criminal Code) or against the rights of workers (Articles 312, 313 and 318 of the Criminal Code).

367. Additionally, Article 89.2 of the Criminal Code establishes that, whenever a prison sentence is longer than five years or if several sentences which if added together exceed that duration are imposed, the judge or the court must agree on the execution of either the whole term or imprisonment or part of it, to the extent in which it is necessary to protect the legal order and to re-establish trust in the legal system. In these cases, the rest of the term of imprisonment will be substituted by the convicted person's expulsion from Spanish territory, once they have served the part of the sentence agreed on and they have been granted open-prison status or conditional release.

368. As in the case of expulsion as an administrative sanction, within the criminal legal order expulsion also entails the filing of an administrative procedure for the purpose of obtaining a residence and work permit in Spain. In addition, and as an added legal effect, expulsion also implies a prohibition to re-enter Spain during a period of five to ten years, depending on the duration of the term substituted and on the foreigner's personal circumstances.

369. If the expelled foreigner returns to Spain before the period of the entry ban has expired, they have to serve the term of imprisonment that was substituted by the expulsion measure, unless, exceptionally, the judge or court decides to reduce it because it is not considered necessary that the whole period of imprisonment is served to protect the legal order and re-establish trust in the legal system that was infringed by the person who committed the crime, if this is dictated by the time that has passed since the expulsion order was executed and the circumstances in which the crime was committed (Article 89.7 of the CC). Nevertheless, should the foreigner be apprehended at the border, he will be expelled immediately by the competent governmental authority, and the period of the entry ban will start again. This is a legal provision that is, in fact, questionable in itself for being disproportionate and unjustified, involving, as it does, the reimposition of the sanction in all its terms.

Chapter 2. Sanctions Against Persons Helping Irregular Immigrants or Residents

§1. Human Smuggling

370. As discussed in Chapter 1 in Part V, the Spanish Criminal Code addresses the question of human smuggling by classifying as criminal offences a series of acts described in Articles 318*bis*. These acts basically refer to two different situations: (a) helping a person who is not a national of an EU Member State to enter Spanish territory or cross it, in breach of the law in force; and (b) helping a person as mentioned in sub (a) to stay in Spain, in breach of the law.

371. As reflected in the heading of the Title that concerns this criminal offence, the integrity of a foreign citizen is protected and, specifically, his right not to be treated as a commodity. Therefore, in the case of the above-mentioned first act, the sentence is increased if it is established that the activity was profit-oriented, while, in the second case, the purpose of profit-making defines the crime itself. This classification is also meant to protect the State's interest in regulating migration flows into Spain and to ensure that the law is respected, by sanctioning all persons who consciously – both provisions make it clear that these must be considered intentional acts – contribute towards non-compliance with these norms and jeopardise the management of migration flows.

372. Helping a foreigner enter or transit through Spanish territory is not considered a criminal offence when it is perceived that the purpose of this act was to provide the foreigner with humanitarian aid. However, in the practice, it is difficult to establish whether the purpose was actually and exclusively humanitarian. Especially the situation described in Articles 318.1*bis* of the Criminal Code does not necessarily imply that the behaviour of the person providing help is profit-oriented – as opposed to that in Articles 318.2*bis* of that code. This is why, every now and then, a debate arises within Spanish society regarding the reasonability of the above-mentioned rule as it is specified and the need to amend it.

373. The consideration of legal persons as criminal subjects was a novelty introduced into the Spanish legal system through a reform of the Criminal Code that was implemented in 2010. Since then the debate on the opportuneness of this decision has been frequent, if only because in the European (Continental) penal doctrine, penal responsibility of legal persons has historically not been supported. In this sense, the sanction initially foreseen, when a legal person is considered to be responsible for a criminal offence, is a financial penalty. However, Article 318.5*bis* of the Criminal Code includes the possibility that the judges and courts can adopt much more incisive measures, as for instance the dissolution or temporary forfeiture of the legal person. However, to this day judges do not seem to be inclined to adopt this kind of decision, if only because there is no tradition in this sense within the Spanish legal system.

§2. HUMAN TRAFFICKING

374. Given Spain's geographical location at the external border of the EU, trafficking in human beings is a reality to which the Spanish legislator has paid considerable attention. In particular, as this criminal phenomenon has reached considerable proportions in Spain during the last few years. As pointed out in Chapter 1 in Part V, Article 177*bis* of the Criminal Code is the provision defining the acts related to trafficking in human beings considered to be criminal offences by Spanish law.

375. As provided for by Directive 2011/36/EU, of 5 April 2011, on preventing and combating trafficking in human beings and protecting victims, replacing Council Framework Decision 2002/629/JHA,[253] the Spanish law uses a concept of human trafficking that goes beyond mere sexual exploitation or forced labour. It states, for instance, that trafficking in human beings, in the terms legally established, is a criminal offence when one of its objectives is to exploit a person in order to perform criminal activities, extracting organs or performing forced marriages.

376. To be a criminal offence according to the Spanish Criminal Code human trafficking must, initially, be carried out using violence, intimidation or deceit, or abusing a situation of superiority or the need or vulnerability of a national or foreign victim, or giving or receiving payments or benefits to achieve the consent of a person having control over the victim. In brief, it is essential that the trafficking takes place against the foreigner's will. In the case of persons under legal age of majority – 18 years old in Spain – this will not be a requirement, because it is presumed that minors are forced to do what they do against their will. For this reason, Article 177.2*bis* of the Criminal Code establishes that, even if none of the above-mentioned means is used, any act described in section 1 of Article 177*bis* of the Criminal Code is classed as human trafficking when it involves the exploitation of youth.

377. Another aspect concerning the penal treatment of human trafficking is that the Spanish Criminal Code punishes not only trafficking in human beings for the above-mentioned purposes, but also the provocation, conspiracy and solicitation to commit this crime. Section 9 of Article 177*bis* of the Criminal Code expressly establishes that the sentences in this Article are imposed notwithstanding those issued in respect of a violation of Article 318*bis* of the Criminal Code – crimes against the rights of foreign citizens – or other criminal offences actually carried out, including those that constitute exploitation.

378. Finally, the Criminal Code includes an explicit reference to the victim's exemption of penal responsibility. In particular, Article 177.11*bis* of the Criminal Code establishes that victims of trafficking in human beings are exempted from any penalty for criminal acts committed when in a position of exploitation, as long as

253. OJEU, L 101/1 of 15 Apr. 2011.

their participation in those acts was the direct consequence of a situation of violence, intimidation, deceit or abuse to which they were submitted and principle of proportionality is observed. Proportionality is assessed by the judges and courts that are competent in each procedure.

Part VI. Legal Remedies and Procedural Safeguards

Chapter 1. Legal Remedies in the Case of a Refusal of the Right to Enter, Stay or Reside

379. Article 24.1 of the SC accords the right to effective legal representation 'to all persons' in the exercise of their legitimate rights and interests, so that in no case a person is defenceless.[254] Therefore, Article 20.1 of OL 4/2000 unreservedly acknowledges the right of foreigners to effective legal representation, which implies not only that foreigner's right to obtain a decision according to law from a judge or a court in relation to a possible violation of his rights, but also the right that these decisions and, ultimately, any act of the Spanish administration in matters concerning immigration affairs are subject to legal review. This right is granted to all foreigners residing in Spain, whether legally or not.

380. As every State that respects the rule of law, Spain not only recognises the right of foreigners to effective legal representation, as set out but also their right to (administrative) appeal of every administrative act adopted by the Spanish administration.[255] Thus, and in general terms, Article 21 of OL 4/2000 states that all

254. In the same sense, Art. 24.2 of the Spanish Constitution SC accords 'everyone' – a concept that includes both nationals and foreigners – the right to have access to an ordinary judge, as determined by law, to the defence and assistance of a lawyer, to be informed of the charge against them, to be tried without undue delay and with every guarantee, to use the relevant means of evidence for their defence, not to be compelled to testify against themselves or to confess guilt and to be presumed innocent.

Ultimately, this right corresponds with the right to an effective remedy, acknowledged by Art. 13 of the European Convention on Human Rights to every person whose rights and freedoms, as established by that Convention, may have been violated.

255. In asylum cases, the legal remedy regime includes the specifications in by Law 12/2009, in particular Art. 29. Basically, the law establishes that decisions issued according to this law exhaust the administrative proceedings. Consequently, the asylum seeker has recourse to judicial remedies – unless he decides to lodge a last appeal to the administration, known as the remedy for revocation. This will be the procedure, unless the foreigner lodges a 'petition of reassessment' of the corresponding administrative decision, as provided for by Art. 21 of Law 12/2009. This implies that the Ministry of the Interior of the Spanish government will reconsider the case, after a hearing with the United Nations High Commissioner for Refugees (UNHCR). This Ministry's administrative decision is the final decision in the administrative proceedings and the opening to appeal proceedings before the Spanish courts. Spanish law recognises, on the one hand, the asylum seeker's right to request the Spanish courts to suspend the execution of the act against which the appeal

administrative acts and decisions concerning the rights of foreigners may be subject of appeal proceedings as provided for by Spanish law.[256] The position of foreigners is thus equal to that of Spaniards in this aspect, to the extent that Article 21.1 of OL 4/2000 establishes that the enforceability regime of administrative acts in matters of immigration affairs is the one generally provided for by law, the only exception being the priority expulsion procedures, which are regulated in a special provision, i.e., Article 63 of OL 4/2000.

381. The right to free legal aid in Article 22 of OL 4/2000 includes foreigners irrespective of the jurisdiction where they intend to act and 'on equal terms with Spanish citizens'. Nowadays, the acknowledgement of this right is neither conditioned by the foreigner's registration as a resident in Spain – as OL 4/2000 initially established – nor by the condition that they are residing regularly in this country – as provided for in OL 8/2000, amending OL 4/2000, which the SCC declared to be unconstitutional in CCJ 236/2007.

382. Currently, Spanish law distinguishes free legal assistance in administrative proceedings from that provided in the context of contentious-administrative legal proceedings. In the first case, Article 22.2 of OL 4/2000 recognises the right of foreigners in Spain to free legal assistance by a lawyer in administrative proceedings that may lead to a refusal to enter Spain as well as in cases concerning their removal or expulsion from Spanish territory and in all international protection procedures. Legal assistance is only free of charge if the foreigner lacks sufficient economic resources to pay for that aid, according to the criteria established by Spanish law regulating the right to free legal assistance.[257] Additionally, the law provides for free assistance of an interpreter if the foreigner cannot understand or speak the language used in court.[258]

383. Regarding the legal contentious-administrative procedure,[259] Article 22.3 of OL 4/2000 provides that, as long as the foreigner thus requests, he is entitled to free legal assistance if he meets the requirements, which are the same as mentioned above for administrative procedures, if the foreigner wants to contest a final decision in cases concerning a refusal to grant entry permission, removal or expulsion decisions. In relation to these legal procedures, the Spanish law expressly indicates

has been lodged, as provided for by Spanish law, as well as his right to request for review of his case whenever new evidence appears that may require a different decision on the application for asylum.

256. The First Additional Disposition 2 d) of Law 39/2015, of 1 October 2015, on the common administrative procedure of public administrations (OSG 2 Oct. 2015, No. 236), establishes that all acts and procedures in immigration and asylum cases are governed by a specific set of rules – i.e., OL 4/2000 and Law 12/2009, respectively. This law is applied subsidiarily in the absence of rules of a specific nature in the aforementioned special laws.

257. In particular, Law 1/1996, of 10 January 1996, on free legal assistance (OSG 12 Jan. 1996, No. 11).

258. Spanish is the official language in Spain, but certain autonomous regions have other co-official languages. Such is the case of Galician, Catalan and Basque (Euskera).

259. In the majority of immigration cases presently fall under the competence of the courts of the contentious-administrative jurisdiction.

that, when the foreigner has a right to free legal assistance and is outside Spain, his request and, where applicable, the expression of his desire to appeal such a decision may be made before the competent diplomatic mission or consular office.

384. According to the Fourteenth Additional Disposition of RD 557/2011, decisions issued by the competent bodies of the Ministries of Foreign Affairs, the Interior, Employment and Social Security, as well as by the Government Delegate's and Sub-delegate's Offices, concerning the granting or denial of visa, the extension of stays, residence and work permits, or registration cards, as well as the sanctions or expulsion measures imposed on the foreigner by the government exhaust administrative proceedings, so that it is possible to seek a judicial remedy according to the law. Administrative decisions concerning a refusal for the foreigner to enter the country and those concerning the foreigner's removal are the exception to this rule because they do not exhaust by themselves the administrative proceedings and may be subject of an appeal in the administrative sphere before resorting to the courts.

385. In general and for the purpose of avoiding unequal treatment in comparison to Spanish nationals, Article 20.2 of OL 4/2000 states that administrative procedures in cases concerning immigration matters must respect, under all circumstances, the guarantees provided for by general legislation on this kind of procedures – basically those in Law 39/2015. This is especially the case where they concern the publicity of the rule, contradictory procedures, hearing the interested party, and the motivation of decisions. In any case, the law recognises the right to intervene in administrative procedures as an interested party to organisations that are legally constituted in Spain for the defence of immigrants and that are expressly appointed by the foreigner to do so (Article 20.3 of OL 4/2000). In the case of contentious-administrative proceedings, the right to intervene is granted to not only the foreigner concerned by the administrative procedure that may be disputed in the court, but also to corporations, associations, trade unions and institutions that may consider themselves affected by the legal dispute, or that are legally entitled to defend legitimate collective rights and interests (Article 20.4 of OL 4/2000).

Chapter 2. Legal Remedies in Case of Detention and Imprisonment

386. Detention and imprisonment are decisions that, undoubtedly, have a very notable impact on the rights and freedoms of the foreigner as a person. This is the reason why the guarantees surrounding these measures need to be strong. From a general perspective, the detention of foreigners, as a measure regulated by OL 4/2000, is affected by the guarantees established in Article 17 of the SC regarding pre-trial criminal detention. This kind of detention is thus limited to seventy-two hours – a time limit that also affects pre-trial criminal detention not related to immigration affairs. It is a ceiling, because, as specified in Article 17.2 of the SC, 'pre-trial detention cannot last more than the time that is strictly necessary' to develop the actions that justified the adoption of this measure, so that, once that period is over, the detainee must be set free or brought before a judicial authority. Additionally, this kind of detention benefits from the constitutional 'habeas corpus' provision in Article 17.4 of the SC. This is a legal procedure that guarantees the judge's review of the detainee's situation, acknowledging as well the detainee's right to be immediately informed, in a language that he can understand, on his rights and on the charges made against him. Amongst those rights is the one not to be compelled to testify against oneself and to be assisted by a lawyer, both during police and judicial investigations (Article 17.3 of the SC).[260]

387. With regard to imprisonment, there is little to be added to what has already been said in § 3 of Chapter 1 in Part V. The judge who is competent to authorise or not follow up the imprisonment order is the one in the jurisdiction where the foreigner is interned. In the case of the CIEs and the non-admission halls at the borders, the competence corresponds with that of the investigating judge in the place where those facilities are located. If there are several courts in that specific territorial jurisdiction, it will be necessary to settle which court is competent for this task. The judges in these jurisdictions are the ones who receive the petitions and complaints that those interned in these facilities may submit in relation to the exercise of their fundamental rights, and they will be entitled to visit those centres and facilities whenever they are informed of serious non-compliance or they deem it appropriate.

388. An interesting aspect of the legal guarantees granted to interned foreigners is that there is what is called a 'status of interned foreigner', as provided for in Articles 62*bis* and 62*sexies* of OL 4/2000. Article 62*bis* of OL 4/2000, for instance, recognises the right of those interned to be informed on their situation; to be guarded; to physical integrity, healthcare, dignity and privacy; to the exercise of the rights granted to them by the law in force with no limitations other than those which are inherent to their status as a prisoner; to receive social, sanitary and medical assistance; to immediate notification of their imprisonment to a person in Spain designated by them, as well as the consular office of their country of nationality and

260. The detainee is entitled to free legal assistance and to the free assistance of an interpreter when he satisfies the conditions subject to which these rights are accorded to him.

their lawyer; and to contact non-governmental associations and national and international bodies represent the interests of immigrants.

389. Interned foreigners are not only subjects of law, they are also duty-bearers. In this sense, Article 62*ter* of OL 4/2000 states that interned foreigners are obliged: (a) to stay in the centre at the disposal of the investigating judge who authorised their stay there; (b) to respect the rules of the internment centre and the instructions handed out by the managers and the civil workers employed there; (c) to have a civil, correct and respectful attitude towards the civil workers and employees of the internment centre, as well as the visitors and the other people imprisoned there; (d) to keep the facilities, materials, furniture and other goods of the internment centre in good condition; (e) to undergo a medical examination at their arrival at and their departure from the internment centre, as well as in those cases where, for collective health reasons, such an examination is required.

390. In addition, Article 62*quarter* of OL 4/2000 acknowledges the foreigner's right to receive, upon arrival at the internment centre, information in writing, in a language that he can understand, on his rights and obligations, general organisational issues, the rules of the centre, disciplinary norms and means to formulate petitions or complaints. The latter can be made, either orally or in writing, to the director of the internment centre, who will respond to them when competent to do so and, when not, will transmit them to the competent authority, usually the judicial one.[261]

391. The security measures in the internment centre, undoubtedly, impact on the coexistence of the interned foreigners. Thus, OL 4/2000 (Article 62*quinques*) regulates the implementation of surveillance and internal security actions in internment centres, which may include, with the regularity that is deemed appropriate, the inspection of the facilities and offices, and, where necessary, the search of persons, clothes and goods. The use of physical restraint is also provided for, as well as the temporary confinement of the aggressor in an individual room to avoid violent acts and injuries, prevent flights, protect the facilities and protect the civil workers in the legitimate exercise of their duties. According to the law, the use of those means must be proportionate to the aim pursued; they cannot constitute a disguised sanction and they can only be implemented when there is no other less drastic way to achieve the aim pursued and for the time strictly necessary. The use of these measures must be authorised by the director of the internment centre, except in the case of an emergency. If this is the case, then the measures adopted have to be communicated to the director immediately. As soon as possible, the use of the aforementioned measures must be communicated by the director of the centre to the judge, who will be informed on the events that led to their use and the circumstances that may require

261. The director of the internment centre is responsible for adopting the necessary measures to guarantee order and civil coexistence between inmates and to ensure compliance with the interned foreigners' rights. He is also competent to impose measures on those inmates who do not respect the rules of civil coexistence or the internal regulations (Arts Article 62*sexies* of OL 4/2000).

continuation of the measures. When the measure imposed is the temporary confinement of the aggressor, the judge, in as short a time as possible, has to decide on the continuation or revocation of that measure.

Chapter 3. Other Legal Remedies

392. Article 65 of OL 4/2000 states that administrative sanctioning decisions in immigration cases can be appealed according to the rules in various acts. The rules on the enforceability of those decisions are the general rules.[262] Therefore, both the enforceability of these decisions and the possibility of appealing them are the subject of the rules especially developed for this purpose by Law 39/2015, that applies to administrative appeals, and Law 29/1998 of 13 July 1998, regulating the contentious-administrative jurisdiction,[263] that regulates the jurisdiction of the Spanish courts. When the foreigner is not in Spain, the law guarantees that he can, nevertheless, lodge his appeal, whether administrative and jurisdictional, through the competent diplomatic mission or consular office that are obliged to send any appeal to the competent administrative or judicial body.

393. Second, regarding the removal and expulsion of foreigners, as analysed in §4 of Chapter 1 in Part V, Article 22.2 of OL 4/2000 grants foreigners who are in Spain the right to free legal assistance in those administrative procedures that may lead to the foreigner's removal or expulsion from Spanish territory. This right to free legal assistance is also considered in relation to those contentious-administrative judicial procedures that the foreigner may decide to initiate in relation to his removal or expulsion (Article 22.3 of OL 4/2000). Expulsion decisions exhaust all administrative remedies and may be brought before the contentious-administrative jurisdiction immediately. Removals have to be appealed first, using administrative routes, and only in second instance does a foreigner have access to judicial remedies (Fourteenth Additional Disposition of RD 557/2011).

262. Governmental sanctions end administrative remedies, and, for this reason, are immediately subject to appeal proceedings before a court of law, *see* para. 384 of this monograph.
263. OSG 14 Jul. 1998, No. 167.

Part VII. Access to the Labour Market

Chapter 1. Overview of Applicable Legislation

394. The legislation that regulates, in general terms, a foreigner's access to the Spanish labour market is basically OL 4/2000 and RD 557/2011. In the case of those to whom the new selective migration channel, established in 2013 – investors, entrepreneurs, highly qualified professionals, researchers, etc. – apply the general rules are found in Law 14/2013. As shown throughout this work, lawful access to the Spanish labour market generally requires the granting of a work permit although there are, of course, exceptions that have been mentioned already. From a conceptual point of view, there are two types of work permit regimes: on the one hand, the ordinary regime, which applies to employed and self-employed workers. On the other, there is the special regime, which is sometimes regulated by OL 4/2000 and its development regulations and sometimes by Law 14/2013 – particularly Title V – that, ultimately, aims at facilitating access to Spain for certain foreigners – usually persons with a high purchasing power or highly qualified – for reasons of economic, labour, social, research and development, or teaching interests – *see* Chapter 4 in Part III.

395. OL 4/2000 is the subject of a quite impressive regulatory development in the current RD 557/2011, which, besides the various additional, transitory and final dispositions, has no less than 266 provisions. In fact, experts have often questioned whether, in its regulatory effort, the royal decree does not go beyond the limits of the law. Considering the volume of legal and regulatory provisions access to the Spanish labour market is basically a regulatory regime that emanates from the Spanish government, albeit respectful of the legal principles established in OL 4/2000 – and when this is not the case the Supreme Court has annulled the contested regulatory provision.

396. Independent of the various considerations that can be made on the technical improvement of the current legislation regulating a foreigner's access to the Spanish labour market, one aspect that may be resolved in the future is the deliberate separation of the normative sources that, since 2013, has configured an ordinary migration channel, regulated by OL 4/2000, and a preferential selective channel, regulated by Law 14/2013. Despite the country's economic interest, which was put forward as the reason to justify the preferential channel – imitating the legislative practices of other countries – the truth is that it is not acceptable that ordinary migration and selective migration are treated as opposing or incompatible concepts. Thus, on the occasion of the next reform of the legislation on immigration affairs, this preferential migration regime should be integrated into OL 4/20000, and the labour needs of the Spanish labour market need to be addressed as a whole, thereby avoiding the temptation to generate first- and second-class migration movements.

Chapter 2. Conditions for Entitlement to Work in the Country as an Employed Person

§1. General Conditions

397. Article 10 of OL 4/2000 establishes that foreign residents meeting the conditions laid down in the law and its regulatory development have the right to carry out a remunerated activity as an employee or as a self-employed person and that they have access to the Social Security system. Therefore, the right of foreigners over the age of 16 years old to work[264] in Spain temporarily is, as in many other countries, conditioned by compliance with a series of legal conditions that can be summarised as the need to be granted previous administrative authorisation to reside and work as an employed person in Spain (Article 36.1 of OL 4/2000).[265] This permit, however, is not effective until the worker has registered in the Social Security system (Article 36.2 of OL 4/2000). The foreigner has a maximum of three months from their entry into the country to comply with this legal obligation and to, eventually, start the labour or professional activity for which he was authorised to enter Spain (Article 25.2 d) of OL 4/2000).

398. There are situations in which a work permit is not required for the performance of a lucrative, labour or professional activity. These situations are identified in Article 41 of OL 4/2000, as mentioned in Chapter 1 of Part III, and concern foreigners who are residing in Spain for the purpose of providing certain services. However, the fact that a foreigner's situation corresponds with any of the cases, as provided for in Article 41 of OL 4/2000, does not automatically imply that he can provide those services in Spain, because Spanish law establishes that he must request the Spanish authorities to officially recognise the legal exception in accordance with the aforementioned rule, a recognition that is issued in the form of an administrative decision.

399. Additionally, the issuing of an initial temporary residence and work permit frequently means that a visa has to be obtained first. This is regulated in Article 70 of RD 557/2011. The importance of a visa lies in the fact that it is the document that enables a foreigner to go to the competent border control authorities and request permission to enter Spain and remain in this territory in an authorised, legal situation, i.e., as a foreigner authorised to temporarily reside and be employed in Spain.

---

264. Temporary residence in Spain refers to the situation in which a foreigner can remain in Spain for a period of more than ninety days and less than five years.

265. If a foreigner aims at pursuing a profession that requires a special degree or certificate, the granting of the permit will depend on the possession thereof or, where applicable, its official recognition as equivalent to the Spanish degree or certificate (Art. 36.3 of OL 4/2000). In order to obtain the permit, a foreigner must have lawful residence in Spain, not have a criminal record in Spain or in any other country where he has lived in the past five years, for acts classed as crimes or offences by Spanish law. Foreigners, who have agreed, within the framework of a governmental programme of voluntary return to their country of origin, not to return to Spain within a certain period of time, will not be issued a residence and work permit until this period has expired (Art. 36.7 of OL 4/2000).

400. The initial temporary residence and work permit, which is issued for one year and may be extended, as mentioned before, is limited to reside and pursue an economic activity in a specific geographical area – a province – and in the occupation specified on the permit. This geographical restriction is directly related to the division of competence as conferred by Spanish law to the AR, which is a consequence of the administrative decentralisation process initiated in Spain in 1978 regarding the issuing of these permits. Evidently, this permit, as described, does not grant the foreigner permission to access the labour market in geographical areas or production sectors other than those authorised, thus restricting a foreigner's possibilities to continue his economic activities on the Spanish labour market if the initial labour relationship is terminated prematurely.

401. To be issued an initial permit, the entrepreneur intending to hire the foreigner has to provide a labour contract with sufficient guarantees that the foreigner will be able to continuously perform an economic activity during the permit's validity period. This legal condition, specified in Article 36.4 of OL 4/2000, is the evidence of more strict conditions to obtain an initial permit. Before the amendment of OL 4/2000 carried out in 2009 – when this legal novelty was introduced, a mere job offer was enough.[266] In addition, the employer must now prove that he has sufficient economic, material or personal means to carry out his entrepreneurial project and to face his obligations towards the foreign worker provided for in the labour contract (Article 64.3 e) of OL 4/2000).

402. As mentioned before, the hiring of foreign workers in Spain is absolutely conditioned by the so-called national employment situation – regulated in Article 38 of OL 4/2000 and Article 65 of RD 557/2011. It is, basically, a technique that prevents any employer from hiring non-resident foreigners when the domestic employment market can provide the necessary workforce itself. Every three months the Spanish labour market is, so to speak, 'photographed' in order to identify vacancies. According to this 'photograph' a 'Catalogue of occupations not easily covered' is drawn up by the *Servicio Público de Empleo Estatal* (SPEE, Spanish Public Employment Service).

403. An exception to this legal scenario that is expressly provided for in Spanish law is that the employer proves that, even if the job that he has on offer is not included in the above-mentioned Catalogue, it is difficult to cover the position using workers from the domestic labour market (Article 65.2 of RD 557/2011). The process must be completed with the issuing by the SPEE of a certificate confirming the shortage of jobseekers in relation to that specific position. In any case, the Catalogue may not include those occupations that, because of their characteristics, may

266. If the foreigner has a part-time labour contract, according to the law the reimbursement has to be equal to or higher than the inter-professional minimum salary that is fixed annually by the Spanish government for a full-day job during a whole year (Art. 64.3 c) of RD 557/2011). It is thus possible to interpret the Spanish law as favouring the hiring of foreigners with higher qualifications because the law requires a salary that is higher than a proportionate correlation between the number of hours worked per day and the salary paid. It does, however, in practice stop employing foreigners who wish to pursue a part-time job in Spain.

be covered by persons registered as jobseekers after participating in the training programmes offered by the SPEE. The purpose is, therefore, to fill those vacancies with persons who are already integrated in the domestic labour market, allowing the extension or renewal of the residence and working permits of foreigners already residing lawfully in Spain. Ultimately, the list of professions in which the national employment situation is not taken into account when hiring a foreigner, which is included in Article 40 of OL 4/2000 and was discussed in Chapter 1, Part III, of this work, also has to be borne in mind.

404. Despite the above said, as analysed in Part III, under certain conditions that are different from those which apply according to the ordinary regime and that may thus be qualified as a preferential regime, Spanish law provides for the issuing of residence and work permits to foreigners whose professional activity is of economic, social or labour interest, or whose objective is the performance of research, development or teaching work requiring high qualifications, or of artistic activities of special cultural interest.[267] This is regulated in both OL 4/2000 and RD 557/2011. At the same time, Law 14/2013 (Article 61 ff.) has established another preferential regime, different to the one just mentioned, to facilitate the entry and residence in Spain and, where applicable, the exercise of a labour or professional activity, for reasons of economic interests, for foreigners who prove to be investors, entrepreneurs, highly qualified professionals, researchers or workers posted in Spain working within the framework of an intra-company transfer.

§2. Administrative Rules and Procedures

405. The procedure to obtain a residence and work permit giving a foreigner access the Spanish labour market is, as mentioned in the previous section, strongly conditioned by the supply of employment already available, known as the 'national employment situation'. This procedure is usually initiated upon special request of an entrepreneur, who personally expresses his will to hire a foreign worker under the terms already explained. In addition to this ordinary individual procedure, there is another one, which has also already been analysed and is the subject of OL 4/2000 and referred to as the 'collective management of hiring in the countries of origin'.[268]

406. The preferential regime is regulated, on the one hand, by OL 4/2000 and RD 557/2011, and, on the other, by Law 14/2013. This regime includes specific administrative procedures for the processing of the applications for a permit. The reader is referred to the procedural sections in Part III.

267. Currently listed in the law are: artists or groups of artists of international reputation or artists participating in an international artistic project that represents a relevant cultural or social contribution, as well as the staff required to carry out their performance, coming to Spain to perform (Art. 178.2 e) of RD 557/2011).

268. *See* the considerations made on this procedure in paras. 146 ff.

Chapter 3. Sanctions Against Illegal Participation in the Labour Market

§1. Sanctions Against Employers

407. The sanctioning regime defined by Spanish law in relation to entrepreneurs has, as pointed out in Part V, a dual nature, both administrative and penal. As regards the administrative sanctioning regime, hiring of workers whose permit does not allow them to work in the occupation or geographical area where they are actually working is considered a minor infringement. The law, however, provides that each foreign worker hired by one specific entrepreneur is a separate infringement (Article 52 e) of OL 4/2000).

408. In relation to serious infringements, the employer's lack of compliance with his legal obligations in relation to a foreigner to register that employer within the Social Security authorities is an infringement, unless there are new circumstances that can explain why a foreigner has not been registered. Not registering a labour contract with the Spanish administration in the form that served as a basis for the foreigner to apply for his work permit is also considered to amount to a serious infringement.

409. The following infringements are also classified as serious: (a) hiring foreign workers who have not previously obtained a residence and work permit – there will be as many infringements as foreign workers hired under those conditions – as long as this is not considered a criminal offence (Article 54.1 b) by OL 4/2000); (b) simulating a labour relationship with a foreigner, when this is done for profit or with the purpose of unduly obtaining the rights recognised in OL 4/2000, as long as this is not considered a criminal offence (Article 54.1 f) of OL 4/2000).

410. The penal sanctions which can be imposed on certain entrepreneurial behaviour in relation to immigration issues are set out in the Criminal Code, especially in Title XV of the Criminal Code Book entitled 'Crimes against the rights of workers', and, more specifically, in Articles 312–314. Thus, Article 312.2 of the Criminal Code classifies as a crime the behaviour of entrepreneurs who employ foreign workers without a work permit and under conditions that may harm, restrict or fully disregard the rights recognised to these foreigners by law, collective bargaining agreements or individual contracts, as well as the behaviour of entrepreneurs who organise or favour the emigration of a person to another country by simulating a contract or occupation, or through any such deceit (Article 313 of the Criminal Code).

411. The behaviour of those who seriously discriminate a person in an occupation, whether public or private, for reasons of belonging to an ethnic group, race or nationality is also prosecuted, unless a situation of equality before the law is restored following a request or after an administrative sanction has been imposed on the entrepreneur and those who have been discriminated against have been compensated for the economic damage suffered by the discriminatory behaviour (Article

314 of the Criminal Code). Discrimination that takes place in an employment situation is a criminal offence, not only at the moment that the person is hired but also during the entire labour relationship.

412. Article 177*bis* of the Criminal Code classifies as a crime the behaviour of a person who, whether in or from Spanish territory, whether across it or on the way to Spain, uses violence, intimidation or deceit, or abuses a situation of superiority or the need or vulnerability of a national or foreign victim, or gives or receives payments or benefits to obtain the consent of a person in control of the victim, were to recruit, transport, transfer, receive, receipt or house such a victim, including the exchange or transfer of control over that person, for the purpose of subjecting the victim to forced labour or services, slavery or practices that are similar to it or to servitude.

413. Regarding the sanctions and procedure to be followed, the reader is referred to the considerations made in Part V on the administrative sanctioning regime. This is also the case for penal sanctions.

§2. Sanctions Against Workers

414. Evidently, the irregular access of a foreigner to the Spanish labour market can generate behaviour that may be the subject of sanctions which can be imposed by the Spanish authorities. The sanction provided for by law is usually of an administrative nature, as the Spanish Criminal Code does not include provisions regarding acts of foreign workers in an irregular situation.

415. The following acts are considered to be minor infringements (Article 52 of OL 4/2000): (a) an omission or delay in informing the Spanish authorities of any changes of nationality, civil status or residence, as well as other relevant circumstances concerning the foreigner's labour situation, if required by law; (b) a delay of up to three months in applying for the renewal of a permit after they have expired; and (c) being employed in an occupation, activity sector or geographical area not included in the foreigner's residence and work permit. Working in Spain without a work permit or a previous authorisation to work, when the worker does not have a valid residence permit (Article 53 of OL 4/2000), is considered to be a serious infringement.

416. On the sanctions imposed and the procedure to be followed in these cases, *see* Part V.

Chapter 4. Legal Remedies and Procedural Safeguards

417. See Part V for the legal remedies and procedural safeguards regarding the interests and rights of foreign workers and the employer who has hired them, in relation to their participation in the Spanish labour market.

Part VIII. Access to Self-employed Activities

Chapter 1. Overview of Applicable Legislation

418. Self-employment by foreigners in Spain is regulated in OL 4/2000, particularly Articles 36 and 37 of this legal act. Additionally, the rules in this act are developed in RD 557/2011.

419. Self-employment in Spain law has a statute of its own. This regime is different from that on employment which is regulated in RLD 2/2015, of 23 October 2015, approving the consolidated text of the Law on the Statute of Workers,[269] and in Law 20/2007, of 11 July 2007, on the Statute of the Autonomous Worker.[270] Article 1.4 of Law 20/2007 expressly establishes that the regime set out in this law applies to foreign autonomous workers who satisfy the conditions set out in OL 4/2000. Additionally, and according to the nature of the self-employed activities to be performed, it may be necessary to also take into consideration the regime established in Law 14/2013 concerning the activities that may be carried out by entrepreneurs, highly qualified professionals, investors or foreign workers posted in Spain in the framework of an intra-company transfer.

420. Finally, OL 4/2000, in particular Articles 50ff, also concerns the administrative infringements and sanctions in relation to the activity performed by the self-employed foreigner Ccriminal offences are the subject of the Criminal Code.

269. OSG 24 Oct. 2015, No. 255.
270. OSG 12 Jul. 2007, No. 166.

Chapter 2. Conditions to Work in the Country as a Self-employed Person

§1. General Conditions

421. As mentioned in §1 of Chapter 4, of Part II, a foreigner who wishes to pursue a self-employed activity generally needs to obtain a temporary residence and self-employment permit as provided for in Article 37 of OL 4/2000 – and its regulatory development in Articles 103–109 of RD 557/2011. These permits are issued to foreigners who are 18 years and older and, in the case of employment, 16 years or older. The treatment of foreigners wishing to pursue a self-employed activity is different from that given to Spanish citizens, because they can be self-employed and perform a professional activity when they are 16 years old if they satisfy the legal requirements (Article 9.1 of Law 20/2007).

422. Modelled on the general conditions to access the Spanish labour market and to be employed, the law in force requires that a foreigner who intends to develop a self-employed activity in Spain obtains a visa in order to travel and enter Spain, as well as to comply with a series of legal requirements which are listed in Article 105 of RD 557/2011. One of these conditions is that there must be evidence that the investment to be made in order to perform those activities is sufficient. There must also be evidence of the potential creation of jobs according to Article 37 of OL 4/2000. The above-mentioned temporary residence and self-employment permit is not effective the moment that a foreigner enters Spain, but requires the self-employed person's registration with the Social Security authorities – usually in the Special Regime for Autonomous Workers. This formality must be completed within three months from the date of entry.

423. A significant issue concerning a temporary residence and self-employment permit is the time and space conditions as provided for by Spanish law. First of all, the above-mentioned permit authorises a foreigner to stay in Spain for a period of more than ninety days and less than five years, even if the validity of the initial permit is limited to one year. When the five-year period has expired, a foreigner, who wishes to remain in Spain, must, if possible, obtain a long-term residence permit. A temporary residence and self-employment permit is only valid in a specific geographical area – not larger than an autonomous region – and for a specific activity/sector. These two conditions clearly hinder, or even prevent, the possibility of changing the foreigner's self-employed activity.

424. Self-employed activities of cross-border foreign workers are a distinct legal situation as was set out in §1 of Chapter 4 of Part II. In addition to compliance with the legal requirements to obtain a self-employment permit, which are specified in Article 183 of RD 557/2011 and common to both employed and self-employed cross-border workers, a cross-border self-employed person needs to belong to a professional association, in the case of certain activities – lawyers, architects, etc. – and has to pursue a productive activity that generates, from the first year, sufficient economic resources to at least sustain the self-employed person, after the deduction of the economic resources necessary to perform the activity.

425. A self-employment permit has a minimum duration of three months and a maximum of one year and is linked to the duration of the self-employed activity and, as with workers, and a specific industrial sector. Article 184 of RD 557/2011 provides that the territorial validity of a self-employment permit is restricted to the autonomous region or autonomous city – in the case of Melilla and Ceuta – bordering the geographical area where the foreign self-employed person resides.

426. As set out in §3 of Chapter 4 of Part II, in 2013 the Spanish legislator established, through the adoption of Law 14/2013, a specific legal regime that favours those foreigners identified as 'entrepreneurs', i.e. individuals whose economic activity is especially characterised by creating jobs in Spain. This explains that amongst the requirements to legally develop an activity as 'entrepreneur' in Spain, consideration is given to the applicant's professional profile, the submitted business plan – including a market, service or product analysis and a financial assessment – and the added value that this activity may have for the Spanish economy or for innovation.

427. According to Article 68 of Law 14/2013 entrepreneurs have to apply for a visa to enter and stay in Spain for a period of one year for the only or main purpose of completing the procedures required for setting up an entrepreneurial activity. They may apply for a residence permit if the entrepreneurial activity for which they requested the above-mentioned visa has effectively started. This permit allows them to develop their activity in the whole of Spain.

428. Spanish law provides for various legal routes to modify the situation of a foreign worker in Spain,[271] which will allow a foreigner to obtain, in certain cases, a residence and self-employment permit – this regime is found in Title XII of RD 557/2011 (Articles 199–204).

§2. Administrative Rules and Procedures

429. In relation to the administrative rules and procedures to be taken into account when pursuing a self-employed professional activity, the reader is referred to the analysis of the different legal regimes provided for by Spanish law on this matter of immigration affairs.

271. *See* §3 of Chapter 2 of Part II, as well as in Chapter 2 of Part III, concerning changes in the legal situation of those foreigners who are staying in this country for the purpose of study, research, training or non-labour training.

Chapter 3. Sanctions Against Illegal Exercise of Self-employment

430. The illegal exercise of a self-employed professional activity in Spain can be sanctioned according to administrative or criminal law. As mentioned above, Spanish law distinguishes between three different types of administrative infringements: (1) minor, (2) serious and (3) very serious.

431. For this purpose here, the following behaviour of foreigners who intend to develop labour or professional activities as self-employed persons is considered to be a minor infringement (Article 52 of OL 4/2000):

(a) The omission or delay in informing the Spanish authorities of any change regarding the foreigner's nationality, civil law status or place of residence, and of other relevant circumstances regarding their legal situation, as required by law.
(b) The delay of up to three months in applying for a renewal of a permit after it has expired.
(c) Working in Spain without having previously applied for an administrative permit to work as a self-employed person, when the foreigner has a temporary residence permit.
(d) Working in an occupation, activity/sector or geographical area that is not specified on the foreigner's residence and work permit.
(e) Hiring workers whose permits do not authorise them to work in that specific occupation or geographical area – there will be as many infringements as foreign workers hired under these conditions.

432. The following behaviour is considered as a serious infringement (Article 53 of OL 4/2000):

(a) Being irregular in Spain, due to not having obtained an extension of a right stay, or not having a residence permit, or having one that expired three months ago without having applied for its renewal as provided for by law.
(b) Working in Spain without a valid work permit or a previous administrative authorisation to work, if the foreigner does not have a valid residence permit.
(c) Being found guilty of fraudulent concealment or a serious misrepresentation of the facts when complying with the obligation to inform the authorities of any changes in certain personal data.
(d) Not complying with the obligation to obtain a foreign identity card.

433. The following acts are classed as very serious infringements (Article 54 of OL 4/2000):

(a) Hiring foreign workers who have not obtained the required residence and work permits, as long as this is not considered a criminal offence.

(b) Simulating a labour relationship with a foreigner for profit or for the purpose of unduly obtaining rights recognised by law, as long as these facts are not considered a criminal offence.
(c) In the case of carriers, who are treated as self-employed persons in Spanish law that explicitly excludes then from the Statute of Workers, not complying with the legal obligations laid down in OL 4/2000 (Article 54.2).[272]

434. There are two types of criminal offences, related to the hiring of foreign employees by a self-employed person: (1) employing foreign citizens without a work permit under conditions that may harm, restrict or amount to a complete disregard of the rights granted to them by law, collective bargaining agreements and individual contracts (Article 312.2 of the Criminal Code) and (b) organising or favouring the emigration of a person to another country by simulating a contract or occupation or through any such deceit (Article 313 of the CC).

435. Regarding the administrative and penal sanctions established for the above-described infringements, the reader is referred to § 1 and § 2 of Chapter 1 in Part V of this monographm.

272. In particular, Art. 1.3 g) of RLD 2/2015, of 23 October 2015, approving the consolidated text of the Law on the Statute of Workers (OSG 24 Oct. 2015, No. 256) excludes from the scope of this law 'the activity of persons providing transport services under the protection of their administrative permits, when this activity is carried out through the establishment of the corresponding retribution and the use of public service vehicles of which these persons are owners or operators, even when the services are continuously performed by the same person'.

Chapter 4. Legal Remedies and Procedural Safeguards

436. On the legal remedies and procedural safeguards to protect the interests and rights of workers carrying out labour or professional activities as self-employed persons, the reader is referred to Part V of this monographm.

Selected Bibliography

Aja, E. (Coord.), 'Los derechos de los inmigrantes en España', Tirant lo Blanch, Valencia, 2009.

Alonso-Olea García, B., 'Extranjería y trabajo', Thomson Reuters Civitas, Madrid, 2011.

Ancizu Beramendi, C., 'Dos regímenes distintos de protección en el ámbito genérico de la protección internacional: el estatuto de refugiado, por un lado, y el estatuto que confiere la protección subsidiaria', *Revista Aranzadi Doctrinal*, nº. 9, 2015.

Boza Martínez, D., Donaire Villa, F.J., & Moya Malapeira, D. (Coords.), 'La nueva regulación de la inmigración y la extranjería en España. Régimen jurídico tras la LO 2/2009, el Real Decreto 557/2011 y la Ley 12/2009', Tirant lo Blanch, Valencia, 2012.

Boza Martínez, D., Donaire Villa, F.J., & Moya Malapeira, D. (Coords.), 'Comentarios a la Reforma de la Ley de Extranjería (LO 2/2009)', Tirant lo Blanch, Valencia, 2011.

Camas Roda, F., 'La política de inmigración de la Unión Europea', in VV.AA., 'Los grandes debates actuales en el derecho del trabajo y la protección social: estudios en recuerdo del profesor Dr. Manuel Ramón Alarcón Caracuel', Consejo Andaluz de Relaciones Laborales, Sevilla, 2016.

Camas Roda, F., 'Inmigración y mercado de trabajo: la gestión de la diversidad como vía para el reconocimiento de un trabajo decente', in Blanco Fernández de Valderrama, C. (Coord.), 'Movilidad humana y diversidad social en un contexto de crisis económica internacional', Trotta, Madrid, 2014.

Camas Roda, F., 'La adecuación de la normativa de extranjería sobre empleo de los inmigrantes respecto de las reformas laborales adoptadas y de la actual situación de crisis económica', *Relaciones Laborales*, nº 2, 2013.

Cavas Martínez, F. (Dir.), 'Comentarios a la Ley de Extranjería y su nuevo Reglamento', Thomson-Reuters Civitas, Madrid, 2011.

Ceinos Suárez, A., 'El trabajo de los extranjeros en España', La Ley, Madrid, 2006.

Charro Baena, P., 'La doctrina unificada del Tribunal Supremo sobre los derechos laborales y de Seguridad Social del trabajador extranjero en situación administrativa irregular', *Revista de Trabajo y Seguridad Social – CEF*, nº 347, 2012, pp. 119 - 146.

Selected Bibliography

Charro Baena, P., 'El retorno voluntario de extranjeros extracomunitarios: configuración general y medidas adoptadas en el contexto de crisis económica: la capitalización del desempleo', *Revista del Ministerio de Empleo y Seguridad Social*, nº 105, 2013.

Charro Baena, P., 'De nuevo sobre el efecto "útil" de la Directiva de retorno. Comentario a la STJUE (Gran Sala) de 7 de junio de 2016 [Asunto C-47/15 Sélina Affum]', *Trabajo y Derecho*, nº 22, 2016.

Cordero Gordillo, V., 'La asistencia sanitaria a los extranjeros extracomunitarios en España', *Revista de Derecho Social*, núm. 78, 2017.

Díaz Calvarro, J.L., 'La Ley 12/2009, de 30 de octubre, de regulación del derecho de asilo y de la protección subsidiaria. Novedades y análisis de su entrada en vigor', *Anuario de la Facultad de Derecho*, Universidad de Extremadura, Vol. 29, 2011.

Elorza Guerrero, F., 'The Regulation of Immigrant Labour in Spain: Ordinary Migration & Selective Migration', *E-Journal of International and Comparative Labour Studies*, Vol. 6, No. 2, 2017.

Elorza Guerrero, F., 'Los trabajadores extranjeros extracomunitarios en situación irregular y su protección por los regímenes especiales de la Seguridad Social', in González Ortega, S. (Dir.), 'La protección social de los extranjeros en España', Tirant lo Blanch, Valencia, 2010.

Faraldo Cabana, C., 'Emplear ciudadanos extranjeros o menores sin permiso de trabajo: ¿un nuevo delito contra los derechos de los trabajadores?', *Revista de Derecho Social*, No. 78, 2017.

Fernández Collados, M.B., 'El estatuto jurídico del trabajador extracomunitario en España', Laborum, Murcia, 2007.

Fernández Collados, M.B., 'Consecuencia de la atribución a las CCAA de competencia ejecutiva en materia de autorizaciones de trabajo de extranjeros', in VV.AA., 'Los nuevos marcos de relaciones laborales en el renovado Estado de las Autonomías', Valencia, Tirant lo Blanch, 2011.

Fernández Fernández, R., 'La movilidad internacional de trabajadores altamente cualificados. (Retos para los juristas a partir de la lectura de los Discussion Papers del Forschungsinstitut zur Zukunft der Arbeit)', *Relaciones Laborales*, nº 4, 2014.

García Árbol, T., 'El trabajo por cuenta propia de los extranjeros en España', *Migraciones*, nº 13, 2003.

García Herrera, V., 'Los menores extranjeros no acompañados en situación de desamparo', *Revista de Derecho Migratorio y Extranjería*, nº 42, 2016.

García Mahamut, R. & Galparsoro, J., 'Régimen jurídico del derecho de asilo en la Ley 12/2009', Centro de Estudios Políticos y Constitucionales, Madrid, 2010.

García Murcia, J. (Coord.), 'Inmigración y trabajo de los extranjeros', Consejería de Industria y Empleo del Gobierno del Principado de Asturias, Oviedo, 2005.

García Ninet, J.I. (Dir.), 'Régimen jurídico del trabajo de los extranjeros en España: estudio tras el Real Decreto 557/2011, de 20 de abril', Atelier, Barcelona, 2012.

González García, J.M., 'Algunas cuestiones sobre el derecho a la tutela judicial efectiva de los extranjeros a la luz de la jurisprudencia constitucional y de la Ley Orgánica 2/2009', *Teoría y Realidad Constitucional*, nº 25, 2010.

González Martínez, J.A., 'Impacto de la nueva ley de emprendedores. Análisis crítico en el ámbito internacional: movilidad internacional, captación de inversión y contratación de profesionales extranjeros en España', *Revista Aranzadi Doctrinal*, nº 9, 2014.

González Ortega, S. (Dir.), 'La protección social de los extranjeros en España', Tirant lo Blanch, Valencia, 2010.

Igartua Miró, M., 'Algunas consideraciones sobre el contingente de trabajadores extranjeros a la luz del nuevo Reglamento de Extranjería', in Alonso Burón, J.C. & Sánchez-Rodas Navarro, C. (Coords.), 'Aspectos puntuales del nuevo Reglamento de Extranjería', Laborum, Murcia, 2005.

Ybarra Bores, A., 'El permiso de los extranjeros en España', in Carrillo Salcedo, J.A. (Coord.), 'La Ley de extranjería a la luz de las obligaciones de España en Derechos Humanos', Akal, Madrid, 2002.

Martí Martí, X. & González García, G.J., 'La política común de visados de corta duración de la Unión Europea: el camino hacia una política inteligente', *Revista de Derecho Migratorio y Extranjería*, nº 41, 2016.

Martín Arribas, J.J., & Suárez Malaxechevarría, A., 'El derecho de asilo y la protección subsidiaria: reflexiones sobre las aportaciones de la reciente jurisprudencia del Tribunal Supremo de España', *Revista de Derecho Migratorio y Extranjería*, nº 43, 2016.

Molina Navarrete, C., 'La dimensión socio-laboral del pretendido – ¿o pretencioso?- nuevo "estatuto promocional del emprendedor"', *Revista de Trabajo y Seguridad Social – CEF*, nº 369, 2013.

Monereo Pérez, J.L., Fernández Avilés, J.A. & Triguero Martínez, L.A. (Dirs.), 'Comentario a la Ley y al Reglamento de extranjería, inmigración e integración social (LO 4/2000 y RD 557/2011)', Editorial Comares, Granada, 2012.

Monereo Pérez, J.L., 'Las políticas de inmigración: la construcción de nuevas formas de ciudadanía y de atribución de derechos para las personas extranjeras', *Revista de Derecho migratorio y Extranjería*, nº 34, 2013.

Montoya Melgar, A., 'El empleo ilegal de inmigrantes', Thomson Reuters Civitas, Madrid, 2007.

Mauro, M.R., 'El sistema europeo común de asilo y refugio, a debate', *Revista de Derecho migratorio y Extranjería*, nº 42, 2016.

Moya Escudero, M. (Coord.), 'Comentario sistemático a la Ley de Extranjería', Comares, Granada, 2001.

Nieto García, A.J., 'Derecho de asilo de menores, menores extranjeros no acompañados y otras personas vulnerables', *Diario La Ley*, nº. 7597, año XXXII, 2011.

Ortega Martín, E., 'Manual práctico de Derecho de Extranjería', 4ª ed., La Ley, Madrid, 2010.

Palomar Olmeda, A. (Coord.), 'Tratado de extranjería. Aspectos civiles, penales, administrativos y sociales', 5ª edición, Thomson Reuters – Aranzadi, Madrid, 2014.

Ramos Quintana, M.I. (Dir.) & Rojas Rivero, G.P. (Coord.), 'Comentarios al Reglamento de Extranjería', Lex Nova, Valladolid, 2007.

Ramos Quintana, M., 'El trabajo de los extranjeros en España', Tecnos, Madrid, 1989.

Rodríguez Benot, A. & Hornero Méndez, C. (Coord.), 'El nuevo derecho de extranjería: estudios acerca de la Ley Orgánica sobre los derechos y libertades de los extranjeros en España y su integración social', Comares, Granada, 2001.

Sánchez Legido, A., 'Entre la obsesión por la seguridad y la lucha contra la inmigración irregular: a propósito de la nueva Ley de asilo', *Revista de Derecho migratorio y Extranjería*, nº. 22, 2009.

Sánchez-Rodas Navarro, C. (Dir.), 'El novísimo reglamento de extranjería', Ediciones Laborum, Murcia, 2011.

Sánchez Trigueros, C. & Fernández Collados, M.B., 'La nueva gestión colectiva de contrataciones en origen', in Monereo Pérez, J.L. (Dir.), 'Los derechos de los extranjeros en España. Estudio de la Ley Orgánica 2/2009, de 11 de diciembre, de reforma de la Ley Orgánica 4/2000', La Ley, Madrid, 2010.

Sardina Cámara, P., 'Comentarios a la Ley 12/2009, de 30 de octubre, regulador del derecho de asilo y de la protección subsidiaria', *Diario La Ley*, nº. 7370, año XXXI, 2010.

Sempere Navarro, A.V., & Kahale Carrillo, D. T., 'Sujetos beneficiarios de la asistencia sanitaria', in VV.AA., 'Reforma de la salud pública y la asistencia sanitaria', Editorial Aranzadi, Madrid, 2012.

Terradillos Basoco, J.M., 'Trata de seres humanos', in Álvarez García, F.J. & González Cussac, J.L., (Coords.), 'Comentarios a la Reforma Penal de 2010', Tirant lo Blanch, Valencia, 2010.

Terradillos Basoco, J.M., 'Inmigración y sistema penal español: últimas estrategias político-criminales', in Gavidia Sánchez, J.V. (Coord.), 'Inmigración, familia y Derecho', Marcial Pons, Barcelona, 2011.

Triguero Martínez, L.A., 'El estatuto jurídico laboral del trabajador extranjero inmigrante', Editorial Bomarzo, Albacete, 2008.

Triguero Martínez, L.A, 'Standars de regulación jurídica sobre los mercados de trabajo en la Unión Europea ante los desplazamientos de asilados y refugiados', *Revista de Derecho migratorio y Extranjería*, nº. 43, 2016.

Ushakova, T., 'Los grandes retos de la migración altamente cualificada: las perspectivas internacional y europea', *Relaciones Laborales*, nº. 22, 2011.

VV.AA., 'Políticas migratorias, asilo y derechos humanos', Tirant lo Blanch, Valencia, 2014.

VV.AA., 'Las Comunidades autónomas y la inmigración', Tirant lo Blanch, Valencia, 2006.

VV.AA., 'Derechos y libertades de los extranjeros en España. XII Congreso Nacional de Derecho del Trabajo y de la Seguridad Social', Tomo I y II, Madrid, Gobierno de Cantabria, 2003.

Vela Díaz, R., 'El nuevo modelo migratorio de acceso privilegiado tras la Ley 14/2013 de apoyo a los emprendedores: hacia una inmigración selectiva de carácter económico', *Revista de Derecho migratorio y Extranjería*, No. 37, 2014.

Index

The numbers here refer to paragraph numbers

www.ingramcontent.com/pod-product-compliance
Ingram Content Group UK Ltd.
Pitfield, Milton Keynes, MK11 3LW, UK
UKHW020143290926
15471UKWH00004B/669

9 789403 508115